ANALYSING THE INTERPLAY OF POWER RELATIONS IN GITHA HARIHARAN'S FICTION

ANALYSING THE INTERPLAY OF POWER RELATIONS IN GITHA HARIHARAN'S FICTION

Dr. Manpreet K. Sodhi

Analysing the Interplay of Power Relations in Githa Hariharan's Fiction

Edition 2024

ISBN 978-93-87537-71-2

Published by:
CRESCENT PUBLISHING CORPORATION
4806/24, Mathur Lane,
Ansari Road, Darya Ganj,
New Delhi - 110 002
Ph.: 011 - 23244131
Mob.: + 91 - 9711991838, 9999021668
E-mail: crescentbook@gmail.com
Website: www.crescentpublishingcorp.weebly.com

Printed at:
Roshan Offset Printers
Delhi

PRINTED IN INDIA

Dedicated to

my father

S. Devinder Singh Sodhi (1934-2015)
who gave

me the wings to fly and showed me a

vision to accomplish cherished

dreams.

ACKNOWLEDGEMENTS

I consider it my pleasant duty to acknowledge the support and contribution of all those who motivated me to accomplish this task.

My gratitude to my mentor Dr. Rupinder Kaur cannot be adequately expressed in words. She has been my guiding light throughout the course of the completion of this project. This book is seeing the light of the day due to her blessings and moral support.

I am also grateful to my family for always standing by me. No words can adequately describe the heartening support of my parents S. Devinder Singh Sodhi and Sdn. Harbans Kaur who have been the pillars of strength and always stood by me in thick and thin. I am also grateful for all the sacrifices they made on my behalf. I seek their blessings in all my endeavours. I also thank my children who withstood my unintentional negligence.

I would like to thank my friends and well-wishers who have always believed in me and inspired me to work on this book.

Dr. Manpreet K. Sodhi

PREFACE

Power has been a subject of interest for many thinkers but in recent times, many major theorists have explored the idea of power relations. Among them Karl Marx, Michel Foucault, Giorgio Agamben, Carl Schmitt and Mahatma Gandhi can be said to have made a major impact in the exploration of the subject. Power plays a significant role in our society as a whole. It has the ability to influence the behaviour of people. It can "modify, use, consume or destroy them." Rather the study of power as it prevails in every sphere of the social setup can be referred to as politics. Power relations comprise an essential component in human communication. Power is never generated from a single direction or source and imposed on the other. Rather it is the collective effect of different sources of power which could assume the form of people, institutions, values, perceptions, etc.

This book aims to scrutinise the novels of Githa Hariharan in the light of the statement which she herself has made: "Fiction has a thousand ways of giving us a new take on the dynamics of power relations." It aims to focus on various types of power relations beginning with the man-woman relationship, political relations, communal relations and the relationship between intellectually developed and underdeveloped sensibilities. Her five novels from *The Thousand Faces of Night* (1992), *The Ghosts of Vasu Master* (1994), *When Dreams Travel* (1999), *In Times of Siege* (2003) and *Fugitive Histories* (2009) and a collection of stories *The Art of Dying* (1993) have been studied in the light of these dynamics. Before embarking upon any analysis of Hariharan's work, it is necessary to understand the basics about the topic of the book and the theories applied to it. Hariharan's writing occupies a distinct place in the literary scenario and her novels reflect a variegated picture of the socio-political conditions. Therefore, her works cannot be studied within the framework of any one literary theory. Rather, a cumulative approach of power relations, feminism and postcolonialism has been applied to it.

Women's writing has picked up momentum in the last few decades and in the present times their writing has diversified into different spheres with multiple themes. Hariharan comes in the category of women writers who are committed to feminist and social issues as well. Her protagonists reflect her mature understanding of the female psyche and portray the subtlety of a woman's mind. Her depiction of patriarchy is based on her clear social observation and realistic social analysis. Her works explore and highlight multi-layered themes of self-discovery, marginalisation, empowerment, pedagogic concerns, communalism and religious prejudices.

This book is a modified form of my PhD. thesis which focusses on the issues of race, class, caste, resistance, fundamentalism and gender and how they affect the power relations in the society. It reflects how these issues are being treated by Hariharan and also attempts to clarify the author's analysis of the power relations in Indian society. Power structures have remained a vital part of our day to day life and they exist in every relationship, political, personal, social or human. Hariharan's work elucidates how the hidden power structures assume the different shapes and faces and become the cause of trouble in the lives of common people. It reflects her concern with the dynamics of power relations. So, a comprehensive study depicting the power relations has been taken up and makes a viable subject for discussion. A study of Hariharan's fiction has proved to be a holistic vision of the dynamics of power relations between different individuals and the society. The connection and commonality between her fictional and non-fictional work clearly shows her sincere intent and purpose to save humanity from the hazards of modern life.

Dr. Manpreet K. Sodhi

CONTENTS

	Acknowledgements	vii
	Preface	ix
I.	Introduction	1-41
II.	Decolonising the Psyche: *The Thousand Faces of Night* and *When Dreams Travel*	42-89
III.	The Siege of the Mind: *In Times of Siege* and *Fugitive Histories*	90-137
IV.	The Societal Ghosts: *The Ghosts of Vasu Master* and *The Art of Dying*	138-183
V.	Conclusion	184-195
	Bibliography	196-208

DISCLAIMER

Chapter 1

INTRODUCTION

> My childhood, my experiences, my political beliefs and the society I am part of are the hooks and buttons that hold together the fictional garment I stitch. But the design and shape and texture of the garment are determined by the imagination. It is this combination – of a writer's data bank of real life, and her imagination or inner life–that makes each writer's voice unique. A writer's gift is her own special voice. My voice, for instance, seems right for a medley. I enjoy weaving both poetry and short stories into my novels. Of course, this also means that I will never be a totally suitable girl whose work is easily classified.
>
> **Hariharan "Discrete Thoughts" 213**

The collection of thoughts put together by Githa Hariharan in the epigraph above reminds one of the commonly used metaphor of stitching or weaving a garment, used for writing a piece of literature. It also recalls to the mind the dohas of Sant Kabir in which he talks of the warp and the woof of weaving the garment of life. The similarity between the two does not end there. Kabir studies and analyses life, points out its irregularities and tells people to beware and avoid them. Hariharan too, (as she claims in many of her works) would want to bring about innumerable changes in the country and in the world around her. Remaining very close to ground realities, she manages to mingle them with her imaginative sensibility to create a unique patchwork design of fiction and poetry. As she rightly claims, it is not easy to classify her work under a single heading because it is pluralistic from the point of view of themes, techniques and designs.

The present research project endeavours to scrutinise the fiction of Githa Hariharan in the light of the variety of power relations depicted therein. Hariharan claims that her works explore and highlight a new arena in fiction and deal with different relations such as the man-woman relationship, political relations, communal relations and the relationship between intellectually developed and underdeveloped sensibilities. In all these relationships, some imbalance of power exists, the contours of which are evident in Hariharan's work. The dynamics that work behind these relationships create crucial situations which interest writers like Hariharan, who combine fiction with the social interest in their works.

It is true that many contemporary women writers like Manju Kapoor, Shashi Deshpande, Nayantara Sahgal, etc. have been portraying somewhat similar relations, but then their range is comparatively limited. Their novels make an attempt to bring out the changing images of women from the traditional to modern and postmodern times. These writers show a deep concern for the problems being faced by women in a male-dominated society. The theme of their novels is to depict the struggle of modern women to elevate their position in a society where they are still slaves to customs, parents, husband and children. Hariharan shines brightest amongst all the writers in the firmament as her scope is more vast and varied. She does not confine herself to the personal and domestic problems of her protagonists. She is a writer with a difference, a social activist, aware of and sensitive to the political and communal disharmonies prevailing in our country. Fundamentalism, the social injustice done both to men and women, the disturbing political conditions that lead to social unrest and riots in the country are all subjects that she deals with. Hariharan's work provides ample scope for a study of this kind as she is an enlightened citizen who is intellectually sensitive and actively involved in the welfare of the society. As Hariharan opines in the essay "Discrete Thoughts":

> Even if a writer does not write what is usually perceived as political writing - direct social commentary, or unbending realism or

> something "authentically" Indian - the writer should aim at revealing truths, questions and/or answers, that are fundamentally political. Fiction has a thousand ways of giving us a new take on the dynamics of power relations."(*Desert* 214-15)

Being a social activist, Hariharan deems it her duty to create awareness among people about the contemporary situation. She has been involved in all kinds of activities related to social welfare. Her passionate concern and involvement in problems related to women are especially noteworthy. When the fact that she was not the natural guardian of her then minor son was disclosed to her, Hariharan challenged the Hindu Minority and Guardianship Act, 1956 and Guardianship and Wards Act, 1890 as biased against women. The case *Githa Hariharan and Another vs. Reserve Bank of India and Another,* led to a Supreme Court Judgement in 1999 on guardianship. A writ petition was filed by Indira Jai Singh and the Lawyer's Collective on behalf of Hariharan and her husband Mohan Rao. The bench presided over by Chief Justice A.S. Anand held in a 1999 judgment declared that under Hindu law, the mother is also the guardian of her minor children along with the father.

Hariharan enjoys a unique position in modern Indian English literature. She is a renowned scholar and well-known writer who presents varied themes in her writings. Her writings reveal her intellectual qualities. Though her birthplace is Coimbatore, India, she was brought up in Bombay and Manila. She has contributed five significant novels during her career between 1992 and 2009. She attained Bachelor of Arts (Honours) degree in English Literature and Psychology from Bombay University in 1974. Thereafter she went to pursue Master of Arts in Communications from the Graduate School of Corporate and Political Communication, Fairfield University, Connecticut in 1977. She also worked for television channels during her stay in the U.S.A. She worked as a staff writer in WNET- Channel 13 in New York. After returning to India, she joined the job for the post of an editor and served for a span of ten long years in offices of Orient Longman in Mumbai, Chandigarh and New Delhi from 1979 to 1984. She was responsible for drawing up the social science, fiction and women's studies lists. She took up professional editing as a freelancer in the year 1985. Her persistent efforts were directed towards becoming a full-time writer which she always wanted to achieve. After her graduation, she had started writing poems and later switched over to writing prose and novels. Presently she resides in New Delhi and was recently working as a writer in residence at Jamia Milia Islamia University, New Delhi.

She began her writing career at the age of thirty after the birth of her first child. She began writing short stories which she contributed to magazines. Much of Hariharan's work has been published and it includes novels, short stories, essays, newspaper articles and columns. She has written five novels till now. Her first novel, *The Thousand Faces of Night* (1992) won the Commonwealth Writers' Prize for best first book in 1993. Her other novels include *The Ghosts of Vasu Master* (1994), *When Dreams Travel* (1999), *In Times of Siege* (2003), and *Fugitive Histories* (2009). A collection of highly acclaimed short stories, *The Art of Dying*, was published in 1993, and a book of stories for children, *The Winning Team*, in 2004. She has edited a volume of stories in English translation from four major South Indian languages, *A Southern Harvest* (1993); and co-edited a collection of stories for children, *Sorry, Best Friend!* (1997). Hariharan writes her stories with unique twists and retellings and mingles them with the myths, legends and fables. She has been a minute observer of Indian society and social institutions which have enriched her experience and outlook. Her novels throb with social and cultural dynamics of Indian life. She also edited and contributed a collection of essays entitled *From India to Palestine: Essays in Solidarity* (LeftWord, 2014). Her most recent book is a collection of her own essays, *Almost Home: Cities and Other Places* (Harper Collins India, 2014 and Restless Books, 2016).

Hariharan's popularity has prompted people to translate her fiction into a number of languages including French, Italian, Spanish, German, Dutch, Greek, Urdu and Vietnamese. Her essays and fiction have also been included in anthologies such as Salman Rushdie's *Mirrorwork: 50 Years of Indian Writing 1947-1997*. She has been writing a monthly column for many years on various perspectives of culture and their political and social underpinnings, in *The Telegraph*, Kolkata. She has been Visiting Professor or Writer-in-Residence at several universities, including Dartmouth College and George Washington University in the United States; the University of Canterbury at Kent in the UK and Italy; Nanyang Technological University in Singapore; and in India, Jamia Millia Islamia and Goa University, where she is currently a visiting professor. She is not just a feminist but she also is a great chronicler as she covers various themes and a lot of ancient myths in her novels. She narrates her stories through mythological examples to provide a distinct and clear understanding of her concepts. Her close observations of social realities and cultural changes find expression in her literary work.

While studying the fiction of Hariharan in the light of the power relations depicted by her, one must keep in mind that differences of various kinds promote the interests of some while controlling the others. How does this happen? How is it that power gets concentrated in the hands of a few people and is wielded over the weaker sections? Thinkers have attributed this to economic, social, cultural, political and gender-based reasons. Ever since the beginning of history, power relations have existed in the world of men and thinkers have pondered upon them and given their own interpretations to explain them. A brief overview would reflect the significance of different theoretical precepts and their relevance to the present study.

Before embarking upon any analysis of Hariharan's work, it is necessary to understand the basics about the topic of the book and the theories to be applied to it. Therefore the first question that needs to be answered is "What is power?" the next "How does power affect the life of an individual?" and "What are the types of power?" For this, one needs to look into the works of great thinkers who have discussed the impact of power and how it pervades the whole society. Power relations are an inextricable part of human history. Power exists in various forms – it can be clearly visible at times and is ambiguous at others. Power relations comprise an essential component in human communication. An analysis of the social environment reveals two types of power in human interactions - individual power and group power. Individual power generally deals with relations between each human being and his/her interaction with others and generally originates from material strength i.e., wealth and riches. Group power entails communication between individuals who belong to different sets and classes. Power is never generated from a single direction or source and imposed on the other. Rather it is the collective effect of different sources of power which could assume the form of an influential individual, groups of people, institutions, values, perceptions, etc.

Many thinkers in recent times have dealt with the idea of power relations. Among them, Karl Marx, Mahatma Gandhi, Michel Foucault and Giorgio Agamben can be said to have made a major impact in the exploration of the subject. The concept of power may be traced back to Karl Marx according to whom it has originated in capitalism. Marx has undoubtedly been a great thinker and he has propagated his economic theories and materialist outlook by bringing to bear on history the underlying economic forces at work in a changing society. The philosophy of Marx occupies a pivotal position amongst the most important ideologies of modern times. M.G. Gandhi opines:

> Marx regards the state as an executive committee of dominant economic class; no matter how cleverly concealed by ideological veils, its real purpose is to keep in power the men who control the forces of production. The class possessing the means of production captures the state machinery and uses it for exploiting the proletariat. (*Gandhi* 28-29)

Marxism refers to a social and radical theory which aims to bring a social change. Its motive is to liberate man from the oppression through the intervention of the revolutionary proletariat. By playing an active role in the human consciousness, this theory can help to usher in a new dawn for the proletariat. The working class moves ahead and surpasses the existing order. Marx termed his ideology as the dictatorship of the bourgeoisie, believing it to be run by the middle and upper classes purely for their own benefit. Peter Singer opines:

> His reasons for placing importance on the proletariat are philosophical rather than historical or economic. Since human alienation is not a problem of a particular class, but a universal problem, whatever is to solve it must have a universal character - and the proletariat. Marx claims, has this universal character in virtue of its total deprivation. It represents not a particular class of society, but all humanity.(*Marx* 30)

Marx predicted that like the previous socio-economic systems, this dictatorship would inevitably produce internal tensions which would lead to its self-destruction and replacement by a new system, called socialism. He argued that society under socialism would be governed by the working class in what he called the dictatorship of the proletariat, the workers' state or workers' democracy. In fact, there is a master and a slave relationship between two economic entities engaged in the production of goods and service for the society. The master is the capitalist who invests money, resources and expertise to which the worker renders his services to earn wages. In this context, Marx employs the concept of "abstract labour" (qtd. in *Marx,* 33) which means the work which is being done by the worker simply to earn wages rather than to work for the worker's own specific purposes. Karl Marx gave a materialistic interpretation of history and emphasised the primacy of matter over idea. *The Communist Manifesto* (1888) categorically states that "the history of all hitherto and existing society is the history of class struggle."(1) Marx gave a clarion call to all the workers of the world to unite under the banner of communism to revolt against capitalistic regimes.

Marx states that power could only be exercised by the rich ruling class who owned means of production. Marx argues that there is a small ruling class that holds power, and a large group of powerless people; over whom the former maintain their power by manipulating the ideas of the latter. Marx insists on the necessity of the class war. He further adds that the conflict between bourgeoisie and proletariat necessarily leads to the dictatorship of the proletariat for the abolition of all classes and creation of free and equal society. Gandhiji's doctrine of *Satya* and *Ahimsa* also aims to bring a stateless and classless society free from all discriminations of caste, creed, colour or sex.

Marxism aimed to change the patterns and recognised the unequal relation of labour. Marx advocated the path of revolution in order to establish a society in which all human beings are equal. Believing in the inevitability of socialism and communism, Marx actively fought for the former's implementation, arguing that both social theorists and underprivileged people should carry out organized revolutionary action to topple capitalism and bring about socio-economic change. Marxist thought implied the need to empower marginalised and dispossessed people. His consistent endeavour to argue in favour of the underprivileged gets reflected in Hariharan's fictional and non-fictional texts.

In the Indian context, power has been interpreted differently by Gandhiji, the father of the nation and the basic concept of his philosophy is Truth. Many socialist writers are now appreciating his great passion for doing service to the poorest of the poor and lowliest of the low. He is also admired for his strong views against all kinds of exploitation, imperialism and colonialism. His contribution to the cause of peace and non-violence is based on his deep humanism and his faith that humanity is one and indivisible. Gandhiji builds a superstructure of social and political thought on the fundamental concept of *Satya* (Truth) and *Ahimsa* (Non-violence) which acts as a fulcrum around which his thoughts on social philosophy and political thinking revolve. He wants to realise the truth in society and politics through non-violent means, i.e., *ahimsa*. To Gandhiji, *ahimsa* is the soul of truth. He further asserts that *ahimsa* and *satya* are complementary to each other and it is practically impossible to disentangle and separate them. His social philosophy aims at the attainment of both material and spiritual prosperity. There should not be any differentiation of caste, creed, colour or sex as he aimed to establish a new society based on love, peace and non-violence. Basavanna predates Gandhiji's philosophical thinking in Hariharan's novel *In Times of Siege* as he aims to bring the general public comprising common men, marginalised groups and the downtrodden together in a congregation. It is an attempt to bring about a social revolution by a thinker who could be seen as a precursor of Gandhi and his philosophy. The ruling elites and the Brahmins of that time could not tolerate the revolutionary ideas which generated a bipolar tension between them and Basavanna.

Gandhiji's views differ from the Marxist doctrine of the predictability of class war. He believes that the capitalist and the landlord will undergo a change of heart through the adoption of concepts like non-violence and trusteeship. He also believes in uniting the workers and believes that if they unite and work with intelligence, they will constitute a great power in themselves and will courageously deal on equal terms with their masters. Elaborating this point he says "Immediately the worker realizes his strength, he is in a position to become a co-sharer with the capitalist instead of remaining his slave."(qtd. in *Gandhi* 16) It has often been stated that Gandhiji was a communist but he did not believe in violent means. The common ground between Gandhiji and Marx is that both were concerned with the upliftment of the suppressed, weak, ignorant, and the starving section of humanity. Both Gandhiji and Marx wanted that people should equally share the gifts of nature and the rewards of human genius.

Thus, Gandhian philosophy is also quite different from Marxian philosophy. The aim of Gandhiji and Marx to achieve favourable conditions and facilities for the masses are somewhat similar but the method adopted by Gandhian philosophy and the Marxist ideology are different. M.G.Gandhi opines:

> Marxism advocates violent methods to overthrow the bourgeois and capitalist classes in a bid to achieve the ultimate goal of classless society. At the first outcome of the class struggle, the dictatorship of the Proletariat must capture state machinery and exterminate all vestiges of capitalism. Gandhi also desires to end capitalism, almost if not quite, as much as the most advanced socialist or even communist. Gandhi favours socialism, provided it is not brought about through violent methods. Communism minus violence is welcome to Gandhi. (*Gandhi* 20)

The main difference between Gandhiji and Marx is the various attitudes about how to deal with life and the universe, and also of political, social, economic or religious ideas. Gandhiji believes in an ideal social order – a classless, casteless, and stateless society based on non-violence and non-centralisation. He named it as Sarvodaya Samaj. The common ground between Gandhiji and Marx is that both are concerned with the upliftment of the suppressed, weak, ignorant, and the starving section of humanity. Both Gandhiji and Marx aimed to uplift the masses but they differed in their methodologies. As O.P. Dhiman opines

> Gandhi has a living faith in living God, whereas Marx emphatically denies the existence of God, rather treat Him 'as an Opium for the Masses.' For Gandhi spirit or soul is the ultimate rather the only reality, whereas Marx believes that the matter is the only reality. Gandhi's Man is Spiritual Man, whereas Marx Man is Economic Man. Gandhism believes in detachment, whereas Marxism is an ideology of attachment. Because of these fundamental differences, Vinoba Bhave calls Gandhi as a great soul and Marx as a great thinker. (*Gandhi* 80)

Foucault has also been influenced by Marx and Weber and takes the power theory further. He has discussed in detail the ideas of Knowledge and Power which are generally referred to the power-knowledge discourse. Power is the ability to influence the behaviour of people. It can "modify, use, consume or destroy them."(*Subject* 786) Rather the study of power as it prevails in every sphere of the social setup can be referred to as politics. Under the influence of power, one group can exert control over another. Inequalities of different kinds result in the domination over weaker groups by the stronger. Lydia Alix Fillingham opines, "Such a science of sex developed as a form of power – a psychiatrist somehow has power over a patient simply by sitting and listening" (*Foucault* 139). Foucault has analysed power in a different manner. He opines in *The History of Sexuality* "Method":

> By power I do not mean "Power" as a group of institutions and mechanisms that ensure the subservience of the citizens of a given state. By power, I do not mean, either, a mode of subjugation which, in contrast to violence, has the form of the rule. Finally, I do not have in mind a general system of domination exerted by one group over another, a system whose effects, through successive derivations, pervade the entire social body. The analysis, made in terms of power, must not assume that the sovereignty of the state, the form of the law,

> or the over-all unity of a domination are given at the outset; rather, these are only the terminal forms power takes. (*History* 92)

Foucault's works analyse power as an ever changing and shifting set of relations. It operates with a different set of force relations that pervade the social body. Foucault has been a great thinker who has been involved in varied activities besides indulging in scholarly pursuits. Mary McClintock Fulkerson and Susan J. Dunlap observe that Foucault's writings and thoughts are postmodern and they possess varied streaks:

> From madness to the "sciences of man" to prisons and sexuality, his writings are rich in the variety of topics they take up and are provocative in their challenges to conventions about truth, power, and the subject. It is difficult, however, to categorize his work. It contains historical, philosophical, and political analyses, but cannot be confined within traditional disciplinary bounds. Foucault's thought is quintessentially postmodern, blurring boundaries between disciplines, theory, and practice, and disrupting fundamental Western truths.(*Postmodern* 116)

According to Foucault, power is what moulds or shapes us and operates on quite a different level from other influences. Foucault expresses that power is exercised by people or groups by way of 'episodic' or 'sovereign' acts of domination, seeing it as all encompassing and discrete. Foucault states:

> Power is everywhere; not because it embraces everything, but because it comes from everywhere. And "Power," insofar as it is permanent, repetitious, inert, and self-reproducing, is simply the over-all effect that emerges from all these mobilities, the concatenation that rests on each of them and seeks in turn to arrest their movement. One needs to be nominalistic, no doubt: power is not an institution, and not a structure; neither is it a certain strength we are endowed with; it is the name that one attributes to a complex strategical situation in a particular society. (*History* 93)

Power is all pervading and a kind of 'regime of truth' that pervades society. It has multiple sources and is "exercised from innumerable points."(94) It is defined in terms of many relations, as ruler and ruled rather than of personal attributes. Power refers to relational fields, i.e., the difference of one field effects the actions or thoughts of other. The power relations can be characterised as dominant-submissive, strong-weak, have-want, etc. Thus it can be said to be a chain reaction – the effect of one person on the second, which affects the third and so on. Foucault opines:

> It seems to me that power must be understood in the first instance as the multiplicity of force relations immanent in the sphere in which they operate and which constitute their own organization; as the process which, through ceaseless struggles and confrontations, transforms, strengthens, or reverses them; as the support which these force relations find in one another, thus forming a chain or a system, or on the contrary, the disjunctions and contradictions which isolate them from one another; and lastly, as the strategies in which they take effect, whose general design or institutional crystallization is embodied in the state apparatus, in the formulation of the law, in the various social hegemonies. (*History* 92-93)

A vital point about Foucault's concept of power is that it goes beyond the politics and considers power as an everyday and socialised experience. This is one reason why revolutions do not always lead to a social change. Foucault, in fact, moves beyond the notion of power and says, "There are power relations. They are multiple; they have different forms, they can be in play in family relations, or within an institution, or an administration- or between a dominating and a dominated class." (*History* 38)

Foucault believes that there is a deep relation between knowledge and power which is inseparable. He feels that any attempt to separate power from knowledge will result in inadequacy between them. Gary Gutting comments on Foucault's analysis of the relation between power and knowledge:

> There is an intimate tie between knowledge and power. This claim develops Foucault's basic insight that changes in thought are not due to thought itself, suggesting that when thoughts change the causes are the special forces that control the behavior of individuals. Specifically, given Foucault's archaeological view of knowledge, power transforms the fundamental archaeological frameworks (epistemes or discursive formations) that underlie our knowledge.(*Foucault* 50)

Power is an anonymous network of relations which are envisioned as a force that functions through innumerable channels. Power/ knowledge, as Foucault says, is not necessarily repressive, prohibitive, negative; it is also positive: "We must cease once and for all to describe the effects of power in negative terms: it 'excludes', it 'represses', it 'censors', it 'abstracts', it 'masks', it 'conceals'. In fact, power produces; it produces reality; it produces domains of objects and rituals of truth. The individual and the knowledge that may be gained of him belong to this production." (*Discipline* 194) Power can affect people adversely but, it can also act as a productive force that makes it possible for human beings to understand and relate to themselves and others, as also to comprehend the meaning of life and existence. As John Gaventa says, "Foucault is one of the few writers on power who recognise that power is not just a negative, coercive or repressive thing that forces us to do things against our wishes, but can also be a necessary, productive and positive force in society." (web *www.powercube.net*)

Theorists like Carl Schmitt and Giorgio Agamben have been inspired by Foucault. Giorgio Agamben admits having learned a great deal from the ideas of Foucault. In his major work *Homo Sacer: Sovereign Power and Bare Life* (1995), Agamben aims to connect the problems of potentiality and power with the problem of political and social ethics emphasising that the latter has lost its previous religious, metaphysical and cultural grounding. His work deals with freedom and human rights within the modern standards of the rule and social sphere as portrayed in Hariharan's novel *In Times of Siege*. In his book *Homo Sacer,* Agamben writes about the person in the Roman Law who has once been accused of committing a certain kind of crime and loses all of his human rights and freedom and cannot even express himself. The individual is expelled from citizenship and is banned from the society. Thus, he becomes a homo sacer or reduced to bare life in the eyes of juridical powers. Homo sacer is a sacred man who is prohibited from being sacrificed in a ritual ceremony but can be killed by anybody without being guilty of committing murder.

Agamben also believes in Carl Schmitt's definition of the sovereign as the one who has the power to decide the state of exception (or justitium), when the law is suspended for an indefinite period and a state of emergency is declared. The concept of the exception plays a central role in Schmitt's constitutional and political theorising. He opines that the exception to comprise sudden, urgent, usually unforeseen events or situations that require immediate action, often without time for prior reflection and consideration. Agamben's text *State of Exception* (2005) also investigates the increase of power structures that governments employ in supposed times of crisis. Agamben defines "state of exception" as "the extension of the military authority's high time power into the civil sphere, and a suspension of the Constitution, in time the two models end up merging into a single juridical phenomenon that we call the State of Exception."(10) This state of exception invests one person or government with the power and voice of authority over others and reduces individual rights, resulting in the marginalisation of the commoners. Thus, it crushes the individual mind and blurs logical thought which leads people to violence. It is, in fact, the indefinite suspension of the law which characterises the state of exception as depicted in Hariharan's novel *Fugitive Histories.* In the Gujarat Carnage, it is witnessed that the state is exercising its power which indirectly curtails the freedom of the persons belonging to the minorities. There is a state of apprehension in the minds of people belonging to these communities, resulting in the fear of insecurity.

Another theory that dwells on the power politics in human society is Feminism. Feminist literary criticism is essentially linked to the political movement for equality of the sexes and seeks to uncover the ideology of patriarchal society in works of art. Feminism has been defined in many ways and approached by different scholars. The word, 'feminism' was invented by a French socialist, Charles Fourier, in the early 19th century. R.S. Tiwari observes and states, "It was used for asking franchise and was later on extended to describe a particular stand in the women's movement that stressed the uniqueness and difference for women rather than seeking equality, even to the extent of claiming superiority of women over men" (*Modernity* 33-34). The word, 'feminism' is sometimes explained as a person's mental state and is confined to the spiritual values which are possessed by women. Feminism is a movement which aims at describing, creating, and protecting equal political, economic, and social rights for women. Feminism also stresses the need to attain equal opportunities for women in the field of education as well as employment. Thus, feminism is a movement for the recognition of identity and self as a woman. The subjugation of women has been a major problem and a cause of many psychic disorders in the society. It has been pointed out: "Feminism is a doctrine advocating social and political rights of women equal to those possessed by men. It is a movement to acquire such rights made by a male in the presence of feminine characteristics"(Oxford Dictionary 276). Literature also focusses on the rights of women and highlights the subjugation and exploitation of women by the traditional parochial system. Feminism is a consistent struggle to bring women at par with men.

The advent of feminism can be traced to the post-war period. The sole aim of the feminist movement was to help women to attain an identity and make them feel safe and secure in the society. In the nineteenth century, people became aware of the fact that women were maltreated in the society. Thus feminism became a movement which was more organised and attained greater recognition. The organised movement commenced from the First Women's Rights Convention at Seneca Falls, New York, in 1848. The publication of John Stuart Mill's *The Subjugation of Women* in 1869 showcased the subordination of women by men, which according to him, was one of the major hurdles for the development and reformation of the society. The Suffragette Movement (1860-1930) was an important development which united women of various backgrounds. The struggle for votes accelerated the development of feminism. Women realised their power through the suffrage campaign. They realised that they could not rely on political parties or the organised labour movement for support. They became aware that they would have to fight for themselves and make an effort to achieve a status of equality and justice. Feminists also criticised the ideas of Freud regarding penis envy, female narcissism, and female masochism because he only based his debates on fixed biological categories of the male and female. He did not try to study the sociological factors involved in becoming a man or a woman. Feminist activity was also stimulated by the works of middle-class writers, particularly by Simone de Beauvoir's *The Second Sex* (1949, 1953), Betty Friedan's *The Feminine Mystique* (1963), Kate Millet's *Sexual Politics* (1963) and Germaine Greer's *The Female Eunuch* (1970). For the first time, a vast range of issues was addressed by women. Githa Hariharan can be described as one of the successors of feminist theorists who is also a part of this process. Abha Shukla Kaushik comments:

> Indian feminism is essentially a by-product of western feminist movement. It has evolved a veritable, unifying force in the present day literature, especially Indian English Literature. As far as the Indian feminist writers are concerned, the Indian woman caught in the flux of tradition and modernity and bearing the burden of past and aspirations of future, forms and crux of their writing. (*Women* 237)

However, the concept of power is interpreted differently as feminists like Millett and Beauvoir regard power to be something as held by men, where men are considered as superior to women. Kate Millett in her famous book *Sexual Politics* writes that "the essence of politics is power", and that the most fundamental and pervasive concept of power in our society is male dominance (25). She insists that the root cause of women's oppression was deeply embedded in the gender system of patriarchy. She says that women can only be liberated when gender discrimination is abolished. Feminists demonstrate how power has been in play under patriarchy and imposed wholly on the women. In the late 1970's, feminists looked beyond the economic, political and legal structures of society and aimed to explain and rectify the inferior status of women. Arpita Mukhopadhyay brings out Simone de Beauvoir's views on Feminism in her book. She states that women were compelled to become the stereotyped homemakers and were denied all social, political and economic rights. She opines:

> Women were compelled to yield to the gender stereotypes of being nurturers and homemakers; they were denied financial, political and sexual autonomy and were discriminated against in the labour market...
>
> Femininity is traditionally conceived as the 'other' in patriarchal societies, as men have dominated the public sphere. Beauvoir emphasises that, in order to perpetuate patriarchal ideology, men have always assumed the position of 'universal subject', denying women autonomy and agency. She underlines the reality that women are complicit in the continuation of patriarchy. (*Feminisms* 30)

Beauvoir's contribution to feminist theory was in highlighting the cultural, psychological and political status of women. Her book *The Second Sex* brings out the existentialist perspective of women's situation. Beauvoir says,

> One is not born, but rather becomes a woman. No biological, psychological, or economic fate determines the figure that the human female presents in society; it is civilization as a whole that produces this creature, intermediate between eunuch, which is described as feminine. (*Second* 295)

The Second Sex argued that there was no such thing as feminine nature. It is not the biology or the physical attributes that makes a woman, it is the social environment which makes her a woman. Fiona Tolan opines in the essay "Feminisms":

> There was no physical or psychological reason why women should be inferior to men, and yet, throughout history and across cultures, women had always been second-class citizens. Even when worshipped and adored, they have had no autonomy and received no recognition as rational individuals, any more than when they have been abused and denigrated...Just as man considers himself superior to nature, so he considers himself superior to woman. Over the centuries, the concept of the female's passive maternal role has become so deeply entrenched in culture and society that it was presumed to be woman's natural destiny. (*Literary* 321-22)

As Tolan avers, with the passage of time, the fixed notions regarding women did not undergo much change. They have always remained the 'other' in every culture and society and on the basis of physical and economic strength they have been made to feel that they have no choice but to be dependent on men. A woman's natural destiny is to be a wife and the child-bearer and rearer in patriarchal societies and she is doomed to a life of subordination to the will of man.

In our own culture and history, woman's position has been shifting as per the circumstances prevailing in a particular era. The paradox of the Indian setting is that though woman was considered a Goddess on the one hand, she was also considered a burden on the other. She was neither given proper education nor was she given any respect in the family. She was regarded as an insignificant person whose only obligation was to attend to the needs of her family. The problems of women have been portrayed in the works of many Indian writers of English literature. R.K. Narayan, Bhabani Bhattacharya, Kamala Das, Nayantara Sahgal, Anita Desai, Kamala Markandeya, Shashi Deshpande, Namita Gokhale, Shanta Gokhale, Shobha De, Arundhati Roy, Jhumpa Lahiri, Mahashweta Devi and Githa Hariharan are a few of the prominent names in this field. These novelists have portrayed the injustice meted out to women and their subordination and subjugation in a callous environment. Their novels reflect feminist leanings.

Usually, their novels have a woman protagonist who rebels and fights against the existing social norms. They shun the idea of being submissive, suffering and sacrificing. But women need to be determined and strong to rebel against the traditional society in order to bring a change. The spirit of revolt arises from the stereotypical routine life where women are considered non-entities as in Kamala Das's *My Story*. The confined and suppressed women can be seen in Bhabani Bhattacharya's *Music for Mohini* and Anita Desai's *Voices in the City*. In *Until Clear Light of Day*, Desai's women characters are sensitive and emotional misfits who try to maintain their individuality. These women writers highlight the oppression and exploitation of women in a patriarchal society. The characters in these novels aspire and attempt to strive hard and also try to revolt against the system. In their varied fictional roles as wives, daughters, and mothers, they are recording their existential struggle on the screen of their fiction. All the major novels of Githa Hariharan amply testify to this phenomenon.

The Marxist analysis develops on the dialectic of base and superstructure. Feminism uses a method through which they oppress women both from the economic or material base as well as from patriarchal or psychological base. In the public sphere, women are paid less, and in the private sphere, they are confined to the household drudgery. Capitalism is similar to patriarchy where men are paid respectably and women are paid less for the same amount of work. They are also expected to fulfil their domestic obligations. In this context, women are comparable to the proletariat in a capitalist system where they are seen as 'dependents'. The relationship between Marxism and feminism is highlighted by Catherine MacKinnon in the essay, "Feminism, Marxism, Method, and the State: An Agenda for Theory":

> Marxism and feminism are theories of power and its distribution: inequality. They provide accounts of how social arrangements of patterned disparity can be internally rational yet unjust. But their specificity is not incidental. In Marxism to be deprived of one's work, in feminism of one's sexuality, defines each one's conception of lack of power per se. They do not mean to exist side by side to ensure that two separate spheres of social life are not overlooked, the interest of two groups are not obscured, or the contributions of two sets of variables are not ignored. (*Signs* 516-17)

In due course of time, Feminists have modified Marxist ideas to explain the phenomenon of women's subordination. Linked with this is the postcolonial theory which is also relevant to the study of Hariharan. Postcolonialism refers to a set of theories in politics, literature and philosophy that struggle with the legacy of colonial rule. The term postcolonial has been used to represent the continuing process of imperial suppression and exchange throughout a diverse range of societies. In many different societies, women have also been relegated to the position of 'Other' and controlled by various forms of patriarchal domination. They share an intimate experience of the politics of oppression and repression with colonised races and cultures. Thus, postcolonialism in the present day scenario is getting all the attention and is affected by these latest developments. As a result, literature is no more written solely for creativity or entertainment, rather it has become the mouthpiece of the writer who highlights the various changes taking place in the society.

Frantz Fanon, Edward W. Said, Gayatri Chakravorty Spivak and Homi Bhabha are amongst the major theorists who have contributed to the postcolonial theory. While Fanon explores the psychological effect of colonisation on the psyche of a nation, Said contributes to the theory with his celebrated book *Orientalism.*(1978). If postcolonial aesthetic owes its origin to Frantz Fanon's book *The Wretched of the Earth* (1961), postcolonial theory is based on Edward Said's *Orientalism* (1978). Said's contribution can be understood in its proper perspective against the backdrop of his concept of 'Orientalism' which has been explained and developed in his major works. The term 'Orientalism' occurs in Said's magnum opus *Orientalism* which refers to cultural superiority of the West over the East which paved way for imperialism. Imperialism actually refers to the authority assumed by one state over another. Said emphasises the relationship between the East and the West and states, "The nations of contemporary Asia, Latin America, and Africa are politically independent but in many ways are as dominated and dependent as they were when ruled directly by European powers." (*Culture* 20) Said's work on 'Orientalism' brings out the idea that the predefined notions of women's discourse produced the foundation and justification of the 'other' through colonialism. He propagates the idea of a discourse of difference and protests against the use of European ideas to represent 'others.' He opines,

> The Orient is not only adjacent to Europe; it is also the place of Europe's greatest and richest and oldest colonies, the source of its civilizations and languages, its cultural contestant and one of its deepest and most recurring images of the Other. In addition, the Orient has helped to define Europe (or the West) as its contrasting image, idea, personality, experience. Yet none of this Orient is merely imaginative. The Orient is an integral part of European *material* civilization and culture. Orientalism expresses and represents that part culturally and even ideologically as a mode of discourse with supporting institutions, vocabulary, scholarship, imagery, doctrines, even bureaucracies and colonial styles. (*Orientalism* 24)

"Postcolonial criticism", writes Homi Bhabha "bears witness to the unequal and uneven forces of cultural representation involved in the contest for political and social authority within the modern world order." (*Location* 171)

If postcolonialism is an offshoot of postmodernism, subaltern studies have their origin in Marxism, post-structuralism and finally become a part of postcolonial criticism. Subaltern studies that were initiated in India in the 1980's, have now become a subject of worldwide significance. Taking the cue from the subaltern studies school in India, Latin American writers and thinkers, African scholars and native writers all over the world began to dwell on issues and questions related to the dominant discourse, the oppressed, marginalised and colonised people. Subaltern Studies received impetus from a group of English and Indian historians who thought of publishing a journal on this subject. By 1986 much of the work that dealt with writings inside and outside the project helped to establish a separate school of research whose adherents were called subalterns. The major issues taken up by these scholars are those of identity, subjectivity, class, gender, race, immigration and diaspora, and historical experiences. Today subalterns include discussion of problems related to dalits, women, minorities, diasporic and partition victims as well.

The term, derived from the work of the Marxist theorist, Antonio Gramsci, entered postcolonial studies through the work of the Subaltern Studies Group. Gramsci uses it as a synonym for proletariat which refers to persons socially, politically and geographically outside of the hegemonic power structure. Originally a term used for the soldiers of inferior rank in the army, the term has now come to include and address dominated and marginalised groups. In the postcolonial context, subaltern is the standard way to designate the colonial subject in terms of class, gender, caste, race and culture. Some thinkers use it in a general sense to refer to marginalised groups and the lower classes - a person rendered without agency by his or her social status while others use it more specifically. It was popularised by Gayatri Chakravorty Spivak's essay titled, "Can the Subaltern

Speak?"(1975) 'Subaltern' means the colonised/oppressed subject whose voice has been silenced. The term has a relevance to the study of Third World countries, especially in India. Leela Gandhi explains the term clearly in the following lines:

> In 1985 Gayatri Spivak threw a challenge to the race and class blindness of the Western Academy/asking 'Can the subaltern speak?' (Spivak1985) By 'subaltern' Spivak meant the oppressed subject, the members of Antonio Gramsci's 'subaltern classes' or more generally those 'of inferior rank,' and her question followed on the work begun in the early 1980s by a collective of intellectuals now known as the Subaltern Studies group. The stated objective of this group was 'to promote a systematic and informed discussion of subaltern themes in the field of South Asian studies.'(*Postcolonial* 1-2)

Subaltern Studies considers that the basis of society is not necessarily put together by reason and logic. This is its theoretical departure from Marxism. Its theoretical relationship to feminism is that the subaltern is like the gendered subject and hence needs to be studied with the help of feminist theory. In postcolonial studies, it is used to address dominated and marginalised groups. The term combines the Latin sub and alten which means 'under' and 'other' respectively. In the postcolonial context subaltern is the standard way to designate the colonial subject. It has been formulated by women theorists and internalised by the colonised subject, it is a word that refers to the subordinate and marginalised section of societies all over the world. The word subaltern has now been adopted as a term in history, anthropology, sociology, human geography and literature.

The quintessence of Gayatri Spivak's essay "Can the Subaltern Speak" is the plight of the woman/subaltern or the oppressed subject who suffers the double bondage. According to Spivak, "...the subaltern has no history and cannot speak, the subaltern as female is even more deeply in shadow." (*Post-colonial* 32) She emphasises that it is impossible for us to recover the voice of the 'subaltern' and to establish her viewpoint. She speaks of widow immolation in India on the plea of performing '*sati*' at the pyre of the husband. Colonialism and patriarchy both oppressed women and it is difficult for the subaltern to articulate her point of view and 'there is no space from where the subaltern (sexed) subject can speak.' The coloniser is both the outsider as well as the male oppressor from within the patriarchal system. Spivak draws attention to the doubly marginalised/ silenced/unheard section of society, the women in the colonised countries.

The theories of feminism and postcolonialism lead us to the fact that gender inequality is not natural, rather there are many varied voices within feminism that bring out the use of power relations. Inherently interdisciplinary, feminism examines the relationship between men and women and the consequences of power differentials for the economic, social and cultural status of women (and men) in different locations and periods of history. Hariharan comes in the category of women writers who are committed to feminist and social issues as well. Her protagonists reflect her mature understanding of the female psyche and portray the subtlety of a woman's mind. She has been a wise observer of cultural issues as a writer. She attacks the traditional notions with humour, subtlety and tenderness.

Today, Hariharan is one of the leading women writers of fiction in English in India. She has her own distinct style and touches the core of social issues. Hariharan is the recipient of Commonwealth Writers Award for *The Thousand Faces of Night* (1992) which made her popular in the world of literature. She has established herself as a top-ranking Indian writer. A.M. Nawale states about Hariharan, "In her work, a prominent aspect is her exploration of issues related to narratives, which is in turn, a strategy to foreground issues relating to feminist and social issues."(*Reflection* 23) Thus, she is not only a mere imaginative writer but also a promoter of ideas. Both her novels and stories showcase feminist elements on an extensive scale. The bond between storytelling and women's writing is part of a historical tradition which Hariharan has continued. Literature is also one of the mediums that portray feminist ideas and values effectively.

All the theories included in the chapter are in some way linked with the works of Hariharan. Marx's emphasis on class-inequality and its repercussions of society gets reflected in many of her works. Gandhian ideology based on *Satya, Ahimsa* and secular beliefs also seeps through the stories of the novels. In her discussion of marginalised people whether they are men or women, postcolonial, subaltern and feminist theories can prove to be extremely fruitful. Foucault, Agamben, Schmitt also enable one to understand that which is between the lines. None of the characters portrayed by Hariharan seem to be in an absolutely difficult situation but all of them are hounded by hidden forces of power structures which emerge from all around. The law and order situation prevailing in the contemporary world particularly in India reminds one of the state of exception where the powerful politicians can suspend all systems of justice that oppose them at will and the individual is no better than a homo sacer who can be readily sacrificed but is considered unfit for any authentic purpose or achievement. Examples of people who are affected by these different systems of power abound in Hariharan's fiction. And of course as a woman, she has concentrated upon issues related to women and encouraged them to emerge from the margins to occupy the centre.

Thus, the present work makes a critical study of Githa Hariharan's novels from a pluralistic perspective. Her reason, wisdom and knowledge are solely dependent on her realistic understanding of social justice in general and gender impartiality in particular. As a writer, Hariharan is involved in observing life in all its details, perusing and narrating stories. She believes that the quality of a fiction-writer lies in narrating different stories of various people. This gives an opportunity to the author to explore the consciousness of her characters. The task of story-telling is a task of great responsibility and an author should always be aware of this. While drawing the characters of her women protagonists, Hariharan displays her talent in expressing the vacuum and silences in women's lives. In an interview given to Arnab Chakladar in 2006, Hariharan frankly admits that during her pregnancy she had various interactions with different women who gave her varied advice. She comments that a lot of that advice was mythical and this is also reflected in her works.

She brings forth social evils like religious and social prejudices, communalism political struggle and violence in her novels and works. She expresses her concern for women and children in her novels especially when they are subjugated and suppressed by the social norms. Hariharan's works indicate the advent of a new Indian woman who is ready to defy the traditional norms and orthodoxy of the patriarchal system. Her women characters are eagerly paving their way to explore and find their identity. Though her women characters are not against the social system in its entirety, they take bold decisions and shun the age-old systems and values to survive respectfully in the society. Her character, Devi, in the novel *The Thousand Faces of Night* is the best example of the revolt of a woman against patriarchy.

Hariharan's novels portray the plight of women of all age groups. Her knowledge and expression of women's lives are quite evident in her works. In one of her interviews by Anuradha Roy, she was asked about having literary models. Hariharan replied:

> I am not consciously aware of models as I write; but certainly I am, like all writers, deeply indebted to the writing I admire. In this sense Coetzee's writing has always been a model for me – and this is true as much of *Age of Iron* as of *Disgrace*. There are chilling, heartbreaking parallels between apartheid and communalism, just as there are between Hitler's fascism and Hindutva. (web *www.thehindu.com*)

Besides writing novels and stories, Hariharan has been an activist, actively participating in women's movement. In her article "Discrete Thoughts", she states that she has been involved in the movement for the last twenty years. Despite her preoccupations as a working woman, mother and a deep fondness for reading and writing, she has been devoting as much time as possible to the movement :

> To begin with, as a student in the mid-seventies, my political concerns were almost exclusively directed and shaped by feminism. Perhaps this was because I was then a student in America, and this was the time of passionate debate of the ERA (Equal Rights Amendment) and so forth. But once I returned to India in 1978, I saw that any real participation in movements for social change had to come to terms with the big

> class-gender issue. It became clear to me that neither class nor gender could be privileged as the central focus of protest and activity at the expense of the other. The struggle to change the quality of political and personal worlds has to be simultaneous. (*Desert* 215-16)

Hariharan has emerged as one of the pioneering Indian novelists of contemporary times. Her fictional works from *The Thousand Faces of Night* (1992) to *Fugitive Histories* (2009) open new vistas and visualize a wide range of power relationships. Starting with the man-woman relationship, she goes on to portray the plight of a woman as an oppressed and suppressed victim of man's desire. A woman is often dispossessed of all happiness in life and undergoes gradual deprivation. Her literary canvas is dominated by the social and political upheavals that affect the lives of people, particularly women. Freedom and self-identity is a theme that lies at the core of her portrayal of all her women characters. Her women struggle against hostile forces that arise sometimes from within their own psyches or are excited by external agencies, which threaten to ruin their attempts at emancipation. She strongly protests the loss of personal freedom, whether it results from human interface or external authority of any kind. This is why her heroines are found resisting and even breaking away from the bonds of marriage to find a life of fulfillment elsewhere.

Hariharan uses writing as a device for highlighting social prejudices. Her work reflects a deep involvement in her own experience of life and the environment. Her fiction questions the oppression of women, the patriarchal setting, the hypocrisy of religion and social injustice. She rejects religious and social prejudices, communalism, fundamentalism and their dehumanising effects and also condemns the corruption and violence which ensues due to these. This is reflected in her novels *In Times of Siege* and *Fugitive Histories*. Her novels and stories showcase the deteriorating picture of the political and social scenario in which the enslaved minds are not independent enough to fight against negativism. Her writing is a medium for the promotion of charity, love, nationalism, freedom and liberty. She accepts the concepts of freedom and equal rights for women and men, protection of civil liberties, social reform and the idea of the autonomy of the individual. She comments in an interview with Bageshree S.,

> All political commitments have to be questioned, strengthened, renewed and made meaningful for different times. It is right now important to debate the way in which walls are springing up to not just divide people, but to keep some people in and some out. (web *www.thehindu.com*)

Hariharan's novels *The Thousand Faces of Night, In Times of Siege, When Dreams Travel, Fugitive Histories* and her short stories collection *The Art of Dying* deal with the plight of marginalised people striving to attain the dignity of individuals who are being strangulated either by the social setup or by male chauvinism. Hariharan's characters like Devi, Sita, Mayamma, Meena, Rekha, Ratna, Shiv Murthy, Basavanna try to move against the tide of traditionalism in order to bring about socio-political change. The characters struggle to attain their rightful honour and dignity through their consistent efforts. Her novel *The Ghosts of Vasu Master* deals with the struggle between the intellects of intelligent and mentally challenged individuals and raises pedagogic concerns. It is a journey of self-discovery of the characters of Vasu Master and Mani.

In her debut novel *The Thousand Faces of Night,* Hariharan attempts to expose the dominating attitude of men and unfolds the plight of Indian women who are affected by the gender bias prevalent in the Indian society. The novel showcases how women are being suppressed and oppressed in the day to day life and forced to play subordinate roles. It highlights the struggle for identity and other problems of women at various levels in society. It exposes the different facets of women's existence and patriarchal callousness through the characters of Mayamma, Sita and Devi. The three generations of women show the struggle for identity to achieve their honour and rightful status in the patriarchal society.

Hariharan's novel *When Dreams Travel* is a reframing of the old story of *The Thousand and One Nights* from a completely different perspective. The novel contains an intermixing of the stories from both texts which provide uniqueness to her work and thus makes it worth reading. It is unique because it undertakes an exploration and revision of the old text to confer a new meaning on it. Ancient myths and legends are incorporated in the novel to recreate the story of Scheherazade which highlights the power structures and politics at various levels. It is a vibrant and inventive story within an old story. The background of the novel is the popular old legendary tale of *The Thousand and One Nights*, and it begins after the completion of the period of thousand and one nights. The legend is at its climax as the emperor admits his crime of killing women after marrying them for a night because of his whimsical desire for new stories. As his present bride Scheherazade has satisfied this urge, he wishes to unite with her. Patriarchal domination is revealed through the characters of Scheherazade, Dilshad and Dunyazad, who appear as women striving for liberation and free thinking. The novel consists of two parts. Part One is called 'Travellers' and Part Two-'Virgins, Martyrs and Others.' Issues like Gender, Identity and Politics are being talked about in the novel. The first chapter of Part One titled 'In the Embrace of Darkness,' the author narrates the story of *The Arabian Nights* as it is in the beginning of the legendary text. Hariharan's story begins in the second chapter 'On the Way to Paradise' which begins the day after the thousand and one nights are over, with the royal couples sitting in the comforting shady bower of the royal gardens.

The Ghosts of Vasu Master is a novel which has drawn critical attention because it is quite different from Hariharan's other novels. Vasu Master is a retired school teacher who is committed to educating a below average student Mani. He takes it as a challenge to teach this child even though he is mentally challenged. The novel reflects how men dominate women and fail to have a congenial married relationship. Vasu Master does not share his teaching experiences with his wife, Mangala, and she too fails to share her childhood experiences with him although they are married for quite some time and are living together, along with their two children. A psychological bridge separates them and they remain isolated from each other. The novel addresses a number of issues such as the man-woman relationship, the father-son and teacher-pupil equation as well as a deep psychological analysis of the retired school teacher's mind. Mangala is shown as a typical Indian woman. Vasu Master explores the nature of teaching in his own imaginative way. He discovers the link between teaching and healing and highlights the pedagogic issues. Hariharan introduces some ghosts from the memory lane of the retired Vasu Master. He uses the term "my feminine ghosts" (131) for Mangala (Vasu Master's wife), Jameela (Mangala's friend) and Eliamma, the real ghost from Mangala's story. The traditional setup and orthodox thinking are depicted clearly in the novel. All this is reflected through Vasu's efforts to teach a mentally challenged child and a deep introspection to discover his own self. It is an insight into the traditional system of education, i.e., the *Gurukulas* which paid focussed attention to the students unlike the contemporary methods of teaching. Hariharan suggests reverting to the traditional method of education through the novel. She also narrates the story of 'The Three Caterpillars' which symbolises the attitude of the people towards life.

Hariharan's novel *In Times of Siege* portrays the struggle of individuals for justice and the assertion of human rights. The novel highlights the present condition of our country where not only individuals but ideas are also under siege. The novel is not only relevant to the contemporary milieu but it anticipates the future as well. *In Times of Siege* narrates the story of Shiv Murthy who raises his voice to "speak up"(27) for equality, freedom or human rights when one of his correspondence lessons is questioned and tagged as controversial. The professor is depicted as the victim of the dominating social system which curbs the freedom of intellectuals. He is compelled to apologise and also withdraw the modules which had been written for the University correspondence courses. The novel is a depiction of communal fascist forces which impart their unnecessary fundamentalism on the individuals. The politics of repression of the communal differences is clearly portrayed in the novel. It depicts the present situation and the troubled times we are living in. It also focusses on different power struggles amongst the communal divide and the social inequalities. It also touches upon the feminist theme through Meena, Shiv Murthy's friend's daughter who is living with him because she has broken a leg and cannot stay in the hostel and also through the occasional references to Murthy's relationship with his wife who is presently visiting their daughter who lives abroad.

Hariharan's collection of short stories *The Art of Dying* is rich in experiences which are concerned with day to day life and its activities. It cites examples from the contemporary life and portrays every trivial matter or event in a realistic manner to make it significant. Twenty short stories of contemporary Indian life which are compassionate yet ruthless in their honesty bring out the observations of Hariharan on various issues. Hariharan highlights the struggle of individuals through the characters of Revati, Rukmini, Patricia, Brenda, Chellamma, etc. who are the protagonists of her stories. The stories highlight the emptiness, rootlessness, yearning, temptation and suppression of human beings. The pathetic plight of individuals has been evoked through these short stories which clearly represent the marginalisation of men and women in the domestic as well as the social sphere. Social evils like casteism, child marriage, dowry system, orthodoxy and widowhood which are evidently responsible for the sorrowful condition of women are also often condemned by Hariharan through the stories in *The Art of Dying*.

Fugitive Histories explores the disastrous consequences of religious and cultural chauvinism. The analysis of the novel highlights certain important issues of culture and identity; and also critically examines the direction where our nation is heading. The novel deals with the issue of some hidden power structures that assume the facades of religion and social welfare and become the cause of trouble in the lives of people. Hariharan's novel *Fugitive Histories* also narrates the story of the Gujarat pogrom in 2002. It showcases the violence and unrest in the state of Gujarat on account of religious prejudices. It is an account of cruelties faced by minority Muslim population. It portrays the sluggishness of the administration. Hariharan writes about inhuman behaviour, cruelty and violence meted out to the Muslims as well as the Hindus of the state and focusses on the Gujarat carnage. Githa Hariharan has drawn this harsh reality of inter-communal and inter-religious riots on her fictional canvas. Hariharan depicts the reality of all the political upheavals and succeeds in presenting the real and hypocritical working of politics in her novel.

Hariharan's book *The Winning Team* is a book exclusively written for different sorts of people in India and narrates their stories. It is a collection of ten different stories meant for children which are either puzzling or sad but also have streaks of humour. Hariharan's stories are replete with the innocence of children and are full of entertainment and pleasure for the young. Hariharan writes about a storyteller who didn't have anyone to narrate his stories. But to his good luck, Kahani Bhai (also called Bhai K) finds a favourable and best audience for himself. He calls them the winning team of friends comprising Nasira, Gopal, Akbari, Veer, Dulari and Ram. It is so amazing like magic that all the old stories coming to his mind and the happy, joyful faces of Tenali Raman, seem to be familiar.

Hariharan's book *From India to Palestine: Essays in Solidarity* is also a collection of essays edited by her which marks her transition from a fictional writer to a non-fictional writer. She stated after the launch of the book at Hyderabad Literary Festival 2014 in an interview with Sangeeta Dundoo, "You can attend lectures, read up or watch movies on Palestine but witnessing the ground reality can be shocking." (web *www.thehindu.com*) She explained the plight of women and children who were not free to move out even to places like schools and hospitals without ID cards. Her involvement with Palestine has been very ensuring in the recent years. The book has essays by different writers which include Meena Alexander, Aijaz Ahmad, Ritu Menon, Nayantara Sehgal and others who delve deep into the issues of foreign policy, occupational dangers, perception on war, etc. This book shows the present condition of India and Palestine.

Hariharan's book *Almost Home: Cities and Other Places* is a collection of essays which is like a complete cultural encyclopaedia. It is a beautifully written memoir about discovering one's place in a global world. It's a unique book which is a combination of memoirs, travelogues, history, fiction, etc. It comprises ten enchanting essays which explore an individual's place in this global world. Each essay adds to the depth of understanding as Hariharan narrates day-to-day moments which brings forth varied experiences. The book is a fascinating story of the concept of home, the essays highlight a cosmopolitan sensibility where Hariharan provides expression to urban people from various places.

Hariharan's novels richly portray varied relations. While the struggle in the domestic relations is evident in *The Thousand Faces of Night, When Dreams Travel* and *The Art of Dying* through the characters of Devi, Mayamma, Sita, Shaharzad, Dunyazad, Ratna, Revati, Rukmini, and Chellamma; *In Times of Siege* tries to highlight the struggle of Prof. Shiv Murthy with the University or the institution which supports fundamentalism and its rigid ideas. Hariharan's novels discuss the social, political and psychological pressures imparted by various power relations that men and women have to deal with. Being a versatile writer, Hariharan has always been experimenting with new techniques in her writings. Her novels *The Thousand Faces of Night, The Ghosts of Vasu Master* and *When Dreams Travel* are richly intertwined with the mythological texts like *Mahabharata, Panchatantra* and *One Thousand and One Nights* respectively. The act of reading and discovering its meaning leads us to trace the relationship between the texts. Hariharan's writing occupies a distinct place in the literary firmament and her novels reflect a variegated picture of the socio-political conditions. Therefore, her works cannot be studied within the framework of any one literary theory. Rather, a cumulative approach to power dynamics, feminism and postcolonialism are applied to the study. Thus, a set of varied theories is adopted for a deeper and extensive analysis of her novels.

A survey of the available critical studies on Hariharan's works reveals that she has been studied mainly from the feminist perspectives, gender issues, search for identity, the study of epics and various other themes. The varieties of relationships that she observes and describes in her novels reflect her concern with the dynamics of power relations. So, a comprehensive study depicting the power relations has been taken up and makes a viable subject for discussion. Hariharan presents the actualities of life and her times. She states in the essay "Discrete Thoughts":

> But writers' voices are heard on the public stage. So they have a special responsibility to discharge, especially in a country like India. I am a writer, but I also live in modern India and am very much an engaged citizen of our multicultural society. So it is inevitable that I am interested in examining certain relevant themes. The tussles between tradition and modernity, or better still, the making of modernity; equal rights for women, in the arenas of legislation as well as social practice; and in recent times, the strengthening of secular ideas and movements to combat growing fundamentalism. (*Desert* 214)

Hariharan is a versatile writer who does not confine herself to a particular type of writing. She is not a staunch feminist, though she feels strongly about exploitation of women and male sarcasm and raises the issue of the identity crisis of women. Her concern for women is more like that of a humanist than that of a feminist. Her novels reveal her broad vision for the society and the rights of men and women as the citizens of an independent India. She has excelled in being more than a social worker and a reformer through her novels and short stories collection which has created awareness about various problems and restraints that tend to crush individual liberty.

Rajul Bhargava talks about the women writers' responsibilities. She opines in her essay "Post-Feminist Configurations in Githa Hariharan's Short Stories in *The Art of Dying*":

> Women as writers have the added responsibility of providing role models for the oppressed of their kind; of reinterpreting old myths to assert if not their primacy at least their coordinate position; of questioning the validity of those traditions and practices that have

> circumscribed them in narrow unflexing slots – pigeon-holed them in unchanging grooves of societal relationships; and of challenging the codes of morality which have subordinated them....they have to do all this very subtly, with exclusive grace and what is more important under circumstances is that they should do so by submerging their aroused egos and manoevouring themselves within their 'given' setups. (*Indian* 224)

In the thesis entitled "Another World is Possible"(2009), Antonia Navarro Tejero takes up a comparative study of the two novels *The Thousand Faces of Night* and *The God of Small Things*. The study portrays the individual's journey towards self-realisation where women protagonists free themselves from all the shackles of the society.

A couple of critical essays are also available which showcase Hariharan's versatility. S. Indira's essay "Walking the Tight Rope: A Reading of Githa Hariharan's *The Thousand Faces of Night*", and Indira Nityanandan's "A Search for Identity: *The Thousand Faces of Night*" showcase woman's struggle in the search for identity through the characters of three women characters in the novel. "In a symbolic gesture", writes S. Indira in her paper "Devi throws her peacock-coloured Sari over the mirror to blot out, true myriad reflections of herself. She is no more a reflection, no longer on the run. She is a survivor now, bent on to become a conqueror."(*Indian* 181) The essays highlight the constant battle of women with men and the social system.

In the essay "Gender Issues: A Study of Githa Hariharan's *The Thousand Faces of Night* and *The Ghosts of Vasu Master*", Dr. M. Murugesan explicates and aims to examine how women try to rise above the male hegemony. He states, "Almost all the women characters in the novels of Githa Hariharan co-operate with other women to achieve their rightful, equal and independent status."(*Critical* 34) Hariharan gives mythological references in both the novels in order to reveal the attitude of modern women.

Dr. Shubha Tripathi in her essay "Voice of Protest and Assertion: A Comparative Study of Githa Hariharan's *The Thousand Faces of Night* and *In Times of Siege*" portray the journey of the feminine progress, i.e., from a submissive Mayamma to a self-confident Meena. Hariharan thus shows the emergence of a new woman and proves the fact that woman has come a long way in the search for her identity. She opines, "It is the sensitive saga of women struggling to survive in a world of shattered dreams...Often their protest is silent and subtle after being subdued and subjected to torture and neglect sometimes it is expressed too, but after a long period of patience and endurance." (*Critical* 136)

K. Damodar Rao highlights the instances of penance in Hariharan's novels in his essay "Penance as Multiple Response in Githa Hariharan's *The Thousand Faces of Night*" which "springs from and results in multiple response ranging from self-inflicted suffering to protest, revenge and violence."(*Indian* 159) Women are the common victims of the oppression and aggression in a power ridden patriarchal Indian society. Thus, they try to be aggressive against themselves which results in self-inflicting masochistic expression.

Dr. A. G. Khan reviews Hariharan's novel *The Thousand Faces of Night* as an epic which has been "capsulized". "It is a Mahabharat of feminism," he writes "in which women fight their wars and become victims to their own ambitions, humility, arrogance and submission."(*Changing* 135) Hariharan exploits the rich reservoir of our collective consciousness by peeping into the psyche of mythical characters - especially the women victims.

Dr. (Mrs.) A. Kala's essay "Flying in New Skies: Githa Hariharan's *The Thousand Faces of Night*: A Feminist Perspective" brings out the predicament of the Indian women. She opines, "The novel describes women's struggle for existence and expression of their individuality in the male dominant society."(*Critical* 37) The novel promotes gender equality and exposes the patriarchal domination in the social setup.

Rama Nair in "The Art of Fiction: A Note on the "Prelude" of Githa Hariharan's *The Thousand Faces of Night*" and Mrs. Bindu Jacob's essay "A Study of the Evolution of Three Generations of

Women in Githa Hariharan's *The Thousand Faces of Night*" give an existential account of the three women characters in the novel, leading them to attain liberation finally. The novel gives an account of the typical parochial society and the male power structures. The female characters are depicted as delicate, lovable individuals aspiring for love and understanding. They attain self-realization and reconciliation through self-knowledge and strive to find a place in the callous society.

Rustam Brahma's research paper "Gender, Identity and Politics: A Study of Githa Hariharan's *When Dreams Travel* and *The Thousand Faces of Night*" and A.S.Mehala's paper "Art – An Act of Liberation in Githa Hariharan's *The Thousand Faces of Night* and *When Dreams Travel*" explore the Indian culture and ideology which has been a major cause for the suppression of women. Women have been treated as subalterns and the papers highlight their silent struggle to attain their self-identity. Both the papers also analyse Hariharan's works in the light of myths and the ancient fables.

Anita Singh's essay "*In Times of Siege*: A Symbolic Declaration of Human Rights" brings out the plight of the protagonist Shiv who is forced to submit as a result of the communist fascist forces. His life goes into turmoil as a result of the fundamentalist group, the Itihas Suraksha Manch. Despite being a Professor in the University, Shiv is not free to express his views. The social barriers of communalism and fundamentalism paralyse his mind and he feels totally helpless. She says,

> *In times of Siege* provides a compassionate but topical look at our collective lives in the throes of saffronization, communal divide and societal disparities...It is against the grammar of Indian politics that this novel is written and dedicated "For all those who stand up *In Times of Siege*". It states Githa Hariharan's honest commitment to the sanctity of human rights to a free and peaceful life (*Indian* 196).

Rajul Bhargava's essay highlights the journey of women in Hariharan's collection of short stories *The Art of Dying*. It is a portrayal of women who try to go beyond the peripheries of orthodoxy. The realistic account of women is being brought out through the protagonists of the stories like Ratna, Sarala, Chellamma, Patricia, Brenda, etc., who shun the social barriers and strive for identity in this male dominated society. Therefore, most of the studies have been undertaken from the feminist and presented in gendered viewpoint. These actually leave out the major concerns of Hariharan which are much more than a simple analysis of the situation of women in this world. Bhargava opines in her essay,

> *The Art of Dying* (1993) has projected the post-feminist ethos with perfection. The main text seems to run smoothly well within the orthodox order as if upholding the traditional power equation, but very subtly she lets us see and feel the simmering ferment just below the surface. The muted subtext, the 'unsaid' seven-eighths of the story speaks louder than the voiced narrative." (*Indian* 226)

This book endeavours to highlight the significance of the power dynamics that lie under the working of all types of relationships in society. It has been divided into five chapters. In the **Introduction**, an attempt has been made to define and clarify the topic along with the discussion on Githa Hariharan as a distinguished novelist and her works with a special focus on her novels. It focusses on the different types of power relations and their social, political and psychological effect on the society.

In the chapter entitled Decolonising the Psyche: *The Thousand Faces of Night* and *When Dreams Travel*, an attempt has been made to highlight the issues related to women characters and their relationship with men. In these two novels, primarily gender issues have been taken up by Hariharan. The novels portray the male power structures that dominate the society. It also discusses the effort made by the women protagonists to restore their identity in the callous world.

In the chapter entitled **The Siege of the Mind: *In Times of Siege* and *Fugitive Histories*,** the Hindu fundamentalism and communal disharmony prevailing in India are being discussed. The disastrous consequences of religious and cultural chauvinism are highlighted through these novels. The thrust of the discussion in this chapter is on how politics affect individual lives.

In the chapter entitled The Societal Ghosts: *The Ghosts of Vasu Master* and *The Art of Dying,* an analysis of the novel and a collection of stories is taken up which abound in a different set of power relations portraying the intellectually developed vis-à-vis the underdeveloped individual. It undertakes the complexity of human relationships studied in the light of the dynamics of power.

In the Conclusion, the findings of the study are discussed. It focusses on the issues of race, resistance, fundamentalism and gender. It reflects how these issues are being treated by Hariharan and also attempts to clarify Hariharan's treatment of the dynamics of power in Indian society.

Works cited

Agamben, Giorgio. *Homo Sacer: Sovereign Power and Bare Life.* trans. Daniel Heller-Roazen. Stanford: Stanford UP, 1998. Print.

---.*State of Exception.* trans. Kevin Attell. Chicago: The U of Chicago P, 2005. Print.

Beauvoir, Simone de. *The Second Sex.* trans. H.M. Parshley. 1949. London: Vintage, 1983. Print.

Bhabha, Homi K. *The Location of Culture.* London: Routledge, 1994. Print.

Bhargava, Rajul."Post-Feminist Configurations in Githa Hariharan's Short Stories in *The Art of Dying.*" eds. Jain, Jasbir and Avadhesh Kumar Singh. *Indian Feminisms.* New Delhi: Creative, 2001. Print.

Brahma, Rustam. "Gender, Identity and Politics: A Study of Githa Hariharan's *When Dreams Travel* and *The Thousand Faces of Night*" *The Criterion.* Web. 6.2 (2015): 179-185.

Dhiman, O.P., *Gandhian Philosophy.* Ambala: Indian Publications, 1971. Print.

Fillingham, Lydia Alix. *Foucault for Beginners.* Chennai: Orient, 2000. Print.

Foucault, Michel. *Discipline and Punish: The Birth of the Prison.* Trans. Alan Sheridan. London: Penguin, 1985. Print.

---.*The History of Sexuality: The Will to Knowledge.* London: Penguin, 1998. Print.

---."The subject and power." *Critical inquiry* 8.4 (1982): 777-795. Web. 26 Oct. 2016. <http://www.jstor.org/stable/1343197>

Fulkerson, Mary McClintock and Susan J. Dunlap. "Michel Foucault (1926-1984): Introduction" *The Postmodern God: A Theological Reader*. ed. Graham Ward. U.S.A: Blackwell, 1997. Print.

Gandhi, Leela. *Postcolonial Theory: A Critical Introduction*. Edinburgh: Edinburgh UP, 1998. Print.

Gandhi, Madan.G. *Gandhi and Marx*. Chandigarh: Kewal Krishan, 1969. Print.

Gaventa, John. *Power after Lukes: a review of the literature*. Brighton: Institute of Development Studies, n.d., 2003. Print.

Gutting, Gary. *Foucault: A Very Short Introduction*. New York: OUP, 2005. Print.

Hariharan, Githa."Discrete Thoughts"ed. Meenakshi Bharat. *Desert in Bloom: Contemporary Indian Women's Fiction in English*. Delhi: Pencraft, 2004. 213-216. Print.

---."A Conversation with Githa Hariharan." Interview by Arnab Chakladar. *Another Subcontinent: South Asian Society and Culture,* 2005. 12 Aug 2005. Web. 8 July 2013. http://www. another subcontinent.com/gh3.html

---.Interview by Bageshree S. *The Hindu* 20 Oct. 2009. Print.

---.Interview by Anuradha Roy. *The Hindu* nd. Web. 8 July. 2013. http://www.anothersubcontinent.com/gh3.html

Hornby, A.S. ed. *Oxford Advanced Learner's Dictionary 8th*. Oxford: OUP, 2010. Print.

Indira, S. "Walking the Tight Rope: A Reading of Githa Hariharan's *The Thousand Faces of Night*" ed. R.K. Dhawan. *Indian Women Novelists*. Set III. Vol. IV. New Delhi: Prestige, 1995. Print.

Jacob, Bindu. "A Study of the Evolution of Three Generations of Women in Githa Hariharan's *The Thousand Faces of Night*" *International Research Journal*. Web 1.5 (2010): 81-84.

Kala, A., "Flying in New Skies: Githa Hariharan's *The Thousand Faces of Night*: A Feminist Perspective" ed. K. Balachandran. *Critical Essays on Diasporic Writing*. New Delhi: Arise, 2008. Print.

Kaushik, Abha Shukla. "Changing Faces of Indian Woman: Bharati Mukherjee's *Jasmine* and Githa Hariharan's *The Thousand Faces of Night*." eds. Malti, Agarwal. *Women in Postcolonial Indian English Literature*. New Delhi: Atlantic, 2011. Print.

Khan, A.G, "*The Thousand Faces of Night:* An Epic "Capsulized". eds. Khan, M.Q. and A.G. Khan. *Changing Faces of Women in Indian Writing in English.* New Delhi: Creative, 1995. Print.

Marx, Karl, and Friedrich Engels. *The Communist Manifesto*. trans. Samuel Moore. London, 1888. New Delhi: Penguin, 2002. Print.

MacKinnon, Catherine A."Feminism, Marxism, Method and the State: An Agenda for Theory." *Signs* 17.3 (1982): 516-17 Feminist Theory The U of Chicago P. Web. 30 Oct. 2014. < http://www. jstor.org/stable/3173853>

Mehala, A.S. "Art - An Act of Liberation in Githa Hariharan's *The Thousand Faces of Night* and *When Dreams Travel*" *Research Journal of English Language and Literature.* Web. 4.2 (2016): 865-867.

Millet, Kate. *Sexual Politics.* Rome: Indiana, 1998. Print.

Mukhopadhyay, Arpita. ed. Sumit Chakrabarti. *Feminisms.* Hyderabad: Orient. 2016. Print.

Murugesan, M. Dr."Gender Issues: A Study of Githa Hariharan's *The Thousand Faces of Night* and *The Ghosts of Vasu Master.*" *Critical Essays on Diasporic Writings.* ed. Dr. K. Balachandran. New Delhi: Arise, 2008. 29-35. Print.

Nair, Rama. "The Art of Fiction: A Note on the "Prelude" of Githa Hariharan's *The Thousand Faces of Night*" ed. R.K. Dhawan. *Indian Women Novelists.* Set III. Vol. IV. New Delhi: Prestige, 1995. Print.

Navarro Tejero, Antonia. *The Fiction of Arundhati Roy and Githa Hariharan: Another World is Possible.* Diss. U de Huelva, 10 July 2003. Web. 24 Oct. 2013.

Nawale, A.M. ed. *Reflection on Post-independence Indian English Fiction.* New Delhi: Anmol, 2011. Print.

Nityanandan, Indira. "A Search for Identity: *The Thousand Faces of Night*" ed. R.K. Dhawan. *Indian Women Novelists.* Set III. Vol. IV. New Delhi: Prestige, 1995. Print.

Rao, K. Damodar. "Penance as Multiple Response in Githa Hariharan's *The Thousand Face of Night*" ed. R.K. Dhawan. *Indian Women Novelists.* Set III. Vol. IV. New Delhi: Prestige, 1995. Print.

Said, Edward W. *Orientalism. The Post-Colonial Studies Reader.* 2nd ed. Ashcroft, Bill, et al.eds. London: Routledge, 2006. Print.

---.*Culture and Imperialism.* New York: Vintage, 1993. Print.

Singer, Peter. *Marx-A Very Short Introduction.* Oxford: OUP, 1980. Print.

Singh, Anita. "*In Times of Siege*: A Symbolic Declaration of Human Rights." ed.Basavaraj Naikar. *Indian English Literature*. Vol VI. New Delhi: Atlantic, 2007. Print.

Spivak, Gayatri Chakravorty. "Can the Subaltern Speak?" *The Post-Colonial Studies Reader*. 2nd ed. Ashcroft, Bill, et al. eds. London: Routledge, 2006. Print.

Tiwari, R.S. "Feminism and Globalisation versus Indian Women Empowerment."eds. Avasthi, Abha and Srivastava, A.K. *Modernity, Feminism and Women Empowerment*. Delhi: Rawat, 2001. Print.

Tolan, Fiona. "Feminisms". ed. Patricia Waugh. *Literary Theory and Criticism: An Oxford Guide*. Oxford: OUP, 2007. Print.

Tripathi, Shubha. "Voice of Protest and Assertion: A Comparative Study of Githa Hariharan's *The Thousand Faces of Night* and *In Times of Siege*." Binod Mishra. *Critical Responses to Feminism*. New Delhi: Sarup, 2006. Print.

Chapter 2

DECOLONISING THE PSYCHE: *THE THOUSAND FACES OF NIGHT* AND *WHEN DREAMS TRAVEL*

> Am I a writer particularly concerned with "women's issues"? And am I a feminist? The answer to both questions is yes. I want to make it clear that in my life my choices have been dictated by what I perceive as the feminist choice... We can't be wary of the word feminist because there are people in the world who misunderstand the word or have done disservice to the word – you can't use most words then!...however you define yourself, all our work is informed in some way or the other by feminism, along with the ideas of Freud and Marx. And this goes for both men and women, of course…I am a writer (as opposed to a woman writer) who is a feminist, along with several other things!
>
> **Hariharan** *www.anothersubcontinent.com*

In this chapter, an attempt has been made to highlight the power dynamics in the man-woman relationship and reveal the feminist elements reflected in two novels by Hariharan *The Thousand Faces of Night* and *When Dreams Travel*. Feminism has a multifaceted representation in literature which touches almost all paths of life. Its progressive elements are visible in varied forms of literature, fine arts and culture. Feminism has wide ramifications, both in short stories and novels of Hariharan. In modern literature, both in the west and the east, feminism has affected various dimensions of writing in a very interesting manner. It reflects upon women's aspirations, their rights and responsibilities through a new progressive outlook. Hariharan's novels *The Thousand Faces of Night* and *When Dreams Travel* reveal the identity crisis of contemporary Indian women. This chapter reflects Hariharan's attempt to portray the condition of the so-called modern woman in India. Every work of fiction by Hariharan truly manifests seeds of feminism, which are deeply rooted in the philosophical base of her mind.

Hariharan's debut novel *The Thousand Faces of Night* and *When Dreams Travel* endeavour to explore and scrutinise the position of women entrapped in typically male power structures. Her novels depict a cross-cultural view of Indian society. She gives voice to women and through her writing, she portrays the plight of her protagonists in patriarchal society. The narratives describe the suffering, humiliation, and alienation of her women characters. The texts deal with feminist analysis based on culture, identity and power which become a vital part of the narrative. Hariharan's novels reveal the psyche of women who are being suppressed, subjugated and reduced to the position of 'Other.' They showcase the shaping of the feminine psyche and feminist politics by tracing the development of women characters in the light of postcolonial theory because women have been compared with the colonised races.

Postcolonialism encompasses the theories in politics, literature and philosophy which struggle and strive to highlight the ongoing effects of the colonial rule. It lays emphasis on the fact that even after the colonisers have gone and the natives are no longer savage, their domination continues. Though the term postcolonial has been used to represent the continuing process of imperial suppression, women have also been doubly colonised by various forms of patriarchal domination. Men occupy a high pedestal in a patriarchal family and are considered superior to the women. The social and psychological social setup rests on the fact that men are superior in the hierarchy and women occupy the second place. The epics, *Ramayana* and *Mahabharata* also reflect patriarchal ideals through different perspectives. With the establishment of strong patriarchal structures that rest on physical and economic strength, the position of women deteriorated. A brief overview of patriarchy and its effects and the relationship between postcolonialism and feminism would be pertinent here before the texts are taken up for discussion. Women's minds are colonised by patriarchal ideology which continues to influence them and are thus unable to decolonise their thoughts to subvert traditions and become modern.

Hariharan has carefully studied the Indian social system and has depicted the effect of patriarchal power in her novels. Her depiction of patriarchy is based on her vivid social observation and realistic social analysis. Hariharan's novels *The Thousand Faces of Night* and *When Dreams Travel* are novels that advocate feminist ideology. Women have often been marginalised and humiliated not only by the callous patriarchal society but also by the larger colonising forces. Women writers have also been sharing their experiences of oppression and repression in the society through their writings. Their works reflect and create awareness in the society and reflect their humanistic concerns. In her article "I'm not a feminist " Shashi Deshpande, whose views match those of Hariharan, writes:

> I'm not a feminist, I am a human being and I write about other human beings who happen to be women.... it is a slow change, but there has definitely been a change, the change is percolating from the urban society to the rural society and the maxim which still holds true - a woman has to do twice as much to prove herself half as good as a man.(web *www.timesofindia.indiatimes.com*)

Patriarchal societies are created by men but the value systems propagated by them are supposed to be followed and maintained by women. This practice is more prevalent in a traditional culture like ours. De Beauvoir has also pointed out that men make the rules but women are to obey them. Patriarchal power politics prevail in every traditional society and the family is the smallest unit of the power structure. Women's priorities are ignored by men even in their marital relationships. In *The Thousand Faces of Night,* three women Devi, Mayamma and Sita are all caught up in the clutches of patriarchy. The variety of problems that they face in the different situations they are placed in, can be seen in the lives of these women in *The Thousand Faces of Night.*

The deep-rooted relationship between patriarchy and culture is recorded by Hariharan who shows how these women sacrifice their personal interests and desires to maintain marital harmony.

Thus, *The Thousand Faces of Night* is a novel which depicts the traditional chauvinism of men and the exploitation of women in the Indian society. The title of the novel 'The Thousand Faces of Night' is quite significant as it signifies the various facades that women have to assume to play different roles in their lifetime. They undergo various ordeals and have to adjust accordingly. 'Night' is a metaphor for the lives of women and it depicts the journey of women towards the day, i.e., towards a better future. Patriarchy has marginalised Indian women and suppressed them to keep them in a subordinated state. The reflections made by Hariharan are true, realistic and fearless. Her major works register the protest against the patriarchal system and demand social justice for women. The condition of women has often been compared with that of the marginalised colonised races and subalterns. Therefore, the study of women requires a pluralistic critical scanner.

In the 1950's Frantz Fanon, an eminent psychologist recorded and wrote passionately about the suffering of the colonised people. He was fascinated by the psychological effects of colonialism on both the coloniser and the colonised. He argued that colonialism destroyed the soul of the suffering and the repressed native who lost his sense of self and identity. As John McLeod puts it, "In a narrative both inspiring and distressing, Fanon looked at the cost to the individual who lives in a world where due to the colour of his or her skin, he or she is rendered peculiar, an object of derision, an aberration." (*Beginning* 20) The colonisers are considered to be civilised, rational and intelligent while the 'Negro' remains 'other' to all these qualities and thus attains an inferior status. They are never accepted at par with their colonisers. This theory can be applied in Hariharan's novel *The Thousand Faces of Night* by replacing the negro with the woman protagonists.

While Fanon explores the psychological effect of colonisation on the psyche of a nation, Said contributes to the theory with his celebrated book *Orientalism* (1978). 'Orientalism' is the European construction of the East as primitive, savage, pagan, undeveloped and criminal. Europe, on the other hand, is developed, Christian and civilised. Said emphasises on the marginality of the East vis-a-vis the West and states, "The nations of contemporary Asia, Latin America, and Africa are politically independent but in many ways are as dominated and dependent as they were when ruled directly by European powers" (*Culture* 20). John McLeod opines

> What critics learned from the work of people like Fanon and Said was the simultaneously candid and complex fact the Empires colonise imaginations ... Overturning colonialism, then, is not just about handing land back to its dispossessed peoples, returning power to those who were once ruled by Empire. It is also a process of overturning the dominant ways which do not replicate colonialist values. If colonialism involves colonising the mind, then resistance to it requires, in Ngugi's phrase, 'decolonising the mind.'(qtd. in *Beginning* 22)

The condition of women can be likened to that of the East in *Orientalism* and hence the need for women to decolonise themselves. In her influential article, "Under Western Eyes" Chandra Talpade Mohanty presents a picture of 'the production of the "Third World Woman" as a singular monolithic subject.' She demonstrates the ways in which such Western scholarship classifies the women of the Third World as a homogeneous group. As Mohanty opines:

> ... a homogeneous notion of the oppression of women as a group is assumed, which, in turn, produces the image of an 'average third world woman.' This average third world woman leads an essentially truncated life based on her feminine gender (read: sexually constrained) and being 'third world'(read: ignorant, poor, uneducated, tradition-bound, domestic, family-oriented, victimized, etc.) This, I suggest, is in contrast to the (implicit) self-representation of Western women as educated, modern, as having control over their own bodies and sexualities, and the freedom to make their own decisions. (*Post-Colonial* 243)

The women characters in Hariharan's novels undergo and experience the oppression like that of the third world women. They are bound by traditions and are victims of their colonisers. The theories of feminism and postcolonialism enable us to understand that gender inequality is not natural, it is cultivated, rather there are many varied voices within feminism that bring out the effect of power relations in creating man as the subject and woman as the 'other.' Both the theories are interdisciplinary. Feminism undertakes to analyse the effects of power relations in the social, economic and cultural spheres of life. Hariharan refers to her various identities in "Discrete Thoughts":

> To some extent, it would seem as if my roles as a novelist and an activist have been fused in the public's perception but deciding which role is more important to me is a little like deciding whether I write as an Indian or as a woman or an activist or a mother. Let me just say that I have a welter of identities and my day-to-day life is all about maintaining an equilibrium - so that I can function as a single, if complicated entity. How can I say which is more important to me - my arm or my leg? (*Desert* 215)

Besides being a writer, she is an activist, an Indian woman - a mother and to maintain a balance in the midst of all these is not easy. She finds it difficult to decide which role is more or less important.

The Thousand Faces of Night primarily highlights the ways in which Hariharan showcases gender, identity and sexuality and its effects on the lives of women. The novel analyses how women in the novel resemble the image of the ideal woman in the Indian social context. Hariharan has lived through the experience of inhabiting a patriarchal Hindu society, she is strongly feminist in her views and she severely critiques the patriarchal power structure of society. Her novel portrays the inner recesses of a woman's psyche, and it reflects how Devi manages to maintain freedom psychologically, economically and physically despite living in a traditional setup.

Hariharan is deeply interested in Hindu mythology and shows a fascination with the epics, the *Ramayana* and the *Mahabharata*, the folktales of India and of Arabia, and many other stories which she uses in her description of the contemporary situation. Both her novels *The Thousand Faces of Night* and *When Dreams Travel* are based on the traditional mythological tales that makes her work different from other writers. She makes use of a great deal of intertextuality in these novels. As Allen Graham puts it, "Intertextuality seems such a useful term because it foregrounds notions of relationality, interconnectedness and interdependence in modern cultural life." (*Intertextuality* 5) Every text has a meaning in relation to other texts and provides a new meaning and vision to it. It subverts fantasy to show the reality with a new dimension. Adrienne Rich described women's writings as re-vision. Re-vision, as Rich defines, is an act of going back to an old text from a new critical tradition. She articulates in her essay "When We Dead Awaken: Writing as Revision":

> Re-vision-the act of looking back, of seeing with fresh eyes, of entering an old text from a new critical direction-is for us more than a chapter in cultural history: it is an act of survival. Until we can understand the assumptions in which we are drenched we cannot know ourselves. And this drive to self-knowledge, for woman, is more than a search for identity: it is part of her refusal of the self-destructiveness of male-dominated society. (*College* 18)

Revisionist myth-making is one of the vital strategies taken up for the liberation of women. Subversion is a technique used for the assessment and feminist re-writing of the old texts. It is through this act of revision that women can make a place in the society, not only as submissive individuals but also being able to express themselves freely. Women writers should subvert the tradition set by the male writers and should create their own. As Rich puts it, "We need to know the writing of the past, and know it differently than we have ever known it; not to pass on a tradition but to break its hold over us." (*College* 19)

Hariharan makes a suitable, revisionary reading of the religious texts of Hinduism and applies them in her novels to the contemporary situations on the lives of women. Indian novelists have often been using Myths in their writings to strengthen the structure of their ideas. The term 'Myth' used in English is derived from the Greek word 'Muthos' which means 'Word' or 'Speech'. According to M.H.Abrams, it is a system of "Hereditary stories which were once believed to be true by a particular cultural group and which served to explain why the world is as it is and things happen as they do to provide a rationale for social customs and observances." (*Glossary* 170)

Myths have a unique place and importance in the traditional Indian families because stories are usually verbally and orally narrated from one generation to another in order to "establish the sanctions for the rules by which people conduct their lives."(*Glossary* 170) Hariharan is well acquainted with these myths and she perfectly intermingles the myth and reality to depict the modern Indian life. Hariharan's novel *The Thousand Faces of Night* abounds with examples of the writers strong awareness of the need for retelling mythology from a feminist perspective. Hariharan looks at these myths through a modern, educated woman's perspective. The patriarchal archetypes in these myths are being challenged by Hariharan in *The Thousand Faces of Night*. *Mahabharata* and *Ramayana* abound with many women characters. Both these epics bring out the male power structures in the society. Hindu Mythology presents women in the ideal traditional manner as submissive, dependent and subordinate to the family.

For ages, the Indian culture has been aping the model presented by the epics. There are many women characters in mythology but 'Sita' in *Ramayana* is regarded as the perfect role model. In Hindu Mythology, the ideal woman is 'Sita' because she is considered to be submissive and obedient to her husband. Wendy Doniger calls Sita the 'official role model' for Indian women and laments, "How different the lives of the actual women in India would have been had Draupadi, instead of Sita, been their official role model! Many Hindus name their daughters Sita, but few name them Draupadi."(*Hindus* 298) As Draupadi is considered an aggressive and defiant character in Hindu mythology, no one in the patriarchal society chooses to name their daughter Draupadi. Rosemary M. George discusses Indian novels that deal with the theme of the search for a feminine self in the midst of a domestic crisis of some sort. She writes of the women protagonists:

> What [they] desire remains undefined and elusive...And yet one can gather that it is a desire for something more than mere material comforts. It is the desire for an imagined self and setting that allows escape from the mundane domestic routine of everyday life and from the usual alternative that a more public life (as working woman or as a socially committed public figure) would provide.(*Politics* 133)

Hariharan talks about ancient Indian myths and turns her work into the restoration of the long lost old tradition. She portrays the struggle of women for survival and self-liberation by weaving texts within the main text and the intertextual narration includes the various mythological stories. Devi in *The Thousand Faces of Night* discusses the importance of mythological stories narrated by her grandmother as,

> My grandmother's stories were no ordinary bedtime stories. She chose each for a particular occasion, a story in reply to each of my childish questions. She had an answer for every question. But her answers were not simple: they had to be decoded. A comparison had to be made, an illustration discovered, and a moral drawn out. (27)

The Thousand Faces of Night is the story of Devi, Sita and Mayamma and it describes how they fare in the journey of the decolonisation of their psyche. The novel abounds in sexual and marital experiences of these women, their emotional turmoil which leads to gradual self-discovery. Self-realisation comes after self-discovery and it is an expression used in psychology and spirituality which denotes that every individual has an inner self which can only be discovered through spiritual self-striving. A person has to accept one's inner self and release it from all inhibitions, mental pressures, fears, desires, etc. in order to understand one's true self. In the era of globalisation, women are still suffering more in a country like India as a result of the impact of traditional ideas and orthodox norms. Hariharan's main focus is on the woman's struggle to release herself from the rigid social structure in which she is perpetually suffering. Hariharan narrates the story of Devi which is intermingled with the experiences related to Sita's and Mayamma's personal lives as well. Hariharan traces the struggle of women in their relationship with man and society, which has reduced them to the status of the subaltern. The main focus is on Devi, the protagonist who undergoes an identity crisis and finally attains intellectual self-realisation. Dr.Sarabjit Kaur opines:

> The novel represents a variety of female characters, mythological as well as real undergoing agony in consequence of their desires and ambitions. These characters are fighting the idea of "an ideal woman"

> which is demanded of them as wives, mothers and daughters-in-law. Hariharan critiques the patriarchal power structure of the Hindu society through these contemporary women. She also shows the reader the position of Indian women in the traditions and culture of this male-dominated society.

Hariharan portrays a true picture of Indian woman to reveal her pathetic plight and to unleash the harsh and truthful realities of her existence. The novel *The Thousand Faces of Night* showcases couples living and adjusting with each other in the rigid institution of marriage in Indian society. Marriage, for them, is a social obligation, a necessity and therefore desirable and inevitable. However, it does not consider love, sentiments and emotions as its essential ingredients. It highlights how a wife is bound to take care of her husband and his family, who in turn have almost no duty or obligation towards her except for accommodating her in the family which she is expected to serve. Hariharan shows that the situation remains unchanged even for an educated woman who has been residing abroad as it was for an educated or uneducated housewife of earlier generations.

The Thousand Faces of Night is based on a traditional structure. Hariharan portrays the images of 'good' and 'bad' women as defined in the Indian social setup. Hariharan's characters are caught between the traditional and modern values and strive to come out of this dilemma of choosing the right path. She tells us the story of five women - Devi, Sita, Pati, Parvatiamma and Mayamma. The novel also comments upon the lives of the mythological female characters, like Sita, Amba, Gandhari, Ganga, Gauri although they belong to the ancient period. Besides this, the women undergo the quest for identity and share their unfulfilled ambitions and emotions. The traditional and contemporary working women are intermingled with the mythological stories. However, Devi does not follow the lessons of these mythologies in a blindfolded manner, rather she tries to interpret the morals of these stories in her own way.

The novel portrays the life of a foreign-returned young girl Devi, her artistic mother Sita and an old caretaker Mayamma. Hariharan blends together the lives of these three women characters to present a picture of the pathetic lives that Indian women lead. Mayamma the old caretaker, and also a cook at Mahesh's house has been living all her life trying to make others happy. She was married at an early age of twelve to a gambler and a useless person who came to her every night, "Her husband woke her up every night, his large, hairy thighs rough and heavy on her, pushing, pushing."(80) Her experience of marriage was unhappy. She had to undergo the wrath of her mother-in-law for not being able to bear any children. She did penance to change her fate, by praying and invoking the names of various gods and goddesses:

> She woke up at four in the morning....She prayed, made vows, dipped herself again and again in the pure coldness. She starved every other day,...She meditated for hours before a pan of clear water ....She fed the snakes her rice and curds, she bathed the all-conquering lingam with sandalwood, milk, and her tears of ardour...She invoked every day the goddess' thousand names; five hundred times she prostrated herself at the feet of the ever-fertile mother. Every six months she renewed her vows; every six months she invited six Brahmins to a feast, and sent them away with the richest gifts she could lay her hands on.(80-81)

Mayamma has learned the art of survival painfully and slowly by accepting what life brings as her destiny. The basic theme of survival is introduced in the Prelude. Devi asks Mayamma, "why she had put up with her life?" Surprisingly the old woman had laughed and said, "'I can see that you are still a child"', she said. She talks of her own tolerance and forbearance, "'When I lost my first baby, conceived after ten years of longing and fear, I screamed, for the only time in my life, Why?'"(vii) The doctor remarked that women must bear pain and attributed her pain to the sins of her previous birth and her mother-in-law had condemned her as a barren witch and had rebuked her for having questioned why the baby born after ten years had died, "The barren witch has killed my grandson, and she lies there asking us why!" (viii) Whatever adverse happens in her life is the outcome of the weak woman's fault. The 'Prelude' thus sets the stage for the psychological development of the protagonist. Mayamma undergoes humiliation at the hands of her mother-in-law for her inability to conceive a child which is highlighted in the narrative. "No, no, Maya. No rice for you today. It's Friday. No rice today, no vegetables tomorrow, no tamarind the day after. Stop thinking of food, daughter-in-law, think of your womb. Think of your empty, rotting womb and pray."(114) This brings us to the unfortunate dilemma which all women must suffer in spite of the modernisation and sophistication of contemporary society. An America returned Devi undergoes the same humiliation that Mayamma an illiterate, ignorant village woman had done a few decades ago.

Mayamma has to deal with a cold and unsympathetic kind of attitude and also the ill treatment from her mother-in-law for no fault of hers. The punishment given to her for not being able to conceive a child is too harsh and pitiless for her to bear. The birth of her son worsens her condition because the son behaves in a shocking way. He hits Mayamma with an iron frying pan for refusing to part with her diamond ring. She faces a life full of struggle and only gets solace in her middle age when she is given an accommodation in Mahesh's house. She is a dutiful daughter-in-law who harbours no grudges against her mother-in-law though she has been humiliating her severely. She rather serves her mother-in-law wholeheartedly even when she is on the verge of death. Her experiences in life make her realise that nothing lasts forever in one's life and that life has to be lived as it comes and it takes its own course.

Devi had gone to America for higher studies where she fell in love with a Black American Dan. However, she refused his proposal for marriage and returned to India for the sake of her widowed mother, Sita. Devi gets into the cocoon of her mother's love and concern when she comes back. In order to make her only daughter Devi settle down, Sita decides to arrange her marriage through *swayamvara.* Though Devi is not ready to tie the nuptial knot, she only agrees to do so for the sake of her mother. She recollects the story of Damyanthi which was narrated to her by her grandmother. Damyanthi's father had arranged a *swayamwara* for his daughter. Damyanthi was quite daring and determined to espouse Nala. So she selects Nala and puts the garland around his neck in spite of all intrigues made by Gods. Devi's grandmother narrates the story to her with the moral, "Because a woman gets her heart's desire by great cunning."(20) Inspired by the story of Nala-Damayanthi, Devi marries Mahesh, a Regional Manager in a multinational company and tries to adjust and fit into the role of a wife and daughter-in-law just as her mother had done years ago, but cannot do so without a sense of frustration. She observes:

> ...this then is marriage, the end of ends, two or three brief encounters a month when bodies stutter together in lazy, inarticulate lust. Two weeks a month when the shadowy stranger who casually strips me of my name, snaps his fingers and demands a smiling handmaiden. And the rest? It is waiting, all over again, for life to begin, or to end and begin again.(54)

The huge, vacant, ancestral house, surrounded by a big, wild garden becomes the centre point of her existence. Her husband behaves like a shadowy stranger, who is always busy with tours. Marriage, for him, is just another necessity. Devi feels that she is an educated, modern girl and is not prepared to accept and succumb to "the vast, yawning chapters of her womanhood."(54) Whenever she expresses her wish to do something that she really desires, like taking up a job or learning to play cards, Mahesh's disapproval is expressed only through his gesture of moving his lips inwards and she says this "weaves a running cord around her vulnerable neck."(56) In an Indian social background, whether it is Maya or Devi – a childless woman loses her right to rule the home. Devi is at this critical juncture where the neglect of her husband almost drives her to desperation. She is alone in the house with Mayamma, the old housekeeper, and Baba's books after his departure for New York. Devi finds herself overwhelmed with a sense of loneliness and futility. She feels that her freedom is threatened and seeks solace and refuge in the stories of Baba, her gentle father-in-law, and in his sweet wisdom. Devi's efforts to become a traditional and idealistic wife get shattered by Mahesh's indifference and his reserved attitude towards love and marriage. But her education helps her to brace herself up to face the situation and does not allow her to succumb to the pressure of her circumstances. She does not conform to the system but does not accept it either.

Devi's grandmother narrates the mythical story of Amba to help Devi to fight against injustices and discrimination. It is the story of the *swayamvara* of three princesses of Kashi - Amba, Ambika and Ambalika. Amba, the eldest daughter, chooses King Salwa and garlands him. Suddenly Bheeshma abducts all the princesses for his brothers but when Amba discloses her marriage, she is sent back to King Salwa. Now the king refuses to accept her as a wife and insults her by saying, ""Do you think I feast on leftovers? I am a king. I do not touch what another man has won in battle. Go to Bheeshma. He won you when his arrow struck my eager hands on your luckless garland. He is your husband. What have you to do with me?"" (37) But as she goes back to Bheeshma, he also sends her away because of his avowed celibacy. '"Bheeshma trembled with desire, but he had spent his youth building thick walls of masculine deafness around himself. The echo that sent a tremor along his spine was, however moving, muffled. He sent Amba away, his face safely averted."'(38) Through the story, Hariharan makes the readers aware of the present condition of women and how they are treated as puppets by men. But the second half of the story asserts that a woman alone can avenge her destroyers. Hearing the story, Devi also learns that "A woman fights her battles alone" (36) through courage and will power.

Devi's inability to conceive becomes a vital reason for her development as an individual. She does not get stuck in social barriers like Mayamma but shuns the traditions. She moves ahead to liberate herself and finds solace in the relationship with Gopal. Her elopement with Gopal is the evidence of her revolt and her urge to lead a carefree life. Her name Devi also symbolises creativity but she does not devote her inner potential to giving birth and bringing up children, rather she leads a free life and gives herself ample opportunities to fulfil her dreams. As S. Indira writes in the essay "Walking the Tight Rope: A Reading of Githa Hariharan's *The Thousand Faces of Night*:"

> Encouraged by this act of rebellion, Devi tunes herself to the "blissful numbness" of Gopal's music, which opens a way out of the "lush prison" (78) around her. She cannot condemn herself to the abject existence like that of Mayamma, a battered wife and mother who suffered at the hands of a domineering mother-in-law and animal-like husband and son. Women like Mayamma continue to sacrifice and live a tortured, humiliating life because they have no option, no way out. Bleeding within, seeking solace in the routine of life and religious worship, they go on. (*Indian* 179)

Sita, Devi's mother, is seen as a cool, self-confident, middle-aged, strong woman. Though she is not attractive physically, her skill of playing the *veena* earns her a good position in her husband's family. She is a woman of conviction and discipline. In the novel, she is compared to Gandhari who played a significant role in *Mahabharata*. Gandhari is married to a very rich prince, whose Palace is double the size and more magnificent than her father's palace. "'The palace Gandhari was now to rule as queen was twice as big, twice as magnificent as her parents' palace. Priceless gems, the size of ripe pumpkins, hung at the tips of chandeliers; the marble pillars shone like mirrors.'"(28) But on meeting her husband for the first time in such a lavish palace, she is taken aback by "the White eyes, the pupils glazed and useless."(29) Gandhari in anger vows never to see the world again when she was married to Dhritarashtra who was blind. Summing up the story Devi's grandmother says: "she embraced her destiny - a blind husband - with a self-sacrifice worthy of her royal blood."(29) This story teaches Devi more lessons of life and she ruminates, "The lesson brought me five steps close to adulthood. I saw for the first time that my parents too were afflicted by a kind of blindness. In their blinkered world, they would always be one, one leading the other, one hand always in the grasp of another."(29)

Gandhari's story resembles the life of Sita, Devi's mother who is compared to the mythological character of Gandhari by her mother-in-law. She is a personification of Gandhari as she too excels in self-sacrifice and discipline. She is expected to give up her personal hobbies and desires and remain busy in the service of her family. Later on, she realises that the patriarchal order gives secondary importance to a woman's hobbies and the domestic work becomes a priority in her life. In the novel, she says that she is a wife and daughter-in-law. The novelist further describes Sita's feeling in an effective dialogue, when she points out, "A housewife should always be joyous, adept at domestic work, neat in her domestic wares, and restrained in expenses. Controlled in mind, word, and body, she who doesn't transgress her attains heaven even as her lord does."(70-71)

Sita loved to play the *veena* and could do it skillfully. When she marries, she takes the *veena* along and continues to practice it daily. However, one day she gets lost in the music of the *veena* and her house work gets neglected and delayed. Her father-in-law is quite upset and rebukes her, "put that *veena* away. Are you a wife, a daughter-in-law?" (30) Sita snaps "in a discordant twang of protest" (30) the strings of her *veena* in shock and disappointment and she swears never to touch it again though she used to play it with perfection in "rapturous flight."(30) Thereafter, she became a "perfect housekeeper, a blameless wife."(101) It is actually the women like Sita who make painful sacrifices to become ideal wives or mothers. Devi too understands the plight of Sita who sacrificed her first love, i.e., the *veena*, along with her dreams of achieving name and fame. Although her position is much better than that of Mayamma, she too, has to undergo pain and suffering all these years of her life being deprived of her favourite pastime. It is only years after when her husband dies that she is able to lead an independent life and enjoy her hobbies of gardening and playing the *veena*. There is a reference to the horizontal growth of the Jasmine creeper in her garden which can also be co-related to the condition of women who are not allowed to grow upwards as per their nature. Sita's sacrifices are made without complaints and she swallows bitter pills of life in silence. Clinging to womanhood comes to her naturally:

> Sita went into labour without a twitch on her dark face; she remained impassive, a model patient, during a childbirth the doctor claimed was the easiest she had ever seen. The minute the baby was laid in her arms, free of the umbilical cord, Sita refused to let any of the nurses

> touch her. She had found a new veena to play on, and this time she was not going to give it up so easily. (104)

As Foucault has pointed out about the normalisation process of power, in the case of women, it is normal to be submissive in a patriarchal power structure. While bringing up Devi, Sita becomes a strict and disciplined mother. She warmly welcomes her daughter when she returns from U.S. and only after a month, plans and prepares a *swayamwara* for her daughter. Devi scrutinizes the lives of these elder women and revisits the stories of women from Indian mythology. She also hears different stories from her grandmother Pati, Father-in-law Baba and Mayamma which add to and affect her growth as an individual. The stories of mythical figures like Gandhari, Damyanti, Amba, Ganga and the devoted wife of the snake husband enlighten her mind about the women who had endured so much for the sake of keeping their marriages intact. The situations affect and disturb her mind deeply. She links all the mythological stories to the contemporary times, i.e., the heroines of yesteryears are linked with the contemporary women. Some streaks of Gandhari's personality are reflected in Sita. Gandhari blindfolds her eyes when she discovers her husband's blindness which is very much like Sita's self-abnegation when she pulls the strings of the *veena* and swears never to touch them again. These women face their fate with bitter acceptance. Amba changes her fate and hatred for Bheeshma who has wronged her and turns feminine fulfillment into sweet revenge and glorious triumph. Devi feels that she too must protest, act and do something subversive like the mythological heroines she grew up with.

Devi, as a woman, is defined as negative as opposed to the man who is positive. As an object of fantasy who occupies the place of the 'Other', she is mystified as the object of male desire. Hindu mythology has created multifaceted goddesses, dichotomizing them into the creative and the terrible - so that men adore mothers but demean other women. Goddesses are one form of primal energy among many. Both men and women have been devotees of the goddesses in India. However, Devi specifically signifies the spouse of Siva, who is the combination of both the ferocious and the sublime. It is only Devi - whether benevolent or cruel - who has a unique and independent personality among the goddesses. Thus, Hariharan gives a symbolic significance to her name, she is a woman who looks for her identity, breaking the social barriers, which try to curtail her personality. Her father-in-law, Baba, keeps her good company with his taste for music whenever Mahesh is on his business tour. Baba also talks about the duty of woman in Hindu dharma and reminds Devi of her grandma, Parvatiamma,

> The path a woman must walk to reach heaven,' says Baba, 'is a clear, well-lit one. The woman has no independent sacrifice to perform, no vow, no fasting; by serving her husband, she is honoured in the heavens. On the death of her husband, the chaste wife, established in continence, reaches heaven, even if childless, like students who have practised self control.'"(55)

Baba quotes Manu, the second century B.C. encoder of Hindu customs and duties, whose patriarchal dictates were markedly anti-women. Baba teaches Devi about Brahminhood and quotes from Manu, "" A Brahmin...shrinks from honours as from poison; humility he covets as if it is nectar. The humble one sleeps happily, wakes up happily, and moves about in this world happily; he who has inflicted the humiliation perishes"" (52). His stories are a contrast to Parvatiamma's, and now Devi dreams of becoming a "*kritya*, a ferocious woman who haunts and destroys the house in which women are insulted. She burns with anger, she spits fire. She sets the world ablaze like Kali shouting in hunger. Each age has its *kritya*...each household shelters a *kritya*"(69-70).

In order to keep women confined and suppressed, old conservative values and ideas have been propagated by the male world and women are forced to practise and keep these ideologies alive. e.g., Parvatiamma, Devi's mother-in-law, a woman of rare beauty was married at an early age. When Mayamma was homeless, she even provided her shelter. Parvatiamma was a simple woman who began to "spend more and more time in the puja room" (63) doing puja and singing bhajans. But one day, she leaves her husband's house never to return again. Baba observes, ""She has made her choice. For a woman who leaves her home in search of a god, only death is a home-coming.""(64) Lakshmiamma, the widowed aunt, close to seventy, lives "alone in a corner of the dilapidated little family house in the *agraharam.*"(125) Parvatiamma's story captures Devi's thoughts as also the mythical tale of Amba. She is fascinated with this ultimate fantasy: "a woman avenger who could earn manhood through her penance."(39-40) All the myths and women that have passed through her life come together in her dreams saying:

> Like Sati you must burn yourself to death, like Sati you must vindicate your husband's honour and manhood.
>
> Like Parvati you must stand neck-deep in cold, turbulent
>
> waters, the hungry, predatory fish devouring your feet.
>
> Like Haimavati you must turn that black skin on your sinful body into a golden sheen of light and beauty. (94)

These are the lessons she has grown up with. Devi is filled with fury when she is expected to forget her hard-earned education and follow her husband's dictates.

Mahesh, eager to see his wife take responsibility of his home, disapproves of Devi's spending so much time with Baba and Mayamma. He discovers one day that she has been reading in one of Baba's books about "a *kritya*". He asks with irritation, '"did your mother need books to tell her how to be a wife? I have never met a woman more efficient than your mother"' (70) and blames Devi's education for her waywardness and discontent. He keeps comparing her unfavourably with her mother, her grandmother and his colleagues' wives who appear more cheerful and efficient, '"This is what comes of educating a woman. Your grandmother was barely literate. Wasn't she a happier woman than you are? What is it you want?"' (74) On another occasion, he pointedly praises his junior colleague Ashok's wife Tara, '"She keeps herself busy but has enough time for her children,'... 'I have never seen such well-behaved children before. Lucky Ashok!"'(56)

Devi is caught between tradition and modernity, loneliness and hollowness. She feels that she is only confined to her house, she yearns to live a free and passionate life and not remain a neglected wife. Condemning Mahesh to a lonely life without wife or child for trampling on the marital vows, Devi goes away with Gopal. She has a feeling of discovering herself through music, which is a powerful medium to express oneself. Her elopement with Gopal, as Hariharan articulates in an interview with Prema Vishwanath, in itself is "a non-conformist mode of spiritual expression." (web *www*. indianexpress.com) In the male-dominated society, women often feel exploited and crushed under the pressure of sexual fulfillment or nurturing and bearing of children. They are not given the opportunity to think or take decisions independently. Devi's extra-marital relationship with Gopal makes us aware of the changed socio-cultural value patterns. K. Damodar Rao opines:

> The act of walking out on Mahesh provides substance to her life and she considers it her 'first real journey.'...as she herself predicts, the affair with Gopal proves to be a short one. He is a flirt with aspirations for an aristocratic way of life. Devi gets disillusioned with him and moves once again...Her life has come full circle with Devi choosing to come back to her mother to begin her life afresh... (*Indian* 168)

Thus, Devi realises that she has been running away from the real track - her American experience, the house on Jacaranda Road, trying to find solace in her relationships with Mahesh and Gopal throughout her life were all methods of escaping reality. She has had enough of drifting between worlds and should find her own authentic "self" now and secure a firm holding to be at peace with her own self. The quest for self-realisation, self-fulfillment and self-identity is strong urge in the modern urban woman which is reflected through the character of Devi. Devi retrospects over the lives of the three women Mayamma, Sita and herself and feels that they have had enough and it's time they stand up for themselves freely with all their dignity without any appendages. As S. Indira writes:

> In a symbolic gesture, Devi throws her peacock-coloured Sari over the mirror to blot out the myriad reflections of herself. She is no more a

> reflection, no longer on the run. She is a survivor now, bent on to become a conqueror. She goes back home to join her mother with an offer of love. And to her surprise, Devi finds her mother's garden "wild and over-grown," not pruned anymore but "lush in spite of its sand-choked roots," and hears the "faint sounds of the veena, hesitant and child-like"(139) welcoming her into the house. (*Indian* 181)

Her mother's warm gesture is a clear indication to Devi that their battle has begun all over again to free the sand-choked roots and to be true to their own "selves", thus ushering in a new beginning. The novel creates a new paradigm for the recreation of a woman's identity. Hariharan's idea behind making and naming the protagonist 'Devi' is to reinforce in a woman the realisation about her inherent powers. Devi represents an Indian goddess who possesses superpower and is strong. Sita proves to be a strong-willed individual who is extremely intelligent and very capable. Devi's grandmother interweaves the tales of ordinary women, Sita, Uma, Gauri and Devi - with mythological heroines, which work as a bridge between the past and the present. Hariharan quotes the Kannada *vachana* by Devara Dasimayya (A.K.Ramanujan's translation) to demonstrate the futility of the feud between the sexes:

> Suppose you cut a tall bamboo
> in two;
> make the bottom piece a woman,
> the head piece a man;
> rub them together
> till they kindle:
> tell me now,
> the fire that's born,
> Is it male or female,
> O Ramanatha? (vi)

Hence, "Devi becomes "Devi" the androgynous principle," articulates Rama Nair " - neither male nor female - but a self in quest of self-hood. Devi, the goddess is *sakti, prakriti* and *maya.* She is portrayed as an overwhelming presence that suffuses the world with vitality, energy and power." (*Indian* 175) Hariharan exemplifies the fact that both male and female are complementary to each other. Devi is a symbol of sublime, power and independence. It is actually the beginning of not only the physical or environmental freedom but freedom of the mind from the age-old customs, beliefs, mental and psychological barriers. Hariharan rewrites Hindu myths to combine revisionism, with a *bildungsroman* plot structure. Hariharan, through her vivid and powerful invocation of stories and women characters from the classical past, attempts to interrupt and redouble Devi's narrative in order to highlight the long history of gender war within Brahminism. Hariharan, in an interview with Joel Kuortti, stated:

> I stumbled onto the idea of the normative myth the kind that tells you what sort of wife you should be, what sort of daughter-in-law and so forth. Of course, once you get onto the normative myth you have to look at the other side of the coin, the subversive myth, the survival teaching myth. (...) In a sense it was unlearning the canon that had been fed to me in college, and relearning these myths and tales so I could twist them for my own purposes.

Women in Indian society have always lived under the protection of husband or children and felt safer in these confined relationships. This confinement has resulted in the dependence of women, on men, whether it is Mayamma, Parvatiamma, Lakshmiamma or any other woman. They have been the victims and losers at the hands of the patriarchal powers. Hariharan's women characters are trapped between traditions, old values, myths and modernity and have become the victims of gross gender discrimination in the male-dominated society. As Baba, Devi's father-in-law says, "The housewife should always be joyous adept at domestic work, neat in her domestic wares and restrained in expenses. Controlled in mind, word and body, she who does not transgress her lord, attains heaven even as her lord does." (71)

Hariharan has described the dilemma of the contemporary Indian woman who is torn between the poles of tradition and modernity. Feminism is generally based on protest and revolt against the established orders. It has been observed, that "Devi internalizes all the pains borne by Sita, Mayamma and Parvatiamma and finally revolts against the social institution of marriage. This was her way of turning the contradictions of life upside down. Hariharan has portrayed Devi's rebellion against the system with a feminist passion. She wants to represent the struggle of women who are in transition from tradition to modernity. Devi faces an identity crisis after following the rules laid down by the Indian patriarchal society. She undergoes the dilemma of making a choice between the traditional and modern. The predicament of Devi is the result of the intermingling of western and eastern cultures and the tussle between the mind (knowledge) and the heart (true knowledge). The major decision to be taken is that of being a good girl or a bad girl. The novel takes us down the lane of Devi's memory, her grandmother's house where this conflict got initiated in her mind. Good virtues and behaviour were put in Devi's mind in her ancestral house. The identity crisis becomes significantly evident in the character of Devi who tries to assess her own situation in the light of the stories of the women who surround her. She realises that each has her own story to tell. Each story teaches her the lessons of patience, forbearance, endurance and the identification of survival tactics by women. She ultimately survives through revolt, unlike the lesser educated women who are taught to comply. She realises that she must assert herself and not allow others to rule over her life. She does not want to maintain the silence that her mother had adopted. Given a choice, Sita too would have been adamant and assertive but the times were not ripe for her or any other woman to protest and lead an independent life.

Hariharan's other text that takes up feminist issues extensively is *When Dreams Travel.* It also deals with the decolonisation of the woman's mind. Hariharan uses the old story of *The Arabian Nights* as an inter-text. She finds this useful for her metafictional schemata. Seen through the angle of modern fiction theory, this double fiction appears to be a story about storytelling. *When Dreams Travel* envisions Shahrzad as the helpless woman caught in an orthodox and patriarchal scheme, who must survive only by means of her consummate storytelling skill. She is the frenzied and compulsive storyteller, imprisoned in the harem during the day, at night in the dungeon of a lecherous, chauvinistic, powerful patriarch. In the grim nuptial bed of the palace dungeon, which reeks of blood, sweat, semen and death of the long line of previous brides raped in the dark and killed at dawn she is forced to create and procreate too in the meantime at sword point. It is with reference to this context that one can understand the feminist-cum-metafictional suggestions implicit in the symbols of palace mausoleum dungeon, bed-harem, and sword blood as the author uses them elaborately in the novel.

Hariharan brings to light a wide range of stories from the medieval to the contemporary times. The famous *The Thousand and One Nights* comprise stories and folktales from the Middle East and South Asia. These tales were compiled in the Golden Age of Islam in the Arabic language. The text is popularly known as *The Arabian Nights* in the English language. The tales have their origin in the ancient and medieval Arabic, Persian, Indian, Turkish, Egyptian and Mesopotamian folklore and literature. The world famous *The Thousand and One Nights* is a typical story within another story abounding in adventure, romances, fables, etc. The frame story is based in ancient Sanskrit literature which made its way into Persian and Arabic literature through the *Panchatantra*. The things which remained suppressed in the original text of *The Arabian Nights* are also foregrounded in the novel. The readers are made to realise the hardcore reality of the new bride and the kind of suffering she undergoes in the patriarchal setup. Hariharan cleverly raises the questions as to how Shahrzad could have such a wide store of knowledge and stories and how she could manage to survive for so long in a world that denied so much to women.

When Dreams Travel presents the popular legendary tale of *The Thousand and One Nights* with a changed design, outlook and narrative which is in some ways different from the source text. Hariharan takes up the challenge to re-explore the marginalised and suppressed female characters and their backgrounds. Rustam Brahma opines,

> Hariharan's *When Dreams Travel* has been a strong feminist critique of the traditional concept of women as mere lustful and traitor or cuckolds, child bearing machine, an object of man's desire, an object of

> use and throw, established by *Arabian Nights*, that has led patriarchal society to disrespect and devalue them in the society. (183)

When Dreams Travel is a sinuous labyrinth of tales, a novel which is beautifully written and narrated in an interesting manner. It is a novel about storytelling as well as storytellers. It is a novel of mystery and suspense which keeps shuffling from reality to the world of fantasy. The whole story revolves around Dunyazad's journey to find out the reason behind her sister's unknown death or perhaps her mysterious disappearance. The narrative technique is similar in both *When Dreams Travel* and *The Thousand and One Nights*. The novel also contains a frame tale and embedded stories like *The Thousand and One Nights*. For example, the mainframe tale is the story of Dunyazad trying to find out what happened to her sister Shahrzad and the embedded stories are different in *When Dreams Travel*. In *The Thousand and One Night* they are told to gain time but in *When Dreams Travel* they are told to unravel the mystery of Shahrzad's death, as it is said in the novel "Will these storytellers be able to resurrect Shahrzad? Persue the fourth player in the room to put down that mirror, come back to life, open her mouth and answer their question? (118) This clearly shows the change in storytelling. Here the storytelling is not done in a life-threatening situation but in a problem-solving manner.

In Hariharan's novel, Dunyazad is said to have explored many lands, "She too can lead an expedition, sometimes more than one, every night to lands beyond seas and mountains - China, Africa, India. Dunyazad savours the names before they slip off her tongue. The names are charms at the head of vivid scenes, harbours, palaces, hovels, cluttered markets."(23) The frame story includes the Far East, Middle East and South Asia which are quite clearly mentioned. Hariharan writes in the novel:

> The city is in the clutches of the dream... from this distance the city is nameless. Or its hushed, remote appearance, its muted suggestion of opulence and ruin, beauty and decay, conjure a range of identities. Samarkand, Basra, Isfahan. A city that can, if it desires, elude the moorings of dates and milestones. Alexandria, Ctesiphon, Baghdad. It

> is difficult to pin a single name on it, locate this mirage-city on a coded map. (29)

The story of Sultan Shahryar of Shahabad and his younger brother Shahzaman, ruler of Samarkand form the basis of the novel. Both were leading happy and contented lives with their subjects. Once after a long span of many years, Shahzaman is invited to visit Shahabad. He is overjoyed at the prospect of meeting his elder brother Shahryar and makes necessary arrangements for the journey. He camps outside his city palace for the night to begin the journey at dawn. He is reminded of a special gift which he had forgotten at the palace and silently returns to it in the dark night. As he enters his bedroom, he is shocked to see his beautiful queen sleeping peacefully in the embrace of a black slave. His senses and vision are paralysed at first but in the next moment, he stabs both the lovers with his sword. Returning to the camp, he immediately orders his men to start their journey for Shahabad, without waiting for dawn.

He is received warmly and with a great honour at his brother's city gates. But Sultan Shahryar feels concerned when he sees his younger brother's pale and sorrowful face. Despite being asked, Shahzaman does not reveal his sorrow to Shahryar. The Sultan, however, arranges for a hunting expedition to entertain his brother but Shahzaman refuses to participate. As he is roaming in the palace, he witnesses a horrible sight. He is shocked to see his sister-in-law, the former queen of Shahabad engaged in sexual activities inside the palace garden along with other slave girls and black slaves. The sight immobilises him at first but then he comforts himself with the thought that he is not the only husband who is betrayed and cuckolded. His elder brother's misfortune is much greater than his own. He is revived and relieved of his grim mental state by these thoughts. The Sultan, returning from his trip, is surprised at the sudden change in his brother's mood and becomes eager to learn the cause. After much persuasion, Shahzaman is forced to narrate everything in detail starting from his own life experiences to what he has witnessed recently in his brother's palace. Shahryar refuses to believe in the infidelity of his noble queen. So, the younger brother suggests that he should secretly spy on the queen. The Sultan is agonised to discover the unfaithful nature of the queen. But instead of resenting to bloodshed, he proposes to renounce the world till he meets another person suffering from such disgrace. Shahzaman agrees to this and both the brothers travel far and wide till they meet a giant who comes out of the sea with a large chest on his head. The brothers are wonderstruck to see a beautiful young lady come out of the box. The girl narrates the story of her being carried away by the giant on her bridal night when she was still a virgin. Since then, she has been befooling the giant, thus being able to take revenge despite being imprisoned. This incident leaves such a deep impact on the two brothers that they decide to return to their royal life.

Hariharan uses her innovation, imagination, vision and power to keep up the challenge of this established ideological text. She rejuvenates the marginalised women characters by giving them new energetic lives, hopes, aspirations so as to bring out their talent and creativity. The structure of Hariharan's *When Dreams Travel* is based on the complex structure of *The Thousand and One Nights*. It is an imitation of primordial traditions of storytelling as is clearly apparent in Indian Literature and the sacred Vedas. The stories in these antique texts comprise a pattern in which one leads to the next. The structure of *The Thousand and One Nights* is just like a gothic novel with many twists and turns. It creates a marvellous and supernatural atmosphere through its narration and exposes the innumerable possibilities of the plot. Rustam Brahma opines:

> Hariharan's *When Dreams Travel* excavates the relics; off-scene backgrounds, hidden experiences, unseen atrocities and injustice, untold stories of danger and fear, struggle and action, unexposed talent and creativity of women in the legendary frame story *Arabian Nights* through a dominant female character, Duniazad, Shahrzad's younger sister and it is exploring the marginalized female characters of the original text. (183)

Hariharan's novel reverberates with echoes from *The Arabian Nights* which take us to the mystical and charming world of geniis, ghosts and magic and thus shows traits of magical realism.

Magical Realism is an art which started in the twentieth century. It was a movement initiated by European artists after World War I. It was later followed by a second phase that began in North America a decade later. The German art critic Franz Roh was the first to use the term "magic realism" in 1925. The movement was actually a reaction to Expressionism and Cubism. Chris Baldick describes magic realism as "a kind of modern fiction in which fabulous and fantastical events are included in a narrative that otherwise maintains the 'reliable' tone of objective realistic report." (*Oxford* 194)

Magic realism is distinguished by two different perspectives - one based on a balanced view of reality and the other relies on the acceptance of the supernatural. Magic realism is different from fantasy mainly because it is set in a normal, modern world with authentic descriptions of humans and society. Magic realism is said to be a synthesis of fantasy and realism. As Maggie Ann Bowers puts it:

> In fact, each of the versions of magic(al) realism have different meanings for the term 'magic'; in magic realism 'magic' refers to the mystery of life: in marvellous and magical realism 'magic' refers to any extraordinary occurrence and particularly to anything spiritual or unaccountable by rational science. The variety of magical occurrences in magic(al) realist writing includes ghosts, disappearances, miracles, extraordinary talents and strange atmospheres but does not include the magic as it is found in a magic show.(*Magic(al)* 20-21)

Hariharan's *When Dreams Travel* is a novel which is framed by fantasy and magic realism. The story also problematises the man-woman relationship, the unfair power exercised by the male and the power of women to survive with the help of their storytelling and imagination. The novel is also about a woman's search for her 'self'. However, what seems to have undergone a sea change is the author's treatment of the subject. Here the author attempts to write a metafiction through an elaborate inter-text that is made to foreground the feminist issue from a fresh perspective. Indeed, the author seems to have set herself a challenging task. Whether she succeeds or not in achieving the goal may be debated; but the way, she grapples with the challenge could itself be an exciting experience. Exploring of *The Arabian Nights* using brightly coloured words with flair and precision, Hariharan provides the sequel to this myth of lust and cruelty, power and magic, as well as the philosophy of feminism. The novel engages with questions of ethics and the importance of aesthetics in relation to ethics.

The high tone of feminism is the real achievement of Hariharan. The novel is a celebration of all womanhood and suggestive of the power of the feminine over male hegemony. The novel offers a subtle critique of the misogynist patriarchal values and sexual morality. The success of Hariharan lies in the creative treatment she gives to the traditional form of storytelling. Hariharan's approach to feminism is very unique. According to her, a woman must be chaste and virtuous even if a man keeps on deceiving her. The medieval tradition of keeping the harem full with thousands of women to satiate the lust of the kings and sultans is also critiqued. The vivid observations made by Hariharan reveal those realities and fantasies but what is more important is her expression of freedom. Hariharan crafts a tale both fantastical and poignantly close to the skin, a story told with such inventiveness, such surefooted style and panache, that it lights up forgotten corners of the reader's mind. The study of this novel must be conducted from a new angle to understand her feminist voices. Hariharan brilliantly reworks the historical tradition with her control of the language and its nuances. The magic touch of this novel depends on beautifully written and obviously deeply felt feelings of humanity. Hariharan's greatest gift is the ability to weave the story, poetry and magic into the simplest of sentences, so that reading her becomes an effortless pleasure. The study of this novel shows that she crafts the tale in a fantastical mode, but it comes poignantly close to the scheme of things in real life. The scheme which she has chosen and crafted well reveals her creative talent which is evident in her unique style. The success of the novel depends on its treatment of the theme with a unique creative force, having its own effect. What Hariharan has ably touched through this work is the magic and mystery of the writer's imagination, her wonderful felicity and image, her wounding wit, her incredible ability to connect this story with any story ever imagined, and heard.

Hariharan retains the above frame as she begins her novel *When Dreams Travel.* The main story of Hariharan's novel revolves around Sultan Shahryar and his adulterous wife. Shahzaman, Shahryar's brother comes to know of his sister-in-law's infidelity and reveals the truth to his brother. Sultan Shahryar is shocked to know of his queen's unfaithfulness. Loathing all womankind, Shahryar orders the execution of his wife, the women-slaves and their black lovers. The sultan is heart-broken and grieved and decides to marry a succession of virgins every night. He deflowers them after marriage and executes them in the morning as a result of his bitterness. Consequently, the wazir, who was put on the duty to provide the virgins, is unable to find anymore. Thereafter, the wazir's daughter offers to become the next bride and requests her father to arrange the marriage. She makes a plan to save herself as well as others from Sultan's mania and terror. According to her plan, she narrates an adventurous story full of suspense and magic to Sultan Shahryar every night:

> If she stops, if she collapses, if she loses Shahryar's interest or attention, the roof could cave in, and with it, all hope of the city's deliverance, or its sultan's redemption. Sometimes, mid-sentence Shahrzad pauses as if to take stock of her audience. Her eyes move from Dunyazad on the floor, crouched like a suppliant, to a half-naked, half-believing Shahryar on the bed, to the unseen Zaman, kneeling behind the door, his breath wheezing with impatience as he waits for her to finish. Shahrzad's eyes turn shrewd; she begins again. (7)

The Sultan is so enthralled by the tale that he suspends the execution of Shahrzad so that he can hear the conclusion. Shahrzad, who had been narrating the tales to save her life, tells the stories in a very engrossing manner. She makes a continuous string of one tale leading to the next, which makes her survive for one thousand and one nights, after which the sultan renounces his barbarous vow. Moreover, he deems Shahrzad the saviour of many other damsels,

> This self-absorbed scene lives on, shamelessly immortal. It unfolds itself every night for a thousand and one nights. It could be the entire

> play itself, all of life compressed into a permanent entanglement - so self-contained does it seem, so complete its power over the players who make up its four limbs. (7)

The prehistoric compilation of stories abounds in the story of Shahrzad and the sultan and provides consistency and continuity to the bulk of different stories. The tales provide a wide variety comprising the history, love stories, tragedies, comedies and poems. It is a unique blend of the past and presents portrayed through the depiction of magicians and legendary places through the techniques of intertextuality and magic realism. The four main characters of the legendary tales - Sultan Shahryar, his brother Shahzaman, and the two sisters Shahrzad and Dunyazad are also the protagonists of Hariharan's *When Dreams Travel*. The Persian names conferred to the characters are also significant. Shahryar means 'holder of a kingdom,' Shahzaman means 'self-willed and self-sufficient,' Shahrzad means 'born from the city,' Dunyazad means 'out of the world,' and Dilshad means 'always happy.' The characters possess the traits that their names suggest in the story.

At the background of the novel is the popular old legendary tale. The actual story of the novel begins after thousand and one nights have passed, when the emperor unites with his bride Shahrzad and admits that his decision of killing women after marrying them for a night was wrong. The novel consists of two parts. Part One is called 'Travellers' and Part Two-'Virgins, Martyrs and Others.' Hariharan introduces epigraphs prior to each part as well as each chapter of the novel. Part One 'Travellers' is introduced with the epigraph taken from Jorge Luis Borges' 'Nightmares' which says, "'...we cannot examine dreams directly,/we can only speak of the memory of dreams.'"(ix) It signifies the plight of women in the patriarchal setup as they are not allowed to express their heartfelt desires. They cannot openly express their dreams. They can only speak about their past and are forbidden to imagine a fantastical world. In the first chapter of Part One titled 'In the Embrace of Darkness,' the author retells the legendary beginning of *The Arabian Nights.* It starts with the epigraph '"Do you not know that a feast cannot be merry with/ fewer than four companions, and that women cannot be/ truly happy without men?'"(3) It signifies Hariharan's humanist concerns. It reflects that she is not a hardcore feminist, but a person who believes in equality of the sexes that her story is different from the legend is clearly indicated in the last line of the first chapter "The story ends on-stage. Off-stage it has just begun."(16) This is when Hariharan's feminist re-writing of the legendary tale starts, exactly at the moment the narrative of the original text stops. Hariharan's story begins in the second chapter 'On the Way to Paradise' which starts the day after the thousand and one nights. The epigraph says, '" O, Shahrazad, this thousand and first night/ is brighter for us than the day.'" (17) The dark night of their life is over and brightness which is the result of Shaharzad's success will follow now. She has succeeded in saving herself and the other women and also saved herself and others from the exploitation. The two titles 'In the Embrace of Darkness' and 'On the Way to Paradise' apparently seem to signify that the characters of the legendary text are emerging from the 'darkness' of patriarchal structures towards a healthy atmosphere of happiness in 'paradise.' It may also be interpreted as a figment of the writer's imagination since the 'Paradise' proves to be an illusion. The royal couples are sitting in comfort in a shady bower of the royal gardens. Shahrzad, who has entertained the king for thousand and one nights and has escaped the sword by her sharp wits is questioned by the king:

> 'Shahrzad,'... 'where did all those stories come from? Shahzaman and I have read and studied more than you have. Certainly, we have travelled more, seen marvels and lands and wickedness you can only imagine.'
>
> She who the repentant sultan has crowned with the words chaste and tender, wise and eloquent, replies, 'I don't have a sword, so it seems I cannot rule. I cannot rule, I cannot travel, I don't care to weep. But I can dream.'
>
> ...'Now tell us - of your own free will - your secret dreams, Shahrzad!'(19-20)

Shahrzad's response is terse and telling and the least romantic as she says:

> 'My dreams? They're nothing - just a rubbishy pile of rough, uncut stones.' She turns to her sister, Dunyazad. Between them passes a swift, secretive look. 'Besides,' adds Shahrzad, darting a teasing look at Shahryar, 'only those locked up in hovels and dungeons and palaces can see and hear these dreams. Only those whose necks are naked and at risk can understand them.'(20)

Her reply hints at the prevalent power structures in the patriarchal system. How patriarchy denounces the ability of women to do anything creative or constructive is reflected in Shahrzad's statement about her dreams which are regarded as a "rubbishy pile of rough uncut stones"(20) in the world of men. Woman and her activity is never given the importance and respect it deserves. She is considered incapable of doing things as well as the men, so Shahrzad modestly describes her dreams as 'rubbishly rough uncut stones.' The novel highlights the injustice and suffering inflicted upon women through magic and varied narrative styles. It is also about a woman's search for her own identity with the help of storytelling and weaving stories within stories. In *The Arabian Nights* the stories are told by Shahrzad and in due course, other storytellers come into focus. In *When Dreams Travel* the story is told through a number of storytellers: at first Shahrzad, Dunyazad and Dilshad. This is because the author's emphasis is more on the speakers and their lives - their dreams and wishes, longings and frustrations. It also portrays the aesthetic style of magic elements which are blended into a realistic atmosphere in order to gain access to a deeper understanding of reality.

The beginning of the next chapter 'Knots in the Afterlife' starts with the epigraph:'"When I am received by the King, I shall send for you. Then,/ when the king has finished his act with me, you must say:/ "Tell me, my sister, some tale of marvel to beguile the night."/Then I will tell you a tale which, if Allah wills, shall be the/ means of our deliverance.'" (27) The epigraph signifies that after she gets the acceptance of the king, Shahrzad can save other girls too. It brings out a relationship of deep female bonding between Shahrzad and Dunyazad too where they come close and share and care between themselves.

Dunyazad remembers her elder sister Shahrzad after *The Thousand and One Nights*, "she sees that it was always Shahrzad who was its central magnetic figure." (105) Shahrzad's question makes every woman think and fight for her freedom. She says "'I fought for myself and yes, for you as well. And you – what will you do when your turn comes?'" (276) Dunyazad's life is an answer to this question. She begins her journey towards Shahabad, her sister's hometown. She sets out on the quest, in order to find out what has happened to her sister. She reaches the palace disguised as a male and meets the old nurse-maid Sahiba. When she makes Dunyazad remove her disguise, the latter looks like an ageing princess. She questions her about the cause of her sister's death but Sahiba cannot give a satisfactory answer.

Sultan Shahryar sends her a message to meet him. Though reluctant at first, she later agrees to meet him. The whole night she keeps dreaming of palaces and tunnels and dungeons as if searching for something. She finds her sister's tomb in the dream and is grieved not to find her name mentioned anywhere on the grave. The next morning she gets ready to meet the sultan with the help of Dilshad, a slave-girl. The sultan boasts of his love for Shahrzad, Dunyazad remains a silent listener. She asks about Prince Umar, her nephew, to which Shahryar starts commenting about the foolish son of Dunyazad. The situation becomes tense when instead of answering Dunyazad's questions, Shahryar starts asking about his brother's Shahzaman's death which adds further knots to their life.

On the other hand, a relationship of bonding is established between Dunyazad and Dilshad. As a result, Dilshad confides in Dunyazad about the wooden chest of Shahrzad which the sultan had gifted to her. Chitra Sankaran observes:

> After the frame story, where the Arab girl narrator's position as the potential victim of a power-crazed, woman-hating, Sultan has been briefly elucidated, the narrative becomes woman-centred. Shahrazad's victimhood is replaced by a version in part two, where two women, Dunyazad, Shahrzad's sister, and Dilshad, a slave girl in Shahryar's palace, who are lesbian lovers, tell each other stories, one tale answering the other's, for seven days and seven nights. Dunyazad

> who was only the secondary, marginalised character in *The Thousand and One Nights* becomes a central character here. (69)

The *hammam* in the palace recalls the old memories of Dunyazad when she is reminded of her sister and her mother Raziya. Both the sisters felt secure in their mother's arms but the sweet memories are transformed into sadness due to their mother's death. Hariharan portrays a silent rebel through the character of Raziya who had yearned to demand the proper rights for herself and her daughters but was silenced forever.

> She saw her mother's heart for a moment before it was shrouded from sight and buried forever. And what she saw was not a broken spring, but a chamber where outrage swelled the air, stretched it to grotesque dimensions till the tightly packed, thin skinned balloon of a place exploded the aftermath of an enraged heart. (84)

Dunyazad meets Prince Umar, Shahrzad's son with the help of Dilshad, the slave-girl. The Prince seems to be a reflection of her father wazir and her mother Raziya and reveres his mother fondly. With the help of Dilshad, he successfully usurps the kingdom and imprisons the sultan in his mausoleum of his creation.

Shahrzad, Dunyazad and Dilshad are the three main women protagonists who have to narrate various stories for survival due to their helplessness in an orthodox patriarchal setup. In the novel *When Dreams Travel* the heroine is virtuous and she becomes a victim as she tries to safeguard the virgins from an unfair, sadistic killer. Hariharan portrays Shahrzad as a woman warrior, striving hard to get deliverance. She is an excellent fighter, intrepid, astute, clever and audacious. Even though Sultan Shahryar is a malicious tyrant, she continues to narrate her story in order to make him a human. She tries to make him realise the loyalty and conviction inherent in woman and her chastity and thereby saves the city and the people. Hariharan narrates:

> The thousand and one nights are done. At the end of the play, a bloodthirsty drama in which swords pierce soft, yielding flesh, a happy conclusion is announced. The sultan, powerful, noble, deluded, has seen the light. He has been brought to his senses by a woman; and

> with, of all things, her stories; her ready tongue, her cleverness. In this abnormal climate where imagination – through the medium of the word – asserts its power over the bloodshedding sword, everyone forgives everyone. (21)

Hariharan has carefully intermingled the text of *Arabian Nights* with her imagination. She has tried to explain the happy tale to make the listener understand the agony of the teller. Shahrzad is always under the threat of death while narrating the story. She explicates her imagination in terms of the terror. Hariharan depicts Shahrzad as the helpless woman in an orthodox man-controlled system. She must survive with her flawless skill. She is forced to make up stories at sword point. In an uninviting nuptial bed, the previous brides are raped in the night and killed at dawn. In order to save all other virgins, she risks her life and undergoes this dangerous experience. She saves herself and an entire world of virgins around her by her overwhelming skill of words. Thus she is able to question the patriarchal system which is against women. Shahrzad represents the spiteful clutches of patriarchal framework which demands that a woman should give herself up completely to man. Shahryar is the symbol of patriarchy, who has illusions about himself and pretends to be a 'god' by taking the lives of the girls as and when he chooses to. Shahrzad does not surrender to the patriarchal tyrant who believes in the power of man. She resists and in fact, fights back not with sword but with her ability to tell stories.

Hariharan has brought out the crudest version of male domination where a woman is literally and purely an object of sexual desires; further, an easy victim of man's cruel power and his ever-growing, insatiable thirst for flesh. Here, a woman is not only deprived of her rights as an individual, but also the fundamental right of living itself. Even if such a thing does not happen in reality, there is a very fine blurred line separating fiction from reality.

They understand the power and pleasure of storytelling and carry out this activity to entertain others, to empower themselves, to manipulate opponents and to liberate themselves as well as others. Shahrzad is a brave and dauntless fighter who held the fate of many women in her tongue. Her creativity was her only happiness and power. It is narrated that "The powerless must have a dream or two, dreams that break walls, dreams that go through walls as if *they* are powerless."(25)

The second part of the novel 'Virgins, Martyrs and Others'is a shift from 'memory-making' to 'story-telling.' The first chapter 'A Dream, A Mirror' starts with the epigraph written by Jorge Luis Borge, "'I thought of a labyrinth of labyrinths, of one/ sinuous spreading labyrinth that would encompass/ the past and the future...'" (111) which hints at many stories told through various storytellers in the novel and form a maze-like structure. It again starts with the four figures in the night's embrace. But this time the ruthless rulers are replaced by two jinns, i.e., Shahrzad and Satyasama. Hariharan discards the cruel, callous, self-centred, insensitive males who do not acknowledge or recognise the creative genius in the women. She replaces them with the creative spirits that lie hidden and unexplored in the women. The story-tellers, Dunyazad and the slave-girl Dilshad are on their way to Samarkand and they decide to re-enact the entire event and share their dreams, pasts and future plans by narrating tales to each other during their journey in the desert. This becomes the forerunner of fresh journeys and new nights. The '*ecriture feminine*' which goes unrecognised in the stories of Shahrzad achieves a status in the 'dreams' and 'mirrors' of Dunyazad and Dilshad, a slave girl. The term '*ecriture feminine*' was introduced by Helene Cixous in her essay "The Laugh of Medusa" which implies female body and her experiences in women's writings and texts. She propagated the idea of writing of the women, by the women and for the women. She proclaims that "women must write through their bodies."(*Signs* 886) and they must write with their mother's milk. (*Signs* 881) It means that they must include their thought process in their literary works. She asserted that women should create new language through their ideas and inspirations in her writing so as to secure their place in the society.

Hariharan also makes Dunyazad who is always quiet, subdued and behind the curtain in *The Arabian Nights* assert her identity as a woman in *When Dreams Travel.* Her role is always to wait upon her elder sister or the king, destined for the requirement of others. She has to dress first as a 'handmaiden' to Shahryar and Shahrzad, and then like Shahzaman's wife and queen. Later like a widow and guardian to the boy-king of her kingdom. Dunyazad and Dilshad, a slave-girl narrates each other their own stories for seven days and nights.

> For seven nights and days, there are dreams in mirrors, mirrors in their dreams. There is a festering memory in Dunyazad's story of the night. Dilshad or Satyasama take this pulpy, oozing memory and transform it in the hard and relentless light of day.
>
> What is it like to talk for your life? For seven nights and days three women play a grown-up version - minus swords - of a dangerous but exciting game, The Martyr's Walk. If you were talking (or writing) for your life, what would you say? Dunyazad, Dilshad and Satyasama take turns playing the woman who saves herself and others through her fiction.(118)

Silence is considered to be a woman's greatest virtue but speech is necessary for survival. The cutting of Satyasama's tongue represents patriarchal control but Shahrzad and Dunyazad are not to be silenced or controlled and they become agents of change in the lives of women. The relationship between the two sisters is that of female-bonding through which they try to find solace in each other's company. The concept of female friendship is a major concern of recent feminists' psychological studies. It is a strength-giving relationship through which women try to create a world of their own. This relationship is an expansion of nurturing and care to be shared between women. Similarly the chapter 'Seven Nights and Days' also begins with an epigraph "'...she threw her arms round her sister's neck, and/ seated herself by her side. Then Dunyazad said to Shahrazad:/ "Tell us, my sister, a tale of marvel, so that the night may/ pass pleasantly."'(119) It again refers to the concept of female friendship, which is likened to the mother-daughter relationship. It is the time when they narrate tales to each other on the way to their journey to Samarkand. They can share their dreams and the heartfelt desires because they are free from the fear of their heads being chopped off. Thus the woman-woman bonding acquires a strong relationship filled with empathy as they could share their past, dreams, plan their future and re-frame their lives accordingly.

The stories of the legend and the novel are totally different in the second part of Hariharan's narrative. The tales are not only simple stories, they are allegorical representation based on modern issues. The tale 'Nine Jewels for a Rani' narrates the story of a monster, Satyasama, who is a one-eyed monkey woman. She was a freak and belonged to the sultan's harem. Her body was wrapped in a sleek, lightweight fur. She was in the habit of climbing tall trees and staring at moonlight. The monster woman belonged to the supernatural as is evident in the text which suggests that the monster was picked like a pawn of God. She would sing truly so that she could provide awareness to the minds of the Eternals. All these characters mentioned in the tales possess a dream-like quality as though they exist in a trance. The stories of *The Arabian Nights* are rich in male adventures and heroism and represent women as wicked, traitors, cruel and witch-like individuals. In the novel *When Dreams Travel,* the stories portray women as the objects of desire who are denied any sort of identity and recognition despite their talents. The rewriting of the legend in the postmodern context of feminism also highlights the cruelty, callousness and pain that women have to undergo in this male chauvinistic world. Hariharan herself is uncertain about a woman's place in the society. The stereotypical patriarchal practices subjugate women and deprive them of their due respect and honour. Thus, Hariharan suggests that women should hold their heads high and raise a voice against the age-old practices. She emphasises that women should critically analyse and understand the disparate distribution of power amongst men and women and finally make efforts to rectify them.

The story "Three Scenes and a Father" portrays Dunyazad's father as the protagonist who experiences three "adventures" in this episode. The adventures expose patriarchy in an allegorical form under the cruel reign of King Shahryar. The first episode explicates the story of wazir, who finds himself in the middle of a dry, endless desert and in the extremity of exhaustion spies "a gleaming, opal-hued pool" (169) in the distance. As he approaches it, he is stopped by a heavy hand that holds him back and the sound of a clear voice. The voice either belongs to his father or his teacher, which rings out with authority, '"No, you haven't finished'.... 'Did you think that was all? A whiff of morality, a pinch of justice, and the task is done? Is salvation to be bought so cheaply?"'(170) The voice, which could be interpreted as the conscience of patriarchy, instructs him,'"The journey, dear wazir, begins here. Be patient; you will have your fill of the pool."'(170) But when the wazir reaches the pool, he discovers it to be a hellish oasis filled with the dismembered limbs and body parts of the virgins executed night after night by the king:

> A whole population of dismembered bodily parts, pickled in a viscous fluid, are floating around the wazir; a long snake-haired, Purple-throated head, a hairless thigh, a lone breast with a hideously engorged nipple. All of the female Shahabad seems to be represented in this hellish oasis. He feels the pain of every severed head, every slit throat, every torn, shrivelling limb. (171)

The second episode is an exposition of the wazir who rushes home to be faced by the sultan's messenger. The wazir buries his eldest daughter in a hole that he digs in his garden. The eunuch returns after prayer and asks the house, '"O mansion of marble columns, do you house a female virgin?"'(173) to which the house does not respond positively. After the eunuch's departure the wazir digs up the ground and finds a plump goat in place of his daughter. This hints at women's fate in a chauvinistic male centred society.

The third episode shows the wazir who is in a hurry to feed his hungry God. He is back in the desert and is carrying the goat on his arm. In the myth, Lord Shiva appears in the form of a mad *Shaivite* to test the faith of his dedicated devotee. He demands that the devotee should kill the most favourite thing in the world to feed him. The devotee, who has vowed never to send away a *Shaivite* unfed from his home, kills and cooks his only son. The ascetic sits down for a meal and asks the devotee to call his son for the meal. The heart-broken devotee pretends to call out to his young dead son and to everyone's astonishment, the son appears before them! Lord Shiva reveals himself to his astonished devotee and praises his dedication for him. In retelling this myth and by substituting wazir and Shahrzad in place of the Hindu devotee and his son, Hariharan exposes the ideological constructions that assert and enforce chauvinistic power structures.

French feminist Julia Kristeva develops the notion of 'abjection', which is important to understand the oppression of women. The term 'abjection' literally means "the state of being cast off." (web *www.en.wikipedia.org*) In common usage, it connotes degradation. Abjection is a psychological process through which subjective and group identity is consolidated. It excludes those elements which dominate the persons or challenge their autonomy. It is a process by which an individual separates one's sense of self - physical, biological, social or cultural. It has been used in post-structuralism and Kristeva's *Powers of Horror*. She writes, "It is simply a frontier, a repulsive gift that the Other, having become *alter ego,* drops so that "I" does not disappear in it but finds, in that sublime alienation, a forfeited existence." (*Power* 18) She promotes the idea that the male supremacy has become dominant in the systems of thought. She believes that it has deeply rooted itself in the Western ideology so that it now appears normal and unquestionable. Society plays a significant role in culturally conditioning women to accept an artificially constructed inferiority. She opines that feminism begins with liberalism when women demand equality with men. The devices of intertextuality and magic realism have helped Hariharan to portray her feminist ideas. She protests against the silencing of the quick-witted talented woman Shahrzad who is doomed to petty domesticity. A woman like Shahrzad who succeeds in saving the whole city with her innovative spirit is reduced to just another queen in the Sultan's harem. Can she happily accept this quiet, static, uneventful life witnessing the harem filling up with queens and slave-girls? Can she remain confined to the walls of the palace dungeon after gaining such love, honour and respect from the country? How could anyone like Shahrzad be content with domesticity, how would someone with the spirit of the most daring warrior cut herself down to the corset of women's protected, quiet existence? Hariharan raises these questions after reading the text between the lines and quite clearly reveals Shahrzad's love for risk:

> Shahrzad, the woman who is talking about her life does not look frightened. She must be though, how can she not be terrified? This could be her very last performance...The sultan may say this morning, or the next: 'That's enough storytelling! Off with her head!' Shahrzad does not betray her fear, but as night nears morning, she stoops now and then, lifts the hem of her robe and wipes the sweat on her neck and face...What she does not swallow she holds for a moment or two, rolling the liquid in her mouth as if she is tasting it for the last time. Then she wets her lips with her tongue and begins again. (6)

In the original text, women are presented as ornate and lustful objects whose only aim is to befool their husbands. But no one tries to reason out why women behave in this manner. It is because the sole motive of the kings is to fill their harems and even ordinary people have many wives:

> All kings are collectors. All of them, whether sultan or raja or chosen leader turned supreme. Their whims and preferences may vary, but most are partial to filling up their treasure vaults - with gems and coins, books copied out by scribes in letters of gold, or stallions, slaves and subjects. But the prize collection is not stowed away in the same vault. It is hidden in the harem, or zenana, or a special palace, or bedchamber. These valuable items are women of all shapes, colours and sizes. (90)

And after putting their "valuable items", they would comment "the harem breeds hungry women, a race of cuckolding subjects."(78) Thus, women are deprived of love, care, identity and space for themselves. As a result of all this, perhaps, the women indulge in extra-marital relationships. The storytelling of Shahrzad is an escape from the patriarchal orthodoxy witnessed in the novel. She is forced to narrate the stories and is robbed of her honour and dignity. She is trapped in her harem like a prisoner and lives in the mire of a dull, monotonous marital life. As Mohua Ghosh writes in "*When Dreams Travel*: 'Writing Back' to the Arabian Nights":

> As a wife, she stands nowhere, just another addition to the line of previous brides who had been raped in the dark and killed at dawn. Even as a mother, the queen fails to attain her selfhood. She is not allowed to experience the bliss and joy of fulfilment of motherhood as the newborn babe is handed over to the nurses to be reared in another corner of the palace. With the sword hanging over the head, Shahrzad is forced to continue her creation and procreation.(*Studies* 123)

The narrator enquires of the mute and docile Shahrzad, "…what will happen to you, Shahrzad, when the urgent need for storytelling, the demand for prolix invention, is withdrawn? Will you be satisfied with bedtime tales to your children?"(133) *When Dreams Travel* begins long after the stories of *The Thousand and One Night* have ended when Dunyazad receives the news of her elder sister Shahrzad's death. She undertakes a long journey in male disguise from Samarkand to Shahabad only to discover her sister left to the care of the slave girls in a remote corner of the palace. This neglected figure is the queen Shahrzad who is supposed and reported to be dead long ago by her husband. In the last chapter "The Morning After" we get a vision of Shahrzad who is happy that her stories had saved many girls from the sultan's lust. Therefore she warns the future generations to take care of themselves and take up the challenge when their turn comes:

> She sees her past, their futures, curving one into the other, a circle with no beginning or end. She says to them, this old warrior in times of peace: 'I fought for myself, and yes, for you as well. And you - what will you do when your turn comes? When the drums roll, and the sword blunted with age, the rusty axe, wake up to be freshly sharpened? '(276)

These two women silenced in the source text take turns to play the roles of saviour queens in *When Dreams Travel.* These two new frame-narrators reconstruct their individual past through their sad, absurd and horrifying magic stories of strange women. However they succeed in asserting their identity as women through their magical-realistic tales. As A.S. Mehala puts it:

> The novel clearly shows that women by nature are not prone to travel and the absence of mobility on the part of a woman is compensated by her skill of articulation which is seen in her narration and description which grab all the attention of the listener to her and finally forge him to listen to her dictation. Shahrzad's story itself is a proven truth that imagination and dreams have the power to liberate anyone and everyone. (867)

Stories, thus, told and retold, create, recreate, form, inform, reform and transform tradition, culture and values. Hariharan hints at the indispensability of weaving tales for healing and liberating the soul. She continuously intermingles and interweaves the two texts and ends the novel ambiguously with some kind of fears and apprehensions by leaving it to the readers to decipher its meaning. As Mohua Ghosh opines:

> Like *The Thousand and One Nights*, we find the characters of *When Dreams Travel* accompanied by the host of jinns and ghosts at every point of their lives. The novel is full of magic and varied narrative styles like that of the old fairy tale. While reading this novel, we can recollect the real and imaginary travels, past and present, glorious etymologies of names of the Arabian Nights. (*Studies* 129)

When Dreams Travel is Hariharan's dynamic avowal on the themes which she voices through her narrators. She dexterously succeeds in depicting the actual and factual issues that are operating in the society. The secondary narratives in the text are shifted to another section of the text (part two) instead of merging them in the main narrative, as is done in the original. This is one of the major structural differences between the ancient anthology and Hariharan's innovative novel. She does not reveal it plainly, rather she employs varied narrative techniques with immense skilfulness. She utilises the techniques of magic realism and intertextuality to highlight the subordinate and subservient position of women. It is no longer a depiction of an Arabian entertainment text but becomes a narrative which centres on women's concerns. It unravels the patterns of misogyny and classism that is totally different from the original tale. The secondary narratives, in the original text, were the tales told by Shahrzad to the Sultan, and are no longer in evidence. In the second part, we come across completely new tales with feminist and ethical agendas, which are very different from the original translated Arab collection. The subversion of the ancient text has been brought into play to foreground and illustrate Hariharan's themes effectively.

Both the novels *The Thousand Faces of Night* and *When Dreams Travel* depict the sensitiveness of women, their vulnerability as individuals and craving for love and understanding. They become the victims of their own gender. In this context, all human activity and expression become symbolic in the realm of existential communication. Their existence shows symbolic transformations in their perspective on life. They prove the strength of women in their struggle for survival by not succumbing to sorrow or despair. The novels move on to arrive at varying levels of intellectual self-realisation which enable the characters to either attain liberation or reconciliation through self-knowledge. It is not just physical or environmental liberation of the mind by cleansing it of the old patriarchal ideals. The centuries-old impact of male dominance of the women's psyche is no less than the imperial influence on the colonised people. To decolonise the psyche is not an easy task for women to undertake and complete successfully.

The mixing of myth and reality in Hariharan's novels is her unique method to deal with the complex issues of women. Her texts usher in a new era in the sphere of women's writing and signify an awakening in the world of women. It seems that she has carefully studied feminism and feminist movements in contemporary India and has treated these complex issues in a careful manner. She is anticipating the arrival of 'New Women' in the new millennium on Indian horizons in a bold manner. The problem faced by new women has been described by Hariharan by juxtaposing different facets of myth and reality. The women in her fiction are progressive, change-oriented, sophisticated and elite. The study of Hariharan's fiction can be interesting if one understands the social fabric on which she has painted her images. The traditional Indian social structure is based on patriarchy, where the role of men is very important and women are given a secondary treatment. This gender bias is truly reflected in her works which record feminist elements in a systematic way. Shobha De opines:

> Eventually every relationship is a power struggle either on an overt or subliminal level....Control over the situation has been a male prerogative over the centuries. Women's destinies have been determined largely in that context alone....It is time they were made aware of their own potential and power. *Shakti* needs to be harnessed, directed and explored for the furtherance of over all human development....It is in maintaining the state of equilibrium between these two opposing forces that can lead to creative and dynamic harmony....Men will have to come to terms with women power. (*Shooting* 112)

With this observation as a basis, it would be interesting to study patriarchy and marital relationships reflected in the novels *The Thousand Faces of Night* and *When Dreams Travel*. India has been known for its paradoxical treatment of women. The woman is worshipped as Goddess on the one hand and dismissed on the other as being the subordinate of man. Hariharan's serious endeavour is to secure the future of women by laying emphasis on their human rights. She believes in liberty, equality, fraternity and social justice for freedom. The author has closely witnessed the miserable conditions of Indian women who are caught between tradition and modernity. On the one side, she has shown the profound impact of epics like *Ramayana* and *Mahabharata* and on the other, being influenced by modern liberal values which have come from the west, she advocates their freedom.

Hariharan has absorbed the new wind of change and rightly incorporated it in her fiction. Her presentations are detailed, creative and carefully constructed. She has ably planned the story and placed her characters in the proper context. Hariharan's meditations are quite balanced and she has succeeded in making the women's voices strong enough to be heard with seriousness and caution. It is an intricate and complicated task to uplift the condition of women in spite of the sincere efforts being made by social reformers because centuries of patriarchy have conditioned the minds of people. Both *The Thousand Faces of Night* and *When Dreams Travel* strive to liberate women from the shackles of male control. The novels describe the hidden power praxis behind the apparently simple man-woman relationship and explain how they need to be subverted.

Works cited

Abrams, M.H. *A Glossary of Literary Terms*. 7th ed. Heinle: Thomson, 2005. Print.

Allen, Graham. *Intertextuality*. London: Routledge, 2007. Print.

Baldick, Chris. *The Oxford Dictionary of Literary Terms*. New York: OUP, 2008. Print.

Bowers, Maggie Ann. *Magic (al) Realism*. London: Routledge, 2007. Print.

Brahma, Rustam. "Gender, Identity and Politics: A Study of Githa Hariharan's *When Dreams Travel* and *The Thousand Faces of Night*." *The Criterion*.Web. 6.2 (2015): 179-185.

Burton, Richard F. ed and trans. *The Thousand Nights and a Night*. 7th ed. Delhi: Jaico, 1999. Print.

Cixous, Helene. "The Laugh of the Medusa." Tr. K. Cohen and P. Cohen. *Signs*. Web. 1.1 (1976): 875-99.

De, Shobha. *Shooting from the Hip: Selected Writings*. New Delhi: UBS, 1994. Print.

Deshpande, Shashi. "I'm not a feminist" *Times of India* Web. 22 July 2001. <http://articles.timesofindia.indiatimes.com/2001022/hyderabad/27243928_1_shashi-deshpande-slow-change-issues>

Doniger, Wendy. *The Hindus: An Alternative History*. Penguin: New Delhi, 1999. p.200-298. Print.

George, Rosemary M. *The Politics of Home*. New Delhi: Cambridge UP. p.133. Print.

Ghosh, Mohua. "*When Dreams Travel*: 'Writing Back' to *The Arabian Nights*." *Studies in Women* Writers *in English*. Vol II. ed. Mohit K. Ray & Rama Kundu. New Delhi: Atlantic, 2005. Print.

---."Feminist Interrogation of a Patriarchal Text: Intertextual Echoes and Departures." *Studies in Women Writers in English*. Vol II. ed. Mohit K.Ray & Rama Kundu. New Delhi: Atlantic, 2005. Print.

Hariharan, Githa. *The Thousand Faces of Night*. New Delhi: Penguin, 1992. Print.

---.*When Dreams Travel*. New Delhi: Penguin, 1999. Print.

---."Discrete Thoughts" ed. Meenakshi Bharat. *Desert in Bloom: Contemporary Indian Women's Fiction in English*. Delhi: Pencraft, 2004. Print.

---.Interview by Joel Kuortti. *The Journal of Commonwealth Literature.* 36.1 (2001): 7-26.

---."A Conversation with Githa Hariharan." Interview by Arnab Chakladar *Another Subcontinent: South Asian Society and Culture,* 2005. 12 Aug 2005. Web. 8 July 2013. http://www. another subcontinent.com/gh3.html

---."Interview with Githa Hariharan." Prema Vishwanath. *Indian Express Sunday Magazine,* Web. 12 Sept 1993.

Indira, S. "Walking the Tight Rope: A Reading of Githa Hariharan's *The Thousand Faces of Night*"ed. R.K.Dhawan. *Indian Women Novelists.* Set III, Vol.4. New Delhi: Prestige, 1995. Print.

Kaur, Dr.Sarabjit. "Journey of Women Characters in Githa Hariharan's The Thousand Faces of Night and Manju Kapur's Home." *IQSR Journal Of Humanities And Social Science.* Web 20.3 (2015): 79-82.

Kristeva, Julia. "The Powers of Horror: An Essay on Abjection." Trans. Leon S. Roudiez. New York: Columbia UP, 1982. Print.

McLeod, John. *Beginning Postcolonialism.* Manchester: Manchester UP, 2000. Print.

Mehala, A.S. "Art-An Act of Liberation in Githa Hariharan's *The Thousand Faces of Night* and *When Dreams Travel.*" *Research Journal of English Language and Literature.* 4.2 (2016): 865-867. Print.

Mohanty, Chandra Talpade. "Under Western Eyes: Feminist Scholarship and Colonial Discourses" eds. Ashcroft, Bill, et al. *The Post-Colonial Studies Reader.* 2nd ed. London: Routledge, 2006. Print.

Nair, Rama. "The Art of Fiction: A Note on the 'Prelude' of Githa Hariharan's *The Thousand Faces of Night*" ed. R.K.Dhawan. *Indian Women Novelists.* Set III, Vol.4. New Delhi: Prestige, 1995. Print.

Rao, K.Damodar. "Penance as Multiple Response in Githa Hariharan's *The Thousand Faces of Night*" ed. R.K.Dhawan. *Indian Women Novelists.* Set III, Vol.4. New Delhi: Prestige, 1995. Print.

Rich, Adrienne. "When We Dead Awaken: Writing as Revision." *College English,* 34.1 (1972): 18-30. 11 Sept 2008. Print.

Said, Edward W. *Orientalism.* London: Routledge and Kegan Paul, 1978. Print.

---.*Culture and Imperialism.* New York: Vintage, 1993. Print.

Sankaran, Chitra. "Narrating to Survive: Ethics and Aesthetics in Githa Hariharan's *When Dreams Travel.*" *Asiatic.* Web. 2.2 (2008): 65-72.

Chapter 3

THE SIEGE OF THE MIND: *IN TIMES OF SIEGE* AND *FUGITIVE HISTORIES*

> Githa declared that she was not a sociologist, a historian or an academic. It was primarily as a novelist that she was responding to serious political issues such as the demolition of Babri Masjid and the Gujarat carnage.
>
> **web *www.thehindu.com***

Hariharan's novels *In Times of Siege* and *Fugitive Histories* explore the disastrous consequences of religious and cultural chauvinism. The analysis of both the novels highlights certain important issues of culture and identity; and also critically examines the contemporary conditions prevailing in our country and where the nation is heading. She concludes that in spite of being in a free and democratic country, Indians remain slaves to prejudices. Unfortunately, the present socio-political system does not allow people to express their opinions fearlessly because of the stereotypical hypocrisy in the society. Hariharan was asked in an interview by Gowri Ramnarayan the reason for being "direct and unambiguous when the trend is for complex, elliptical, magical." Hariharan thus replied:

> There is no place or time in this book for magic, it was important to me to address the problem head-on. But "In Times of Siege" is carefully structured, with unlikely links between different kinds of time and space, its complexity may not be obvious. I've gone backstage to look at several people, their fears, apprehensions, nobilities, deceptions. I've done this with the dubious magic of day to day life. (web *www.thehindu.com*)

This quotation explains the meaning of the title 'The Siege of the Mind' as it shows how the minds of people are haunted by the fear of being annihilated as they are being conditioned by the prevailing communal tensions.

Hariharan's novel *In Times of Siege* deals with the analysis of political power relations among people belonging to different religious and social groups. The struggle for power is usually between two socially exclusive groups, and in this novel, it is caused by the struggle between religious ideas and ideologies on one hand, with the liberal and secular ideas on the other. With the passage of time, it becomes a tussle between the fundamentalists whose ideas get crystallized over a period of time into prejudices, dogmas and hypocritical notions. Hariharan highlights the Indian culture and contemporary Indian scenario and also explores the various aspects of religious fundamentalism through this novel. It also presents the plight of the people who cherish secular ideas and are put to test because they go against the traditionalists. Hariharan is a human activist who believes that as a writer, it is her responsibility to highlight the wrongs which are prevalent in the society. While talking about a writer's responsibility, Hariharan states in her interview with Chitralekha Basu, "Our work has to reflect the troubled times we are living in. The battering rams are at the door and we have to think of protecting the cushioned writer's space."(web *www.the statesman.com*) Hariharan believes that being a writer means she has an edge over the power relations which are being practised in the society. In reaction to the controversy created by Sarkar's and Panicker's book on the freedom struggle, while Hariharan was writing *In Times of Siege*; she states in *The Deccan Herald*:

> Over the last several years, along with a lot of other writers, artists and film-makers, I have felt very strongly that we are travelling in a direction that is deeply regressive, and both as a citizen and a writer I have felt that I must take this head on, and that was the general background that was going on in my head...I was midway through my novel, when to my shock I found that eminent historians Sarkar and Panicker had their volume on the freedom struggle recalled. In fact, I had to stop writing for a few weeks because it was almost as if the media coverage and the kind of historians' fear was both similar yet different from my fictional situation. (web *www.githahariharan.com*)

In Times of Siege is a novel set in New Delhi which highlights the power politics prevailing in 1990's. It can be read as a commentary on the political situation in India. Delhi is deeply embedded in politics and power and history is shown as a divisive force in the novel. It reflects a complex relationship between power and cultural pluralism. The plot of the novel is built on the ideological war which came up in the late 90's. BJP (Bharatiya Janta Party) had gained a majority in parliament in 1998 and this victory was repeated in 1999. When NDA (National Democratic Alliance) under the leadership of BJP came to power in 1999, the government tried to replace the Marxist individuals with right-wing scholars in curriculum agencies at the national level. They believed in Hindutva which is the ideology of the right-wing BJP.

A real-life incident from the life of Kannada poet and playwright H.S. Shivaprakash formed the basis of the novel. He wrote an award-winning play *Mahachaitra* in the 1990's based on the life of Kannada saint Basava, the medieval social reformer and founder of Veerashaivam. The play was prescribed as a textbook in three different universities. It was almost a decade later that it was prescribed in Gulbarga university as a textbook which led to a horrid controversy raised by some so-called preservers of history. The controversy resulted in the withdrawal of his award-winning play from the university syllabus on the grounds that it presented Basava in an unflattering light. As a result of all this, a legal battle ensued resulting in the play being withdrawn from university curriculum. It was this controversy that seems to have inspired Hariharan to write the novel *In Times of Siege*. Shiv Murthy, the protagonist, is a counterpart of H.S. Shivaprakash. Hariharan also creates a young student activist, Meena and her radical friends who represent the Left wing. Hariharan opines in *The Deccan Herald*, "History, with all its ugliness and achievements, is something that we should have access to explore, debate. This is what I wanted to focus on, because I think history is not just something that we study in school. It is a tool of analysis for us to know our past." (web *www.githahariharan.com*)

The novel is a portrayal of a middle-aged professor of medieval history Shiv Murthy who teaches at an open university located in Delhi. He is leading a quiet and comfortable life, writing modules, attending staff meetings and taking things in his stride. The novel projects a male character in the pivotal role. On being questioned about the idea of choosing a male protagonist, Hariharan states, "Yes, I have portrayed a man at the centre, but it is a man with a large female component in him. He transcends gender, I want to show that the complex male figure is as much a victim of society." (web *www.thehindu.com*)

Shiv gets into an unexpected and awkward situation when a friend's daughter Meena, a college student, comes to stay in his home. She is the daughter of his childhood neighbour Sumati, who suddenly calls upon him for help. She requests temporary shelter for her daughter Meena in Shiv's home as she has broken her leg. Meena is to stay with him for a few weeks even though they hardly know each other. She barges into Shiv's life unexpectedly, "How do I get in? These are Meena's first words to him. Only now it occurs to him that they have not greeted each other, nor has she thanked him for coming."(7) Shiv has gone to pick her up from her hostel. He takes her home expecting that her mother Sumati will take her away soon or will come to look after her, but he is surprised as Meena says, "Look, I know you plan to call my parents. I'd rather you didn't. That you didn't worry them. I'll be all right here. You don't mind, do you?"(13-14) The fact is that Shiv's wife Rekha is in Seattle visiting their daughter Tara. Since Meena is unable to work independently, Shiv helps her with daily chores. He washes her hair, buys Asterix comics and a walking stick for her. Hariharan writes in the novel:

> And Shiv – for the first time in his life he makes breakfast for two; tea for two; snacks for two. He goes to markets he has not been to for years, unlikely shopping lists to hand. A white plastic stool for Meena to sit on while bathing. A shower head and a tube he attaches to the bathroom tap so that Meena does not have to bend for a bucket bath. (28)

Both Shiv and Meena spend peaceful, cosy and intimate moments together in each other's company. Meena is a sociology student, who is pursuing research on what she calls women's stories. She is working on the aftermath of "women affected by the anti-Sikh riots after Indira Gandhi's assassination in 1984."(28) She is a voracious reader and admirer of radical texts such as *The Politics of Hate, Onward United Action, Women's Voices and The Communist Agenda* and forms her worldview based on them. She is impressed by Martin Niemoller, the German pastor who was the victim of the Nazi concentration camp and puts up a huge poster in her room "...in screaming red: **Speak Up! Before It's Too Late**"(27), which speaks volumes for the agenda of Hariharan's works. The lines on the poster (written below) clarify Meena's viewpoint:

> In Germany, they first came for the communists, and
> I did not speak up because I was not a communist.
> Then they came for the Jews, and I did not speak up
> because I was not a Jew.
> Then they came for the trade unionists, and I did
> not speak up because I was not a trade unionist.
> Then they came for the homosexuals, and I did not
> speak up because I was not a homosexual.
> Then they came for the Catholics, and I did not speak
> up because I was Protestant.
> Then they came for me... but by that time there
> was no one left to speak up. (27)

Meena is a courageous young woman who believes in action and not in passive and complacent acceptance. The story of what happened in Germany highlights the fact that if one finds excuses to remain passive in the face of any crisis, he/she is not necessarily out of danger. Because he/she has remained passive when others were attacked, there is no one to protect him/her when he/she is in danger. Meena, therefore, wants to remain actively involved in the world around her. Though she is physically confined to her bed with her leg encased in a cast, she is mentally quite active and "talks of causes and street theatre, 'gender' and 'courting arrest' with the ease of a veteran."(31) She likes to champion political causes through poster campaigns, "sit-ins" and demonstrations. As Anita Singh opines:

> The cast around Meena's leg is also employed as a metaphor. It is symptomatic of the three R's-restriction, regression, repression – a woman is subjected to all her life. Meena has an indomitable spirit and is not mired by the constricting conditions. The communal fascist forces also function as cast 'incapacitating' and ruthlessly paralysing people's rights. (*Indian* 199)

The novelist emphasises that despite the cast, Meena is presented as a feminist who refuses to abide by the norms of the society. She believes in living independently and asserting herself. She believes in the inherent power lying latent in the downtrodden people and helps them to cope with difficulties. Hariharan portrays the concerns and perceptions of a free-thinking woman and shows how she is not satisfied with playing just the role of a weak, suppressed and subdued individual. She smokes, drinks and even goes on to have a sort of physical intimacy with the man who is almost her father's age, thus moving against the tide of traditionalism. Permanent relationships like marriage are not the priority on her mind, "clearly she is the competent sort who always knows what she is talking about."(7) Shiv's wife Rekha also represents the class of a woman who is not satisfied with the status of a domesticated housewife bestowed on her. She is physically absent and is visiting her daughter in Seattle, so she is unable to participate in the events in the novel but her presence is quite obvious through the authoritative phone calls that she makes to Shiv. She is a modern woman who can balance both home and work perfectly. She is quite concerned about Shiv's safety when she comes to know about the protest and requests him to settle the matter and give up struggling against the fundamentalists. She has a premonition that it can bring a big loss to Shiv and her family,

> 'It's not as if I don't see the principle of the thing. But to be idealistic at such a time, and with such people!' Her voice shook again, then fell almost to a shamed whisper. 'Don't forget, you're dealing with hoodlums who have pulled down mosques and churches that have stood for so many years. They've engineered riots, for god's sake, what's a little violence to them? And they're so powerful now. What can we do – Shiv, don't you understand? I'm afraid. (154-55)

Shiv sometimes feels incomplete and lacks self-confidence. Rekha is quite dominating and efficient in her office "the efficiency that makes her an administrative asset in her office." (4) She almost resembles Meena in the matters of authority, intelligence, competence and common sense. Both Meena and Rekha belong to the contemporary class of women who believe in themselves and in action.

The incident that disrupts Shiv's life is the uproar that arises about the lesson that he prepares for one of his B.A. History courses. He dares to write a chapter about Basavanna in which he brings forth the truth about the religious structure of his time. He presents Basava as a secular human being rather than as a Hindu demigod and this is not acceptable to the fundamentalists. He is condemned by some hypocritical people for writing about the dominance of the Brahmins at that time. He is considered to be an anti-Hindu and is advised to leave India and go to Pakistan. Though Shiv has collected facts and references after thorough research, still he faces hatred, criticism and the protests of the Itihas Suraksha Manch. All this opposition creates a commotion in his peaceful life. In an interview with Luan Gaines, Hariharan clarifies what she had in mind when she took Shiv Murthy, a middle-aged professor as the protagonist:

> One thing about being middle-aged is this sense that this may be the last chance to act, to change, to experience something that you have not before. Usually, in a cliché sense for a man at least, this means some little affair. But in the novel, Shiv is actually challenged on both personal and political fronts, and both aspects come together in the person of Meena. (web *www.curledup.com*)

The lesson which is being questioned is based on Basavanna, the legendary figure of the twelfth-century Karnataka history. Shiv has written about the Vijaynagar Empire and its finance minister named Basavanna, sometimes also called Basava who questioned everything traditional. He strived to create a free society without any caste barriers or differences:

> Basava gathered around him a unique congregation of mystics and social revolutionaries. Together they attempted a creative, courageous experiment: a community that sought to exclude no one – not women,

> not the lowest, most 'polluting' castes. Poets, potters, reformers, washermen, philosophers, prostitutes, learned brahmins, housewives, tanners, ferrymen - all were part of the brief burst of Kalyana's glory. All were equal in that they were veerashaivas; warriors of Siva. (60)

All this became a part of Kalyana's (capital of Vijaynagar) glory and fame for the freedom and equality which prevailed there. The elite of the Vijaynagar kingdom which was dominated by the Brahmins could not tolerate the movement which is primarily constituted by the masses of the society. "The people became a movement; the movement swelled and surged, a wave that threatened to swallow social conventions and religious ritual, staple diet of tradition."(61) This movement may be seen as a precursor to the Gandhian philosophy which aims to coalesce workers and commoners to form a mass movement to fight for freedom and equality. Trouble arises in Vijaynagar when the marriage of a Brahmin girl is solemnized with a cobbler's boy, and this acts as a catalyst for the city of Kalyana. The King's relationship with Basava, which is soured under the tremendous pressure from the so-called guardians of the society, reaches a breaking point. The marriage is challenged by the traditionalists and condemned by King Bijjla, who thereby orders special deaths for the fathers of the couple. People get agitated and retaliate despite Basava's call for non-violence. "His charisma was no longer enough to keep the moderates and the extremists among his followers together." (62) The king is assassinated by Basava's followers and soon Basava too dies under mysterious circumstances. Basava's dream of equality and democracy is broken but the questions he poses remain relevant till date. Hariharan's discussions on the religious fundamental attitudes and liberal ideas begin and end with history. As she opines in the text:

> Each of us carries within ourselves a history, an encyclopedia of images, a landscape with its distinct patterns of mutilation. A dictionary that speaks the languages of several pasts, that moves across borders, back and forth between different times. (104)

Shiv is accused of deforming history and historical figures and condemned by the Itihas Suraksha Manch. He is alleged to have undertaken deliberate exaggeration of the problems of caste and of writing in a prejudiced way about Brahmins and temple priests. It is described as an unpatriotic and unholy act where Hindu saints were projected as cowards and failures in exile. It undermined Hinduism and hurt the sentiments of Itihas Suraksha Manch. Hariharan writes:

> History, its layered terrain of past merging into present, shrinks to the size of a module, a black-and-white booklet of lessons. Then that too goes. There is only a lone, orphaned atom left behind, a sullen, impoverished particle of knowledge. The world and its multitudinous mysteries are reduced to precarious survival on a crude seesaw: saint versus leader, saint versus man. Golden Age versus Dark Ages. Hindu versus Muslim, Hindu versus Christian, anti-Hindu, pro-Hindu. Secularist, pseudo-secularist, soft Hindu, rabid Hindu. (150)

Many newspapers and news channels wish to interview Shiv. Trapped in a very difficult situation, he tries to find the person who may make this article seem non-controversial. Division among the staff into two groups is quite evident as the Left and Right Wings - Dr. Arya is the leading Right whereas Menon and others signify the Left Wing. Shiv is sceptical about the orthodox thinking of his colleague, Dr. Arya and Hariharan also exposes the orthodox thinking of some stereotypical people through his character. Dr. Arya presents an article entitled 'Problems of the Country and Their Solutions', in a meeting in the university through which he expresses orthodox Hindu sentiments. He reads out a paragraph:

> 'Our land has always been a temptation to greedy marauders, barbarous invaders and oppressive rulers. This story of invasion and resistance is three thousand years old. Lakhs of foreigners found their way to India during these thousands of years, but they all suffered humiliating defeat. Some of them we digested. When we were disunited, we failed to recognize who were our own and who were foreigners, and we were unable to digest them. Today, apart from Muslims, even Christians, Parsis and other foreigners are also recognized as minority communities. But in many of the states the Hindus have been reduced to a minority, and the Muslims, Christians or Sikhs are in a majority.' (19)

Mrs. Khan, the secretary of the Department of History who is also a Muslim feels uncomfortable after Dr. Arya's speech. During his speech, Dr. Arya refers to Muslims as foreigners in India. Shiv hates Dr. Arya for his orthodox attitude and for being a supporter of theocratic beliefs. Professor Arya is annoyed because of Shiv's article on Basava, since Shiv has highlighted the Brahmin's dominance in Kalyana city and Basava's struggle against them. Mrs. Khan goes on leave and Hariharan aptly articulates:

> Obviously the leave was planned many days back. But now she has a week to recover from the new status thrust on her - Muslim Mrs. Khan, Foreign Mrs. Khan. Mrs. Khan, a woman who has travelled leagues from her grandmother's and mother's lives to work in an office and make a modest contribution to the family income. Now she is being pushed back to square one, to the old diminishing religious identity. She has seven days to examine her new status and, hopefully, shed it. To come back the same sweet, helpful secretary they know, incorrigible only when it comes to telling n's and u's apart on her typewriter. (20)

The insecurity and horror of not being considered as being a part of the setup she has inhabited for so many years is indeed shocking for Mrs. Khan.

Shiv is accused of misleading and giving a false account of history and historical figures by the Itihas Suraksha Manch. He is shocked to know that an objection is being raised against his article despite the fact that Shiv had written the chapter after a thorough research. He had conscientiously studied the books available on Basava before he proceeded to write that article. *The Hindu* remarks:

> In taking as her protagonist Professor Shiv Murthy (The protagonist of the novel *In Times of Siege*) of the imaginary Open University of Delhi, named Kasturba Gandhi Central University (which seems to be a combination of JNU and IGNOU), she was trying to play up the subtle use of and the assorted systems of coercion and restraint. The discussion after the reading centered around issues such as the novelistic decisions Githa made, that liberal response to national/international crises and the inadequacy of the liberal discourse. (web *www.thehindu.com*)

Shiv is really traumatized to hear such charges being levelled against him from the head of his own department. He is forced to re-think about himself and his personal values. He defends himself stating emphatically that his article is authentic, and is drawn from different sources, "'Part of the challenge of getting to know Basava's life and times is reconstructing it out of literary texts, legends inscriptions and other records. The bibliography for the lesson includes all the major sources that have been used for quite some time now by medieval historians.'" (68)

The Chair of the Department, Dr. Sharma and the Dean are harassed by the attention of the national media and attempt to persuade Shiv to revise the lesson and sign the apology that is being demanded of him. The Chair's complaint against Shiv is a nice caricature of bureaucratic absurdity. The head of the department gives his views about Shiv's lesson:

> 'Yes, we've read the lesson, Dr. Murthy. The problem is not the text itself but the implications. What can be read between the lines? I have gone through the lesson carefully and I have made a list of the phrases and sentences that lend themselves to misinterpretation. I am afraid these lapses are what we will now have to explain.' (67)

The protest against Shiv gives rise to an agitation and the agitators come to destroy Shiv's room and his belongings. They are the goondas hired by Arya, Shiv's colleague. Hariharan describes their ghastly deeds thus:

> ...the tables and chairs and bookshelves are broken, the walls defaced. There are torn books everywhere, cupboard and files open-mouthed and in shambles. A jumble of crumpled paper. His nameplate is on the floor in a heap of little pieces, like a jigsaw puzzle that will need patience and imagination to put together again. (130-31)

Arya and his cronies have ultimately made the history professor "a full-time fugitive."(131) The protest results in Shiv being forced to go on leave which is later extended by the university. When Shiv is on leave, a reporter comes to question him about his controversial article. It is from the reporter that Shiv comes to know that the university has extended his leave. "Did the university ask you to go on leave or is it voluntary?"(51) Menon informs Shiv that his lesson has been sent to the committee for review. It becomes evident that Shiv would have to resign. He receives letters which are threatening. Shiv is charged with destroying the "Great Hindu Past," and is advised through anonymous hate mail to go to Pakistan, "If you want to rewrite Indian history with our Hindu saints as cowards and failures in exile, why not go to Pakistan and do it? They will welcome you and give you all attention and praise you are desperate for." (78) The Manch President and Vice President call for the revival of Hindu courage. The novel describes how the eminent Leftist historians condemn Kasturba Gandhi University and fight against Hindu organisations. It is an ideological war going on between the Leftist group and the Right wing. In an interview with Gowri Ramnarayan, Hariharan articulates, "Shiv began as a liberal but with ideas never put to the test. Ideas can get tested only in times of siege - the Emergency, after Babri Masjid, the Gujarat carnage or the Iraq war. Then people have to reclaim these ideas and discover whether they really own them or not." (web *www.thehindu.com*) In these chaotic circumstances and during Shiv's crisis, Meena becomes his torch bearer. She tries to boost him and takes charge of the situation. She guides him through the difficult times and arranges for a Press Conference with the help of her friends. She arranges a TV show and circulates leaflets attacking RSS and their ideologies through them. An ideological war ensues in the newspapers about the biased approach of historians in the editors' column. Using Meena as her mouthpiece Hariharan writes, "The link between fascism and the ugly faces of Hindutva unveiling themselves around us is the regimentation of thought and the brutal repression of culture."(101)

Hariharan thinks that our utmost effort needs to be directed towards those forces which are bent upon striking at the root of our efforts to survive and emerge as a modern nation-state. Meena belongs to the newer, politically aware generation. When Shiv discloses the details of the controversy to Meena, she retorts, "The protection of history! Whoever heard of history having to be protected?"(55) Meena motivates him and guides him not to surrender in front of the fundamentalists. "'Protect?' says Meena with a knowing sneer. 'The minute they use the word you know they mean attack.'"(55) Since she is an activist, she is aware of how such protests are to be dealt with. "...Meena is a step or two ahead of Shiv. 'What are you going to say tomorrow? You will have to chalk out a plan. Obviously, you can't apologize or take back a word of the lesson'"(55). Meena's mind is full of plans to fight for Shiv, and she doesn't want Shiv to surrender in front of the Manch. When crisis befalls Shiv, she itches for a fight, '"What's the plan of action? How do we beat your fundoos at their game?"'(57) She defies social constraints, religious bigotry and challenges fundamentalism portrayed through the "*fundoos*"(57). Meena acts as a catalyst in the vortex of feelings/ and thoughts of Prof. Shiv and gives him solid support to fight back the forces of fundamentalism. It is Meena who teaches him to confront the challenges bravely and always to stay happy. She goes about distributing leaflets, posters, and arranging a public meeting in a bid to rescue Shiv. She does not shy away from the prospect of violence. "Her brief history, a history of doing."(111) She drums up support for Shiv, they put up a sea of placards, "STOP TALIBANIZATION OF INDIA to HISTORY DESTROYED! to WHO'S AFRAID OF THE MANCH?"(145) Anita Nair opines in her official website, "The book begins quietly enough. But as I read on, I realized that the quietness was a deceptive calm ... like the ominous silence before a storm, the beginning of the book lulls the reader into an acceptance of a sedateness. So that when the storm arrives, its fury is that much more intensified." (web *www.anitanair.net*) There is no doubt that a text which apparently seems to be a simple rendition of a university teacher's life, turns out to be one of the most meaningful and probing texts. It not only describes but also raises a number of questions regarding the 'secular' 'democratic' nature of the Indian Republic.

Meena acts as Hariharan's mouthpiece where she uses the novel as a medium to comment on her ideological opponent – Hindutva Brigade. She coins a new name – "*Fundoo*" for a fundamentalist and uses it frequently:

> Fundoos. How familiar Meena's generation is with the word *fundamentalist*. So much a fact of life that a nickname, *fundoos*, rolls off

> Meena's tongue with ease. A nickname for a pet, a pet enemy. The familiar garden-variety hatemonger, inescapable because he has taken root in your own backyard. Fundoo, fundamentalist. Fascist. Obscurantist. Terrorist. And the made-in-India brand, the communalist - a deceptively innocuous-sounding name for professional other-community haters. (57)

The author's hatred against her enemies is evident through both the groups in the novel. In addition to all this, the author also quotes a few lines from Madhav Sadashiv Golwalkar's book *'We or Our Nationhood Defined'* which describes the past, present and the future for India - a Hindu Rashtra. Golwalkar was the second sar-sanghachalak of the RSS and took over the organisation for nearly 33 years. His thoughts are quoted by Hariharan:

> "Foreign races in Hindusthan must either adopt the Hindu culture and language, learn to respect and hold in reverence the Hindu religion and must entertain no ideas but those of the glorification of the Hindu race and culture...or may stay in the country wholly subordinated to the Hindu nation." (100)

Shiv finds himself caught up in a strange situation and feels that "...he is in a play, miscast as a protester marching down the road"(142) He yearns to remain a simple academician and does not attend to any of the interviews, meetings, telephone calls and hate mails. He feels like a "body in a lawless country, a body that has somehow unlearnt the law of gravity."(131) His books and room are stripped naked. "A sullied place, no longer anyone's refuge" (130) Shiv is in a perplexed state and asks himself: "What makes a fanatic? A fundamentalist? What makes communities that have lived together for years suddenly discover a latent hatred for each other?"(129) He tries to imagine what Basava would have done in these circumstances. Shiv could not think of anything in this bizarre state of affairs that he is caught in. He sees two images side by side "condemned to be coupled forever. There, to the left, is Basava confronting his Manch, standing up to what he passionately believes in ... To the right is the second image, inexorably tailing the first."(136) Girja Kumar describes the similar plight of Shivaprakash in his book:

> All this controversy had been upsetting for Shivaprakash. He was to ask this question of himself repeatedly. Why did he have to be victimized? How come he was victimized by those who were never going to read the book? After all, he was rendering a service to seer-saint by interpreting his life and times in a new light. (*Censorship* 91)

The fundamentalists hire the services of proficient "*goondas*" to aggravate the political stir against professor Shiv and to harass the university authorities. The university succumbs to the pressure which is being built up by the manch and withdraws the history lesson, which consequently leads to protests by the university professors. They collectively stand against the despotism and dominance and uphold their intellectual freedom at the altar of a so-called culture which propagates 'One Language, One Nation, One Religion.' The Professors condemn the university's failure to take a firm stand against this kind of intellectual censorship which can also lead to a further targeting of secular historians. Girja Kumar comments on the similar state of affairs which affected the socio-political situation at the time of the protest against Shivaprakash:

> While the politicians deserted the author en masse, the literary community responded magnificently. It closed its ranks behind the author. Readings from the play were held all over the place and discussions were organized to explain the content of the play and its importance as a social document. Pro-book demonstrations were held at several places. The association of college and university teachers in Karnataka also condemned the governmental interference in the affairs of universities. Newspapers and periodicals were flooded with articles and "letters to the editor," and both for and against the book. (*Censorship* 85)

Shiv undergoes a lot of mental stress during this hard time. He has to face the opposition and allegations from a group of religious bigots regarding the article that he has written on Basava. The *fundoos* make a lot of fuss and the media also gets interested in the incident. Shiv picks up courage and makes some bold decisions pertaining to his career. He is too troubled when he is asked to give an apology which he refuses plainly as he says, '"I will not apologize."'(69) It is under the influence of Meena that the professor neither apologizes nor withdraws his lesson. Shiv thinks of an action plan to go against the Manch after consultation with his colleagues. At this point, Shiv is getting emotional support from the teachings of his father (who had been a freedom fighter and has gone missing) and also the poet-saint Basava. His father's legacy to Shiv is only a faint presence and "the gift of remembrance." (193) The haunting memory of his father and the ghostly intervening of Basava coincides with his shift from ordinary and simple middle-class professor to a subversive political thinker. Meena also gives her full support to Shiv along with her friends Amar, Jyothi and Manjar. Amar had been an active and committed member of many citizens' groups along with his comrades. The head of the department is pompous though a timid person who states that there was no need for Shiv to give such details in the correspondence lessons. He elaborated that the students only need to know the important dates and achievements of the great personalities and that there is no need to make history interesting and fascinating for them. He further accuses Shiv of having deviated from the truth:

> 'One: Backward-looking. Two: Contradictory accounts of Basava's life, conflicting narratives. Three: Birth legends fabricated. Four: Called a bigoted revolutionary by temple priests. Also called a dangerous man, a threat to structure, stability and religion. Five: The comfort of faith was not enough for Basava. Six: There were rumours that Basava used money from the royal treasury to look after his followers. Seven: The lines of social division in the great city of Kalyana were sharply drawn. Caste was a dominating factor. Eight: There was tension between the Brahmanical religious orthodoxy and the popular religious reformers and saint-poets. Nine: Basava met and could have been influenced by the 'mad men from Persia', the dancing, drinking Sufis. Ten: Bijjala, the king of Kalyana, was pressured by brahmin leaders to commit atrocities on low-caste devotees, especially untouchable devotees, were shown to be superior to Brahmins.'(68)

The list of objections formed by the Head reflects the religious bias and political pressure being put on him. Shiv had always been a peace-loving and subdued professor. Suddenly he acquires courage in his middle age due to Meena's support. He tells Meena,'"Courage is a strange thing, isn't it?"'(34) His behavior undergoes a tremendous change. He startles the Dean and the Head of the Department as he resists and puts his foot down.

He refuses to apologise which is unbelievable for them because they had never seen Shiv behaving adamantly. Shiv has suddenly developed the guts to enter headlong into the battle as he has decided that "he will pick up a spear and a shield and rush headlong into battle"(57) against the *fundoos*. There are lots of discussions in the form of attacks and counter-attacks. Hariharan comments in an interview by Luan Gaines,

> The point is that if a college-a place of learning, debate, openness of mind-is actually taking mob censorship seriously, we really are living in times of siege. And the siege is not just external-the mob or the fundamentalist or the terrorist-but within minds. (web *www. curledup.com*)

How deeply the academic environment is affected by clever political manoeuvres of the powers that beget reflected in Hariharan's comment. How severely they attack the human psyche and besiege the mind is also evident in the statement. The manch is determined and strident in their condemnation as well as in the assertion of their own 'truths', "The truth is that these minorities will be safe in India only if they share our vision of our country and culture. Then we won't mind accommodating two more gods (Allah and Christ) along with our thirty-three crore gods and goddesses. "(118) These nativists, as Said points out, imagine a world without any "warring essences"(*Culture* 277) and such a world is only a fabrication of imagination because, in reality, no such perfect and uncorrupted world exists today. He writes:

> One should not pretend that models for a harmonious world order are ready at hand, and it would be equally disingenuous to suppose that ideas of peace and community have much of a chance when power is moved to action by aggressive perceptions of 'vital national interests' or unlimited sovereignty. (*Culture* 20)

Hariharan is an objective writer who critiques the fundamentalist tendencies and tries to assert the idea that in the name of national interest democracy is being threatened. The novel is a satire on liberalism in India and other places. By bringing in examples from other parts of the world through the books that Meena reads and citing the German story, Hariharan brings out the fact that from time to time human history reflects the violation of human rights. We should try to learn lessons from the past rather than propagate the same denial of freedom to people in the contemporary age. Shiv is caught up in the circumstances that bind him and do not allow him to act or think freely. As Hariharan writes in the text:

> ...a cast like the one on Meena's leg is being wrapped around Shiv, a cast that immobilizes him completely. It is not as if he is just being asked to prove he is a historian. It's the other demands of proof – from two different corners of the ring – that freeze Shiv, slow his heart to a standstill. Proof on the one hand that he is patriotic, Hindu, Indian; proof on the other that he can say and do the right things, transform himself into a twenty-first-century echo of the dissenting Basava.(88-89)

Shiv inherits the values of truth, secularism and freedom from his father who was a freedom fighter and had fought throughout his life to achieve them. His father's words resonate in his mind, '"You must mine the truth. If you settle for safety, if you choose to go along with whatever makes your life comfortable, truth will escape you completely. Shiva: there is a kind of person who lives like this. He is called an opportunist. Repeat the word after me so you remember it. Op-por-tun-ist."'(82) Like Gandhiji, for him too, *Satya* is all important.

In Times of Siege is not just the story of Shiv, it is the story of any individual who tries to "speak up" for equality, freedom or human rights as propagated by Gandhi and Marx; for they believed in a free and classless society. The novel is a criticism of communal fascist forces which impose their fundamentalism on the individuals. It highlights the politics of oppression and repression initiated by the communal forces. Anita Singh articulates the queries raised by Hariharan in the novel:

> ...*In Times of Siege* triggers a slew of questions, both to the individual reader and to the body politic. Who are we, as people? What are we headed for? What defines an individual within the bounds of nationhood? Is secularism a valid ideal as the ground shifts beneath our feet? Human rights are they safe today or are they being trampled upon everyday? (*Indian* 196)

The novel provides a look at the troubled times we are living in and focusses on various power struggles going on amidst the communal divide and the societal inequalities. The world around Shiv is actually a picture of the degeneration in the world today where even an educated Professor like Shiv is not free to express his views. Anita Singh opines:

> Admittedly, the writing has been undertaken for the purpose of stating a message. Political statements can be made in different ways, and a novel is a way of reaching out to a wider audience. It is about the perils of being a liberal in degenerate times. The world, which collapses so abruptly around Shiv, is a world we see coming apart in India today; the polarization is total, and the divide absolute. To be liberal is asking for trouble, to try and teach the values of liberalization might cost you your life, as Shiv learns. This work is a progressive criticism of communal fascist forces. (*Indian* 206)

The irony of the situation lies in the fact that a man with logical and practical thinking becomes a misfit - a kind of outcast, somewhat like Agamben's *homo sacer* in this world. Hariharan has highlighted the fact that there should be some solution for the problem of the growing violation of human rights in the world. The novel presents a picture of the conditions prevailing in the contemporary world. There is actually an absolute divide in the country and a violation of human rights which has virtually taken the whole country under siege – a siege which has acquired a global significance.

Hariharan has started her novel with three epigraphs which are ironical. All three reflect upon the power relations prevailing in the society where the weak are suppressed and repressed by the powerful. The epigraphs ironically refer to the futile effort of man to preserve history or culture because time marches on and people change. The first epigraph is a *vachana* by Basava which refers to the power relations between the fundamentalists and the common people indirectly. The '*fundoos*' belong to the Itihas Suraksha Manch in the novel. Ironically, they are protectors who have turned destructive. They are trying to fight for the preservation of old beliefs but even if they make an iron frame to do so, they will not be able to prevent the bubble from bursting.

So, Hariharan is critiquing their effort to do so. They assert for the protection of historical beliefs but it seems to be useless because these things are ever changing and ever flowing. These beliefs are short lived like a water bubble which bursts even on a delicate touch. It states:

Look at them,
busy, making an iron frame
for a bubble on the water
to make it safe!

-- Basava, Vachana 162

The second one by Zbigniew Herbert articulates that these religious beliefs and ideologies are not necessarily shortlived. Even if a whole city is destroyed and a single person survives, he will carry the flame of those ideologies in his heart. He will have the ability to even set up or reinstate a new empire. So one must not be disheartened and must learn to fight rather than fall before negative forces. Hariharan quotes:

and if the City falls but a single man escapes
he will carry the City within himself on the roads of exile
he will be the City

-- 'Report from the Besieged City', Zbigniew Herbert

The last one is a quote from Basava's *vachana* which is a warning saying that if anyone takes up issues with the fundamentalists, one will have to bear the consequences. It says:

If you risk your hand
with a cobra in a pitcher
will it let you
pass?

-- Basava, vachana 212 (vi)

On being questioned by Gowri Ramnarayan about quoting the *vachana*, Hariharan herself explains, "I'd say the cobra is the unilateral worldview of bigotry, prejudice, ignorance ... Our *fundoos* are made of venom. I'd say the minute you try to co-exist with a cobra you'd get bitten." (web *www.thehindu.com*) The caste system has always plagued the Indian social setup and any effort to solve this problem is commendable. One can find instances in history where *Bhaktas* of various parts of India have tried to resolve the issue and Basava is one of them. So his *vachanas* pithily and suitably sum up the need of the hour. Hariharan states that she chose Basava's *vachanas* because they are appropriate and continue to pose a challenge to our society till the present time. She articulates in *The Deccan Herald*:

> When I wanted to show that a history professor gets into trouble for a lesson he wrote years back, immediately my choices were Vasava and Hampi. I first came across the *vachanas* of Vasava and others when I was 17 years old. In case of Vasava, there is sharp questioning, rejection of caste, which is something we cannot simply forget today. This is a tortured soul, who is trying to understand how he is part of this kind of a society where there is such blatant injustice. Then the fact that the whole movement was absorbed - everything he stood for, Vasava's ideas continue to challenge our society today. (web *www.githahariharan.com*)

In the contemporary context, Hariharan's novel comes as a warning against religious fundamentalism and its power when it gets into wrong hands. Hariharan cautions against fundamentalism of any religion be it Hindu, Christian, Muslim, Sikh in an interview with Vaishna Roy. She says, "I think that we need as many warnings as possible in all kinds of ways possible. Whether it is through art or literature, or journalism or in the classroom or courtroom. To say that any kind of prejudice, bigotry, warspeak, fundamentalism, obscurantism is going to diminish our lives, impoverish our lives." (web *www.outlookindia.com*)

Hariharan's novel *In Times of Siege* highlights that all individuals must speak up and assert to achieve their rightful honour and dignity to live in this callous and prejudiced world. The novel tends to bring out the idea that human rights must be protected not only for the sake of the individuals or the countries but to preserve the human race in totality as propagated by Gandhian philosophy and Marxist ideology. It is a call for attention for each individual to sit up and fight against the rising tide of communalism, intolerance and bigotry so as to achieve an equal, fair and independent world. There is need to bring about a pluralistic vision of the world where people of different origins, castes and nationalities can come together and live in peace.

Hariharan's novel *In Times of Siege* is prophetic as it highlights and predicts what can be seen in the present day scenario. It presents a pathetic, degenerating and deteriorating picture of the society - a society affected by communalism, fundamentalism and false prejudices. It has taken the whole world under siege which paralyses the mind and its thought processes. In an interview with Preeti Lal Verma, Hariharan says that she felt compelled to write the novel because:

> ... The book is my writer's equivalent of shouting a slogan; and a writer's slogan is something more than mere rhetoric. It explains why the writer is issuing a warning, a call to understand what is besieging us, and why we have to resist. A writer's "slogan" challenges comfortable middle class placidity and asks dangerous questions.
>
> In the last several years all of us know — as citizens, as people with high stakes in the place we live in - that the world as we know it, the country we think of as ours, is falling apart.
>
> The best way to describe what we feel - the state we are in - is siege. Our spaces, as citizens, as writers, as teachers, as students, as rational people, are shrinking all the time. (Web. *Literary World*)

This is the reason why Hariharan set the novel at the University - a place of learning where ideally the process of learning should wipe out all the differences and enlarge the students' mind, but power relations prevail in educational centres too. Free-thinking and independence are discouraged and the greatest research is condemned if it happens to hurt the religious sentiments of the prevailing powers.

Hariharan's novel *Fugitive Histories* which deals with the Gujarat carnage abounds in the depiction of religious and social contradictions in Indian society and carries the argument of *In Times of Siege* further. It continues the legacy of *In Times of Siege* and Hariharan once again skillfully presents the social and political problems prevailing in the country. The novel reflects the intermingling of the personal lives of her characters and political conditions of the country. Religious prejudices are the negative attitudes or behaviour bred by people belonging to different communities because they practice different faiths, beliefs and religious ideologies. The analysis of the novel highlights certain important issues of our culture and identity; and also critically examines the way in which the nation has always been led by scheming politicians. A fugitive is actually a person who is hiding from law enforcement in intolerable circumstances or taking refuge in different places to avoid being arrested. The word fugitive is also used for persons who are trying to avoid dangerous situations. The title *Fugitive Histories* thus signifies the plight of the people taking refuge wherever they find it to save their lives during the Gujarat carnage. The extreme violence and devastating circumstances caused by religious prejudices force people into hiding for safety. It represents the struggle to survive and save one's beliefs, faith and identity.

Fugitive Histories deals with the scrutiny of power relations which perpetually prevail in the society on the basis of religion. Power is generally seen as a tussle between two socially exclusive units or individuals. It is, in fact, a scuffle between the fundamentalists who have fixities developed over a period of time in the form of bigotry, narrow-mindedness, intolerance and the worldly, liberal and secular ideals in this particular text. Hariharan highlights through her novel that in the contemporary Indian scenario, dogmas, prejudices prevail and also that religious fundamentalism is gaining ground. *Fugitive Histories* describes the condition of people who believe in secularism but find themselves in the midst of trying times when the state of Gujarat is burning with commotion due to riots and communalism. The novel shows the persistence of Hariharan and her versatility to present the story of communal differences, horror and prejudices in her own way which lends it a colour of authenticity.

The state of Gujarat witnessed genocide against the Muslim community in 2002. It began as a collective punishment - as a reaction to the burning of the Sabarmati railway coach carrying fifty-three Hindu pilgrims. The Gujarat pogrom was a spontaneous act of revenge meted out by the Hindus. As

Arundhati Roy writes in the essay "Listening to Grass-hoppers: Genocide, Denial and Celebration":

> In a carefully planned orgy of supposed retaliation, two thousand Muslims were slaughtered in broad daylight by squads of armed killers, organized by fascist militias, and backed by the Gujarat government and the administration of the day.
>
> Muslim women were gang-raped and burned alive. Muslim businesses and Muslim shrines and mosques were systematically destroyed. One hundred and fifty thousand people were driven from their homes. (*Listening* 136-37)

The root cause of the Gujarat pogrom described in *Fugitive Histories* is believed to be the burning of the train from Ayodhya in Godhra. The Sabarmati Express which was returning from Ayodhya to Ahmedabad was stopped near Godhra railway station on the morning of 27th February 2002. Four coaches of the train caught fire under mysterious circumstances and many people including women and children were trapped and finally succumbed to burns. This incident took the lives of fifty-three Hindu pilgrims who were returning after a religious ceremony performed at the site where the Babri Masjid had been demolished. Despite the tragic background of the story, the novel reveals some streaks of human sympathy and female bonding along with the ugliness of the communal violence it portrays. As M. Ronak Soni opines:

> Marked by an astonishing clarity of observation and deep compassion, *Fugitive Histories* exposes the legacy of prejudice that, sometimes insidiously, sometimes perceptibly, continues to affect disparate lives in present-day India. In prose that is at once elegant, playful and startlingly inventive, Githa Hariharan portrays with remarkable precision the web of human connections that binds as much as it divides. (Web *www.githahariharan.com*)

Fugitive Histories exposes communal prejudices which extend to the homes of common people and adversely affect their lives in India. The burning of the bogies of the Sabarmati Express ignited the Hindus. From the next day onwards i.e. 28th Feb began the planned genocide of Muslims in the different cities of Gujarat. Ahmedabad was the worst affected of the eighteen districts of

Gujarat which were involved in violence. Mobs comprising two to three thousand people were seen armed with swords, *trishuls* (tridents) and agricultural implements for killing the Muslims. The rioters were callous and behaved like butchers. They attacked the Muslim minorities and burnt their business properties like shops, godowns, restaurants and hotels. They behaved in a ghastly manner and poured petrol in a little boy's mouth and lit it up with a matchstick. On being asked for help from policemen, the victims were rejected plainly, "'The better policemen simply said we can't help you'. . .'They said we have no orders to help you, you better learn to protect yourselves if you want to live in Hindustan." (160) People lived in the graveyards for weeks, "'The relief camp we went to was in a graveyard. We were still living but we had to sleep where the dead sleep. We had to sleep between the graves'." (161)

The novel reiterates the theme of *In Times of Siege* by highlighting how communal prejudices have often affected people's lives in India. Their obnoxious behaviour is reflected in the cruelties inflicted by them. The places of religious worship like *dargahs* were also targeted. They were destroyed overnight and roads or temples were built in their places. Women and children were the special targets. The little boy's example cited earlier reflects that they did not spare anybody irrespective of age. The denial of help to the Muslims by the policemen and the remark made by him reveals the fact that the government of Gujarat was indifferent to their suffering.

The novel revolves around the lives of three women characters belonging to different generations, residing in three different cities, which are in one way or the other connected with the Gujarat incidents. Hariharan presents the stories of Sara who lives in Mumbai, Mala who lives in Delhi and Yasmin who lives in Gujarat. These women are also symbolic of the trapped sensibilities and fugitive, marginalised communities in the larger social scenario. Sara is the pivotal character in the novel and Mala is her mother and Yasmin is a young Muslim girl who belongs to one of the victimised families. The novel is divided into three sections: 'Missing Persons', 'Crossing Borders' and 'Funeral Rites'. 'Missing Persons' refers to those who actually disappeared from the scene during the carnage. 'Crossing Borders' refers to the development of sympathy between opposing forces. 'Funeral Rites' ties up some loose ends. In the first section, Mala and Sara are introduced, the death of Asad and how it affects their lives is also described. The second section gives an account of Sara who leaves for Ahmedabad to help her friend and room-mate Nina to prepare the script of a documentary on the people of the city affected by the riots. During the making of the documentary, Sara and Nina visit Yasmin's home and meet other Muslim women of the locality. The third section of the novel reflects how religious prejudices affect the common man who is generally secular in his attitude but is forced to follow them. It highlights the suffering and death of Asad and Mala's bonding with her daughter, Sara.

The novel runs on two parallel tracks. The psychological journey of Mala in her house in New Delhi runs parallel to the physical journey of Sara from Mumbai to Ahmedabad and then to New Delhi. Another character Yasmin who is the victim of the pogrom narrates her story in the novel. All the characters in the novel are like fugitives who are trying to find an escape from their present lives. Hariharan does not delve deep into the history but takes the story of the recent past, i.e., of the year 2002 Gujarat carnage. Gujarat - the birthplace of Mahatma Gandhi – the torch bearer of *ahimsa* and *satya*, was burning with fury and flames due to the pogrom. The '*fundoos*' of *In Times of Siege* acquire the name of 'fanatics' in *Fugitive Histories*. India, which is popularly known as a secular country, ironically has the largest number of instances of communal disharmony and religious prejudices that tear people apart.

Fugitive Histories presents women not as weaklings but as strong and capable individuals. The relationship of Mala and Asad who have had inter-religious marriage forms the backdrop of the whole story of the novel. Various problems dealing with their marriage in particular and the man-woman relationship, in general, are taken up in the novel which also takes up the cause of women. Mala indirectly represents all the women characters in the story. The women's stories also highlight the themes of religion and fundamentalism which are central to the novel directly and indirectly. She is not over sensitive but has the power of clear thinking. She is not selfish but individualistic and is making an attempt to discover her own self and identity. She is not an utterly domesticated woman whose role is confined to getting married and rearing a family but is also dedicated to the service of the community. For example, since childhood, Mala was a kind of a tomboy. She loved to indulge in adventurous activities like climbing trees, riding a bicycle at a fast speed and picking coconuts from the trees. But she is not allowed to do any of these things because these activities are not girlish. Her grandfather is a conservative and strict man who wants each person of the family to follow his orders. Mala is often jealous of the boys who ride fast bicycles and pluck coconuts. She is deeply disturbed and harbours rage in her mind because, "Being her seemed to mean being inept, her fear of failure making her taste failure even before she had actually failed"(14) She wants her life to be independent, so that she can live freely according to her will:

> For some years, her ambitions centered on trees and bicycles. But anything would have done as long as it let her be one of *them*, those fearlessly joyous children she watched secretly, obsessively, from a distance. What she wanted was to find a place to be in or a thing to do that would set her free from her family, her home and school in the city, her annual summer home in the village. What she wanted was to be set free from herself. (14-15)

Mala's grandfather is a man of principles but he does not treat his wife Bala in a respectable manner. He often bullies Bala as a result of which she suffers from hysteria. She is like a prisoner in the family. She feels nervous due to the harsh behaviour of her husband. Therefore she ignores others and does not pay heed to anyone except Mala. Even after her marriage, she has not attained any kind of freedom. Rather she remains confined to the house and is never allowed to go out:

> Bala was barely twelve when she came to the house, a week after she began menstruating. Her husband was only five years older, but

> already he had firm ideas on who fits where in his household and his life. It didn't take long for him to decide that this childish, flat-chested, chattering girl was not the bride he deserved. But still she was *his;* he had to make the rules, she had to follow them. Bala was never allowed to step out of his house, not even to visit her parents. She *belonged* to the house. (15)

The mental state of Bala might have triggered Mala's desire of living independently. She wants to live a carefree, independent life but it is not possible for her to leave her mother, "It's unfair, horrible, this price to be paid for being reborn. She will be free, but so free that even her mother will have let go of her. Mala burst into tears."(17) She loves her loving and caring mother so much that she cannot stay away from her, "The thought makes her a little sick because she knows she can *never* be someone else. All her life she has to be Mala, all the days till the day she dies. And in between, home will be like this big room, the people in it her family. When she grows up she will be one of them."(17)

Just like Mala, Bala also harbours a desire in her heart to attain freedom. She calls her husband "hairy old bastard, the big boss"(23) At one point, Bala goes on the rooftop to comb her hair and watch the unknown streets and nearby houses of the strangers but gets panicky when she sees her husband walking on the street and coming back home. She is sure that he will rebuke her:

> From the roof, Bala could see unknown streets, unknown houses full of strangers, a whole new life waiting to be lived. But then she saw *him* walking down the street toward the house, she saw the enraged disbelief on his face as their eyes met. Even before it happened she could feel the rough arms pulling her away from the roof, protecting her from the hungry eyes of strange men, eyes that may slide down the length of her wet, naked hair. (21-22)

Through the character of Bala, Hariharan showcases the plight of Indian woman and the place they get in the family. Despite being old and having grandchildren, Bala still remains a slave to her husband. She has to abide by all the rules set by the family and is locked inside the storeroom. She is not even allowed to meet anyone in the house and exemplifies Simone de Beauvoir's description of the situation of women:

> ...man does not make his appeal directly to woman herself; it is the men's group that allows each of its members to find self-fulfilment as husband and father; woman, a slave or vassal, is integrated within families dominated by fathers and brothers, and she has always been given in marriage by certain males to other males. In primitive societies the paternal clan, the gens disposed of woman almost like a thing: she was included in deals agreed upon by two groups. The situation is not much modified when marriage assumes a contractual form in the course of its evolution; when dowered or having her share in inheritance, woman would seem to have civil standing as a person, but dowry and inheritance still enslave her to her family. (*Second* 446)

Hariharan's female characters are mostly educated and possess an independent thinking. The family and parochial society hardly understand their struggle to be free and attain an identity for themselves. Mala, who is senior-most in age has a complicated past. She is a girl belonging to a South-Indian Brahmin family who fell in love with an artist Asad and marries him. She recalls the memories of her past life. She lives alone in Delhi after the recent death of her husband. Both her children Sara and Samar are staying away from her and settled in cities which are far from Delhi. Though Mala often feels lonely she never expresses her pangs of depression and loneliness to her children. Mala, who works as a librarian in a school, finds her only company in the life sketches left behind by her husband. Mala remembers the long-lost memories of her childhood when she used to visit her grandparents' house in the village in the summer vacations. She opens the tin trunk and finds Asad's sketches which were related to their past lives and memories. The only solace she has that she feels close to Asad through his sketches:

> She opens the trunk, expecting a mess. But unlike the cupboards, it's tidy. There are sketchbooks inside, what at first sight looks like dozens of them, packed tightly, row after neat row. Rows, piles, enough to encompass a lifetime. She suppresses this unlucky obit-like thought almost immediately, touches her head in place of wood. How can anyone's life, even a few decades of it, fit in a tin box? Still, what is biography - or its less disciplined relative, memory - but a reckless attempt to fit chunks of a life into a box, whether she calls the box 'the times' or 'the works' or 'the love story'? There are those usual official signposts: *born in, born on, born to, married on, had a son by, had a daughter called."* (5)

Mala lives alone in her apartment and keeps looking at or arranging and rearranging relics from her past. In order to break her loneliness, she does household chores like cleaning and shifting things in the house. Asad's sketchbook makes her feel alive. "Maybe it's something as simple and indescribable as that secret that can sometimes reveal itself, become an open secret for a brief and piercing moment: I am *alive*! *We* are alive! (7) It signifies that Asad is still alive through his art. While accomplishing her tasks of washing dishes, putting them away, watching TV and checking her mail "She can feel the air of anticipation in the empty rooms, the sense that someone is waiting for her. She has to finish what she's doing so she can get back to him." (11) Asad is waiting for her. Or at least his diaries are. She constantly thinks about him and feels comfortable even though Asad is not near.

Going through Asad's sketchbooks, Mala finds one page that was marked with the year 2002 – "There's a caption below the drawing and, again, a date. *Broken Home, February 2002.* There's no doubt what the date refers to. It's the year Gujarat burnt, the month it burst into flames."(198) Mala remembers the evening when they were all listening to the news of the Gujarat pogrom, everyone was hurt and frightened. Since Mala was not born in a Muslim family, Asad and his family may have thought that she could not feel the way all of them were feeling:

> Asad is disturbed, but they're *all* disturbed. Mala is as sick and grieved about it as the rest of them in the living room that evening. But is there something, some evil canker that has planted itself in the room, planning to grow between her and everyone else? A growth that may make all of them believe, herself included, that she can only be a sympathizer, she's different from the really beleaguered? (202)

Having been brought up in a Brahmin family, Mala recalls certain memories of the biased viewpoint of her mother. Hariharan showcases the religious prejudices and the superiority of Brahmins through the instructions given by Mala's mother to make her a good Brahmin girl.

> *Don't use your left hand like a bazaar Christian!*
> *Don't show off like an uncultured Punjabi!*

Don't part your hair on the side like a Muslim!
Push the fa-a-a-t slaving pa-a-r-i-aa-h out of the game! You're the stupid pariah this time, you're thrown out of the game! (203)

It is through the memories of Mala that the reader learns about her past. Mala comes to Mumbai for higher education, she visits Dilkush Mansion (her friend Nasreen's house) where she happens to meet Asad, an artist. Asad is a man of liberal views who believe in secularism and the equality of religion. Thus, he marries Mala who is a Hindu. Mala's parents do not approve of the marriage due to religious prejudices. As a result, days pass in silence between Mala and her parents. They do not even face each other. The parents indulge in loud pujas to various deities to bring back the peaceful atmosphere at home. Religious bias prevents them from seeing that even if he is Muslim, Asad is a sensitive artist and a good human being too. Mala finally elopes with Asad which is something scandalous in Indian society because every sect and religious group puts strictures on women and wants to confine them to their own faith and religion. Some of Mala's cousins pretend not to recognise her because she had eloped with a Muslim.

Indian society never accepts inter-religious marriage even though times have changed now. Inter-religious marriages have also resulted in honour killings where parents do not hesitate to kill and punish the child to save their reputation. While endorsing a secular attitude towards inter-religious marriage, Hariharan also realistically examines the result of such a union through Asad and Mala. Mala's parents express their feelings, "You're killing us! You'll marry this man, this foreigner, and you'll be lost to us, you'll kill us!" (69) It so happens that after some time they accept the marriage and send for her though with a little reluctance. When Mala is invited by her parents to come to their house, "Asad is not invited; but if they haven't disowned their daughter, things can't be as bad as they seem. They assure their sudden influx of visitors that Asad's family is not religious, they are *quite* modern. Mala's father even adds that Asad is secular" (72) When she comes to her parents' house, Mala's mother angrily says "'I hope you're happy.'" (72) Her mother throws a silk sari at Mala instead of giving it to her and says "'I hope you're satisfied everyone is talking about us."(73) Her mother is irritated by the coming of one of her great-grandaunt who especially comes to meet Mala, "Now this horrible woman is coming to look at us like we're animals in the zoo." (73) Mala's grandaunt tells Mala to leave Asad because of the cultural differences between them. She opines that it is next to impossible for Hindus to adapt themselves to the Muslim culture and people who ate meat and read namaz five times a day. The grandaunt whispers in her ear "'Don't they do it differently? And more often?' Her eyes glitter as if on the verge of discovering how to live another twenty years. 'How many times a night?'" (73) The questions disturb and hit Mala deep in the heart.

Mala and Asad try to defy the norms but succeed in doing so but only outside their social circles. Asad is a man of liberal views who believes in the equality of religions. The married life of Asad and Mala is challenging in many ways - the chief one being the religious differences. They belong to the lower middle class, so financial paucity is also one of the problems they face. Asad, who is an artist, lives an impoverished life. Mala suffers the pangs of poverty in her marriage after having enjoyed a comfortable childhood. Even though Mala stays with Asad in a dirty rented room, she wants to enjoy her life with him. The inter-religious issue arises during the naming ceremony of the baby that is born to them. Initially, Asad overrules all debates by saying that if it is a boy, he will be called Ahmed or some other good name that begins with A. It is then decided that if the baby was a boy, he may be called Samar. But now Mala's mother insists that the new baby should be named Rama or Krishna, or Ramakrishna. When Mala's mother finds that Mala is not interested in the naming ceremony, she scolds her. "'First you come up with a strange name we've never heard before,' . . . 'Then you don't want a naming ceremony. What do you think, this boy is going to live in a world all by himself?'" (32)

The identity crisis faced by Sara who is Mala and Asad's daughter also arises out of the religious differences between her parents. Her dilemma is that "'I have Muslim relatives and

Hindu relatives. I'm neither. Sometimes I think I'm Indian. But most of the time I'm just Sara.'" (167) "And my father's family is Muslim, my mother's family is Hindu." (179) So it becomes difficult for her to identify with either. The story of Mala and Asad suggests that if left alone people of different religions would live together in harmony. It is when authority is wielded on them by social, religious and other institutions that complications arise.

Hariharan assesses the pros and cons of such inter-faith relationships objectively. Other stories get connected with the lives of Mala and Asad. Mala is now living alone with her memories and as her story unfolds, other characters and their stories merge with it. Sara wants to maintain her faith in her own and her parents' secular ideals. She comes to Ahmedabad in search of a purpose and meets Yasmin - a survivor of the mayhem, whose missing brother miraculously returns after a long time gap. She comes across people whose minds are full of anguish and hatred and yet they are trying to maintain their hope and fulfil their dreams valiantly. The novel exposes how the legacy of prejudice continues to influence the Indian people. Hariharan, however, does not despair; she shows how human connections can go beyond religious biases to bind as much as they divide humanity. These ideas form the backdrop of Hariharan's *Fugitive Histories.*

Inter-religious marriage also has its repercussions in the lives of the children born out of them. The spiritual or identity crisis which is faced by Sara reflects these. When Sara is travelling in a train, a man asks her about her origin. But Sara can hardly answer that simple question. Her friend's husband Rajat is confident enough to say "'I can *make* what I am, I'm not just some inheritance'." (178) Although he hails from Lucknow, he admits himself belonging to Mumbai. Unlike him, Sara says "'I don't really know' . . . 'I live in Mumbai, but I've lived in other Indian cities. I was born in Chennai, and my parents are from different parts of India. And my father's family is Muslim, my mother's family is Hindu.'"(179) One day even her school going friend Tripti asks her about her identity "'So what are you then?'

Sara couldn't answer her.'"(179) Although Sara is perplexed about her identity at times yet she is happy about her secular beliefs. She keeps wondering on the way in the train as to who she is and what would others say about her condition. Sara's great-grandfather called her a "Muslim Indian. Or Indian Muslim"(180). She feels good as he opines "...she's her parents' daughter, she's secular."(180) She resembles her mother more, "she is clearer about what she is not rather than about what she is. Sara could be both Hindu and Muslim, the kind of person who announces that she celebrates all festivals with equal fervour."(180) At last Sara realises that being a woman determines her status in the world just like her name, religion or social stature. She is not anything but a young woman with a body. As she arrives home in Delhi and is loved and cared by her mother, she feels blessed. She realizes the unconditional love and affection of her mother as she kisses her. Sara tells her mother, "'Good thing Asad and you married when you did'. . . 'How lucky I am.'" (184) Mala could not make out why she is calling herself lucky."'Lucky?''Yes, I'm beginning to realize how lucky I am. How *glad* I am that I'm a hybrid.'(184) Being one she knows the religion and culture of both major communities of India. Sara drops her gaze, and adds almost shyly, "'I wish I could tell Asad that.'"(184) When she looks at her mother, she sees that Mala's face is glowing and she seems to be happy inside. "'Maybe he knew it anyway,'she tells Sara." (184)

The threat to secularism is highlighted through the character of Asad who had a clear vision of it and the equality of all religions before the Gujarat pogrom. But the riots shatter the illusion of secularism and Asad realizes that a Muslim will remain a Muslim because people are prejudiced, biased and divided on the basis of their religious sentiments. He is deeply hurt and shattered because the carnage breaks his faith in the equality of religions. He expresses his feelings through his sketches. The pogrom has a deep impact on his mind. He is a changed man, he does not interact with Mala as well, instead, he dedicates most of his time in his studio and focusses on his drawings. He says to Mala, "'We've marched all our lives and nothing has changed.

Or it's changed for the worse'."(215) He gets so depressed that he stops listening to the news and going outside his house. He cannot bear the cruelties which are inflicted on the Muslims. Mala tries to comfort him and supports him in every possible manner:

> She no longer goes to school. The two of them are caged together with a heavily coiled creature too somnolent to move. The flat feels overused; there's no air in the place. She has to inhale what there is of it, process it so it's easy to swallow, then feed it to Asad so he can continue to breathe, think, talk. Continue to suffer. If only she could open all the windows and the door of the flat, let the air outside come in! But what will she do if it brings Asad news of new terrors? (216)

Asad is much too sensitive to this situation and develops heart disease. Though Mala tries her level best to console Asad she fails to do so. Asad feels too deeply about the dehumanizing experiences inflicted by the powerful majority. He feels degraded and humiliated and is made to feel helpless and powerless. He also feels himself to be a victim due to his minority status. Eventually one morning, he is found dead in his bed because of heart failure.

Sara starts working in Bombay in an NGO named *Sangam* and shares her room with Nina. As their relationship matures, they develop a very close bond with each other. Sara accompanies Nina to Ahmedabad and is helping her in writing a script for a documentary on the Gujarat pogrom which is being produced by Nina. The city of Ahmedabad unfolds the story of the Gujarat pogrom, which remains centre stage in the second section of the novel. Sara and Nina visit the victims of Godhra tragedy to document its impact of it on their lives. They intend to bring on screen the faces behind shrouds and muffled reality. They act as agents, conveying reality in a fictional manner to the readers. They interview families and individuals who lived through the brutal catastrophe. Noorjehan, another interviewee of Sara and Nina wails:

> 'They burnt my husband, they burnt my father, they burnt my son. His name was Shafiq, he was just fifteen years old. If only I could have buried them properly, with some dignity . . . if only I could have given

> them the respect everyone should have in death . . ."Now give us our men back, give us our children back. All those they took away with made-up charges. Give us our missing ones, our lost ones.' (162)

The investigations reveal how Muslim women were the worst affected in the communal disturbance either as rape victims or because of mutilation and murder. The novel narrates the subjugation of women in a multifaceted manner. Many women were gang-raped and thereafter had their heads shaved by the rapists and "Om" was cut into them with knives. There were other instances of "Om" being engraved on women's buttocks and back and they were even murdered. Another instance is about a woman in Vadodara who had her "stomach being ripped open and stuffed with burning rags."(*Listening* 3) Hariharan narrates the aftermath of these brutal acts in her novel and reveals the inhumanity women were subjected to. Sexual assault on women and young girls is the most brutal outcome of such communal riots. Zulekha, a victim from Ahmedabad talks to Sara and describes their condition during the mayhem, "'Those girls were screaming, they were begging us to remove the stumps of wood that had been pushed into them. Each one was crying, "Me first, remove mine first."'" (160) Zulekha feels her blood boiling whenever she recollects their screams. On reading texts like Hariharan, it seems that religious fundamentalism which is the superficial cause of creating divides is only the tip of the iceberg and it hides beneath it a host of deeper animosities and differences at the socio-political level. However, humanity and humane attitudes somehow manage to survive the ravages of such violence. The lesson learned is that prejudices must not condition our responses to the trouble caused by hidden forces and agendas. It becomes disparaging and brings forth hostility and misery. As Hariharan opines in an interview given to S. Bageshree,

> ...Fugitive Histories looks at these familiar ideas in a more personal, private way. It presents the mosaic of lives that collide in unhappy ways, but also in ways that produce love, passion and tenderness. After all, shrinking of public spaces also shrinks private spaces. The novel says that we can no longer be satisfied with overused rhetoric. A lot of people with liberal ideas would not hesitate to formally

> condemn prejudice against a community. But what happens to that same middle-class person in day-to-day life when he or she is continuously exposed to the profile of a community? There is a need to not just define prejudice but also fears in our individual lives. Prejudice is not just something that comes up only when we are in public meetings. (web *www.thehindu.com*)

While on the one hand, it is through these women that the terrible consequences of the carnage are revealed, on the other the detailed story of Yasmin raises another significant question. How safe are minorities in a so-called secular, democratic country? *Fugitive Histories* describes the tendency among people to indulge in anti-human activities to destroy an entire community. The people who were victims of the riots had to undergo immense physical and mental ordeals. The extreme poverty they had to face is evident through the plight of Yasmin's family in the novel. Yasmin has a father, mother and a missing brother, Akbar. Mohan Ramamoorthy opines in the article "A novel discord", "Missing is a strong metaphor she (Hariharan) uses deftly. From Mala's missing twin to Yasmin's brother who went missing during the riots and now presumed/confirmed dead, they add a real/surreal dimension to the narrative." (web *www.indian express.com*) Her family exemplifies the people who are trying to find a secure place as the foundations of their lives have been shaken. All their lives they believed that they were in a safe secular haven but all of a sudden this belief is shattered. They are in search of a society that is more human. The novel is a powerful narration of the historical events which have left an indelible impression of cruelty and fear on the minds of the people. Yasmin also emerges as a helpless young girl who wants to set everything right. She is only seventeen years old, a school-going girl and Sara has to coax her tactfully into sharing the past trauma with her. Sara writes about Yasmin in her diary:

> Yasmin, seventeen years old. Yasmin's father had a shop downstairs in the house where they used to live. Yasmin's mother used to be a housewife, now an NGO helps her and other women in the area sell the skirts they stitch and embroider. Yasmin's brother was in college when the trouble started, he did not come back home. He's still missing. Her father was forced to sell their house for whatever he could get and

> move to a safe area. He's trying to set up a small business but is often sick. Yasmin is in the last year of school. She wants to go to college, but she failed her boards last year. (114)

A sense of fear and insecurity haunts Yasmin who is able to win Sara's sympathy and love. Yasmin's profile arouses interest in both Nina and Sara, they notice that "The daughter, Yasmin, has a thin, watchful face, She lets her mother do the talking, but she doesn't leave the room...When Nina talks to her, all she does is nod or shake her head."(111)

When Sara and Nina pay their first visit to Yasmin's house, Nina shows her concern by carrying some vegetables and fruits from Mumbai and hands them to the mother in the family who is very careful, alert and attentive. Her mother stitches clothes and trains a few girls in the art of sewing. Yasmin wishes to pursue higher studies and take up a career to support her family. Though she failed last year in her higher secondary exams, but she is a courageous girl, who works hard to pass her exams this year:

> She has to pass because Akbar-Bhai is gone. Earlier she used to think it was only till he came back from wherever he was hiding that she had to be Abba and Ammi's daughter and son. Now she knows he will not come back; she has to be their daughter and son forever...everyone who tells Ammi and Abba she shouldn't go to school will never be able to open their mouths again. They'll know they're wrong, they won't say it's not safe for girls, *anything can happen*. They won't say it's no use, it's better she goes to sewing class like Sultana, it's better she does some work right now. It's better she helps you. (116-17)

However, the indelible impressions left by the riots make both her vision and mission blur and slow down. She is a sensitive girl who lives with her parents in the riot-hit state. She has lost her brother Akbar and is emotionally wounded by the ruthless rioters. She assists her mother and tries to make a living so that she can continue her education. She tells her father, "'I don't have to go to Mumbai, Abba. I just want to go to college.' *Teach me to be brave, Allah. The wall has cracks, it may break any minute. But it's still high. It's still hard to see what's on the other side.*" (228)

Yasmin is a silent, shy girl, a dreamer who is interested in Bollywood films. She is an ardent admirer of Shabana Azmi and she believes that Shabana will come and save her from the adversities of life. She asks Sara whether she is in the film industry and knows the actress. Yasmin's mother tells Sara that Yasmin has seen all of Shabana's films. The extreme suffering of Yasmin's family and their fugitive status after the riots is highlighted through Yasmin who reflects the dilemma of people who are trying to find a foothold in a world that is lost. Everything changes for her and her family and nothing remains the same due to the riots. There is death, poverty, fear, doubt, destruction, death and helplessness in place of a normal life. As Hariharan writes in the novel:

> 'What do you call what happened here in 2002? Just communal violence, the bland, zipped-up phrase the government prefers? Or danga, riots? But it's all too obvious these were not riots. Then there are those slightly desperate phrases journalists cooked up. *Dance of death. Season of hate. Inferno of hate and horror.* But we have to call it what it was, we have to use hard words even if they're frightening. Pogrom. State-sponsored terror. Carnage. *The Gujarat carnage.*' (234)

Bloodshed and never-ending tears are the only visible results of violence in the name of religion. The suffering and pathetic condition of the affected people are highlighted in the novel. It shows that even the police officials had connived with the rioters and the public was immensely insecure so much so that they had to hide in the graveyard! In fact they were so insecure that they hid anywhere and everywhere they could think of:

> 'We had nothing but stones to pelt them with.'
> 'We could do nothing but hide.'
> 'We hid in the toilets.'
> 'We hid on the roof.'
> 'We hid in our neighbour's house.'
> 'We hid in the fields.'
> 'We hid in the well.'
> 'We hid underground, in the water tank.' (163)

Fugitive Histories narrates personal and communal histories of victims and witnesses who happen to see and suffer the unthinkable atrocities. They are haunted by the bloodthirsty cries of rioters which keep echoing in their ears. They continue to shout "'Kill them, kill all the Mian! Burn them alive!'" (162) The wretched and pitiable nature of the Gujarat pogrom is evident in the novel's description of the way in which the girls and women were molested brutally. As a result, even today many of the Muslim families live in ghettos – near garbage heaps with no basic amenities like water supply, drainage, street lights and in unhygienic conditions, "ghettoized, socially and economically ostracized." (42) They live an inferior life, boycotted socially as well as economically. The Gujarat genocide was not the first of its kind in India. In 1984, three thousand Sikhs were killed on Delhi streets in almost the same manner, by killers who were not brought to book for the Congress party. But the Gujarat genocide was much bigger and more complicated. One of the accused persons of Gujarat genocide Babu Bajrangi was caught in a sting operation and his statement was recorded in Indian news magazine *Tehelka* "We didn't spare a single Muslim shop, we set everything on fire, we set them on fire and killed them .... hacked, burnt, set on fire .... We believe in setting them on fire because these bastards don't want to be cremated, they're afraid of it...." (qtd in *Listening,* 139)

Fugitive Histories thus showcases the violence and unrest in the state of Gujarat in 2002 resulting out of religious prejudices. It is an account of cruelties faced by the Muslim minority. It portrays the sluggishness of the administration. Hariharan writes about inhuman behaviour, cruelty and violence meted out to the Muslims as well as Hindus of the state by focussing on the Gujarat carnage. Hariharan has drawn this harsh reality of inter-communal and inter-religious riots on her fictional canvas. She tries to expose the reality of the Godhra tragedy in this novel. It portrays the Gujarat violence in which Muslims were burnt alive and slaughtered for the sake of fulfilling political aims to establish a state cleansed of the non-believers (Muslims).

Towards the end of the second part of the novel, Hariharan introduces another happy smiling face whom Sara happens to meet in the city in the Sabarmati Ashram. This is an ironic reference to the fact that the city which houses the ashram – the abode of the man who preached non-violence, has been plagued with so much violence. "Like Akbar, he is now a missing person."(170) But he became a father before he went missing. He is unforgettable among the masses. Though he is not around any longer, his ghost can be seen. But it is ironical that the ghost seems like he is starving and pale and not happy and contented in the free country:

> Why should this ghost look like it's starving, why should it shudder and grow paler under such a bright, hard-working sun? The ghost has been fed, it's been *well fed* by its descendants. It's been fed with laminated calendars, framed and garlanded photographs and paintings, road signs, rupee notes from five to a thousand, doggerel, bronze and iron statues, shelves of hardbound books, Oscar-winning films and banned plays, monuments and memorials, cartoons and politicians' speeches. The ghost should be fat, it should be a huge gas balloon floating high above the city rooftops as if advertising his brand of wares. It shouldn't be lurking alone and unhappy, a mere shadow in a villager's cottage in a shady old ashram. (171)

There was a rumour that he has come back to the ashram. Sara visits Sabarmati Ashram which is also known as Gandhi Ashram. She discovers it to be a very peaceful, serene and a beautiful place. It is surrounded by tall trees and various types of birds like parrots, koels, parakeets, bulbuls, mynas, golden oreoles and drab sparrows. The environment is opposed to what has been seen in the rest of the city and the two contrasts of the same place are emphasised. It is worth observing that the birthplace of the great leader Mahatma Gandhi, who was the propagator of non-violence, is filled with turmoil and extreme violence and unrest. It is ironical that a place which should be reverberating with peace and love is burning with hatred, violence, abuse, rape and molestation. Sara observes the Ashram where everything is dusty. There are eight oil paintings which are lying for exhibition, one of them being "*My Life is My Message* and another called *Gandhiji in Ahmedabad.*"(174) Sara goes to the river bank and enjoys the serenity of nature. She closes her eyes and sings "*Ishwar Allah tere naam, sabko sanmati de Bhagwan*"(175) which is a prayer for peace in the world. After her stay in Ahmedabad, she moves to Delhi to join her mother Mala.

The third part of the novel "Funeral Rites" brings out the stark realities of the circumstances and portrays how the characters cope up with them. Sara's mind is deeply influenced after her trip to Ahmedabad. She hears strange voices in her dreams shouting that *Muslims in India have only two places: Pakistan and kabristan.* (192) She even sees Laila and Yasmin suffering in her dream in which the former is burnt and the latter is molested. The cover page of the novel is also quite meaningful. It depicts the three cities Mumbai, Ahmedabad and Delhi on a soiled map along with a pair of hands of a person with 'stand at ease' position. It signifies that the country is trying to be at ease under the adverse circumstances. India has been witnessing such situations throughout different periods of history. Ever since the foreign rulers adopted a policy of divide and rule, outbursts of communal violence have occurred - the mutiny of 1857, the partition in 1947 and innumerable other instances of communal violence can be cited from the pages of Indian History. This is chiefly because of the scheming leaders who follow the example set by the British rulers. People are not allowed to express their opinions fearlessly because of the stereotypical psyche and hypocrisy of the society promoted by religious bigotry.

Communal differences have always been a trump card in the hands of politicians who exploit people on the basis of religion. Indian history is replete with references to occasions when religion has formed the basis to exercise power over the masses. Divide and rule have been a major tactic in the governance of the country. Differences are created between two communities to attain political ends. This policy has its roots in the colonial period of India. It results from power relations between communities, and a strong will to dominate over others. Communalism has varied streaks-political, economic and social and it aims to dominate the people belonging to different communities. Religion has always played a dual role in the Indian scenario; it brings faith, hope and consolation to people and also becomes the source of commotion, tension and conflict. Hariharan depicts the true motives behind the political upheavals and succeeds in presenting the inner truth that underlies the politics in the novel taken up for study. Aamer Hussein in a review of the novel in "Tehelka" writes:

> To Githa Hariharan's great credit, she looks unflinchingly into the ugliness of sectarian destructiveness and strife with an almost photographically realistic lens but always remains within earshot of her protagonists' small personal voices... As subtly constructed as a Chinese box, concealing narratives within narratives and yet remaining blindingly clear in its exposition of public and private realities. (web *www.githahariharan.com*)

Fugitive Histories like *In Times of Siege* describes how the hidden power structures assume the facades of religion and social welfare and become the cause of trouble in the lives of people. Power structures have remained a vital part of our day to day life and they exist in every relationship, political, personal, social or human. Communal discourses have been affecting and injuring the sentiments of people in India especially the minority communities and women have been the worst sufferers. They have been used as pawns in political games, they are the victims of rape, mutilation and have been exploited as well as brutally murdered. They have been playthings in the hands of patriarchal and colonial powers and are prone to become victims in every critical moment of history. These adverse experiences affect their minds and downgrade them socially, economically, politically, and also psychologically. India has witnessed communal tensions since the Muslim invasions. These continued to affect human relations during the colonial period, the era of the freedom struggle and even later. The nation witnessed sexual violence and killings in the last sixty-five years or so a number of times and these were mostly based on religious differences. The 1984 riots are an example of extreme violence and unrest based on communal issues in the country. Sikhs were brutally murdered and killed. As Ajoy Ashirwad Mahaprashasta and Venkitesh Ramakrishna cite Jarnail Singh's example to show that only the victimised community keeps raising its voice while the government remains inactive. (web *www.frontline.in*) This was repeated in Gujarat about a score of years later when religion became the basis for exciting hatred among people who had lived together for innumerable years. Hariharan has always considered it to be the duty of a writer to expose the reality of the situation. She is a human activist and a writer who highlights the contemporary situations that the "liberals" are facing. She states in the interview with Anuradha Roy "Resisting regimentation":

> YES, to the extent that it is possible for many people to be "liberal" because they are not directly, painfully affected by the oppression of the authorities they are critical of. Recent experiences - Gujarat for example - show that the times of siege we are talking about have stripped the cushioning of even this usually comfortably placed class. The liberal in the novel Shiv, says... "Forget your little arguments, the enemy is almost at our heels! If this can happen to an ordinary, cautious man like me, what about you ideologywallas?" But the novel is also saying that when pushed to a point where a choice has to be made, ... "just ordinary, decent people" will speak up for the fundamental values that hold their world in place... This is what happened during the Emergency, after the demolition of Babri Masjid, and after the Gujarat carnage. (web *www.thehindu.com*)

Power has been wielded in the name of religion to exercise control over the society and the conduct of other individuals. Power can be generally seen as immoral or unreasonable but it is widespread and prevalent when implemented. Power, however, never originates from a single source and is contingent upon other sources. Rather it is a collective effect of varied power sources which could reside in a person, an organisation, perception, etc. Power is analysed as an itinerant and constantly changing set of relations that become apparent in every social communication and thus encompass the social body. Foucault states, "Power is not something that is acquired, seized, or shared, something that one holds on to or allows to slip away; power is exercised from innumerable points, in the inter-play of nonegalitarian and mobile relations." (*History* 94) *Fugitive Histories* reflects such relations that are created by the religious controversies.

The analysis of the novel re-interrogates issues of religious prejudices, identity and communalism. It highlights the vicious nature of religious fundamentalism. The Gujarat carnage portrayed in the novel brings out the political, cultural, racial and gender issues, as also the physical and mental wounds inflicted on people on the basis of these. While reading the novel one wonders whether the country is actually a secular and democratic nation. One is reminded of some pertinent questions raised by Arundhati Roy in her essay "Introduction: Democracy's Failing Light":

> Could it be that democracy, the sacred answer to our short-term hopes and prayers, the protector of our individual freedoms and nurturer of our avaricious dreams, will turn out to be the endgame for the human race? Could it be that democracy is such a hit with modern humans precisely because it mirrors our greatest folly - our nearsightedness? (*Listening* x)

In the contemporary context, Hariharan's novel comes as a warning against the religious fundamentalism and its power when it gets into corrupt hands. It has been a part of India's polity since freedom. Our political leaders have been creating divides in order to enhance their power. They have been sticking to age-old systems and trying to uphold one religion against another. The novel highlights the traumatic circumstances and the plight of the people who are victims of communalism and religious prejudices. It portrays a picture of India which is completely sieged by fanaticism, hatred and mistrust. It highlights the lives of ordinary men and women who are not stuck up in the religious prejudices and are struggling to make a better nation. The novel is a writer's warning to the masses, a call for people to understand why they are under siege. The writer poses some challenging questions pertaining to the seriousness of communalism. She asks whether India can rise above communalism and live in perfect harmony leaving aside politics. Hariharan suggests that the need of the hour is to educate and create awareness among the masses through various mediums, i.e., literature, films, media, etc. so as to remove all prejudices of religion, bigotry and fundamentalism from the society. She advocates the building of a country where perfect peace would prevail. She confesses in an interview with S.Bageshree, Hariharan says, "All political commitments have to be questioned, strengthened, renewed and made meaningful for different times. It is right now important to debate the way in which walls are springing up to not just divide people, but to keep some people in and some out. (web *www.thehindu.com*)

Hariharan suggests that the need for today is a long-term vision for the sake of improving this planet and preventing the damage and devastation that threatens it. It seems like democracy is a failing light which cannot be relied upon to provide freedom, justice and stability which was dreamt about by the leaders who struggled for India's independence. Hariharan comments in an interview with P.Anima:

> As both author and citizen, I can say that despite fears like my character Shiv, I would not be able to live with myself if I didn't speak up about prejudice and injustice. I think the best way to begin doing this is the tried and tested method – to be part of concerned groups. Later, you develop the toughness to disagree with them if you must! (web *www.thehindu.com*)

The novel highlights the undercurrent of hidden power structures that can ignite an issue to such an extent that the situation ultimately gets beyond the control of the persons who incited people to rise up against one another in the name of religion. Hariharan seems to be pointing in the direction that Indian politics are heading towards – the establishment of a Hindu *Rashtra*. She hints that minorities are being forced into extinction and oblivion as part of a program designed to trample down their power and identity. Through her women characters, she is portraying the trapped, silent and unrecognised sensibilities of people and present a counter-hegemonic discourse. Hariharan also questions the validity of a democracy which is redundant in the hands of power players who are continually manhandling it and weakening its power. Like T.S. Eliot's reminder to the people "HURRY UP PLEASE IT'S TIME" (*The Waste Land* 55) Hariharan is asking questions and inspiring people to raise their voices and articulate queries regarding the future of democracy in India. Hariharan also wishes to arouse awareness about the fact that a designed endeavour to incite one community against another has been a pattern which has been followed. This has helped to create fear in the minds of people. It is a shame to live like fugitives in one's own country. As she says in an interview that even though liberal thinkers would not hesitate to condemn such prejudices, how can people resist their influence when they are exposed to a continuous 'profiling of a community?'(web *www.thehindu.com*) Thus, it is necessary to fight prejudices at all levels.

Works Cited

Agamben, Giorgio. *Homo Sacer: Sovereign Power and Bare Life.* trans. Daniel Heller-Roazen. Stanford: Stanford UP, 1998. Print.

Bajrangi, Babu. "'After Killing Them, I Felt Like Maharana Pratap'" *Tehelka.* 1 Sept. 2007.

Beauvoir, Simone de. *The Second Sex.* trans. H.M.Parshley. 1949. London: Vintage, 1983.

Eliot, T.S. *Selected Poems.* Great Britain: Penguin, 1951. Print.

Foucault, Michel. *The History of Sexuality: The Will to Knowledge.* London: Penguin, 1978. Print.

Gowalkar, Madhav Sadashiv. *We or Our Nationhood Defined.* Nagpur: Bharat, 1939. Print.

Hariharan, Githa. *In Times of Siege.* New Delhi: Penguin, 2003. Print.

---. *Fugitive Histories.* New Delhi: Penguin, 2009. Print.

---."Resisting Regimentaton" Interview by Anuradha Roy. *The Hindu* nd. Web. 8 July. 2013. http://www. anothersubcontinent. com/ gh3.html

---. Interview by P. Anima. "Going Strong After Decades of Writing." *The Hindu.* 19 Mar 2007. Web. 20 Nov. 2013. <http:// www.thehindu.com/2007/03/19/stories/20070319 0533 0200.htm>

---. Interview by Bageshree S. *The Hindu* N.p. 4 Aug. 2009. Web.10 Mar. 2013. <http:// www.thehindu.com/mp/2009/08/04/ stories/2009080450050100.htm>

---. The Siege of The Mind." Interview by Vaishna Roy. *Outlook* 23 Apr. 2003. Web. 22 May, 2014. <http// www. outlookindia. com/ article.aspx?219912>

---."Plea for pluralism." Interview by Gowri Ramnarayan. *The Hindu* Web. 22 Apr. 2003. Print.

---."An Interview with Githa Hariharan." Luan Gaines. Web. 25 Feb. 2011, Print. <http://www.curledup.com/githaint.htm>

---."Our Spaces are Shrinking All the Time." Interview by Preeti Verma Lal. *Literary World.* Web. 19 Mar. 2003.

---.*The Deccan Herald.* Interview. n.d. Web. 12 Oct. 2014 www. githahariharan.com/downloads/selected_ interviews.pdf

---.*The Hindu.* n.d. Web. 25 Apr. 2012 http://www.thehindu.com/ thehindu/mp/2003/04/22/stories/200304220046 0100.htm

Hussein, Aamer. *Tehelka.* Rev. Web. 22 July, 2016. <http:// www. githahariharan.com/books/fugitivehistories>

Kumar, Girja. "Bhakti Movement and politics in Karnataka."*Censorship in India: Studies in Fundamentalism, Obscenity and Law.* New Delhi: Har-Anand, 2009. Print.

Mahaprashasta, Ajoy Ashirwad and Venkitesh Ramakrishnan. "Wounds of 1984." *Frontline.* 26.24 (2009): Web. 28 Nov. 2017. <http://www.frontline.in/static/html/fl2624/stories/20091204262410000.htm>

Nair, Anita. "In Times of Siege: Githa Hariharan" Rev. Web. 15 Mar. 2011. <http://www.anitanair.net/reviews/review_ 14.htm>

Ramamoorthy, Mohan. "A novel discord". Rev. n.d. 2009. Web.12 Oct. 2013. <http://www.indianexpress.com>

Roy, Arundhati. "Listening to Grass-hoppers: Genocide, Denial and Celebration" *Listening to Grass-hoppers: Field Notes on Democracy.* New Delhi: Penguin, 2009. Print.

---. "Introduction: Democracy's Failing Light" *Listening to Grass-hoppers: Field Notes on Democracy.* New Delhi: Penguin, 2009. ix-xxxvii. Print.

Said, Edward W. "Culture and Imperialism." *Modern Literary Theory.* ed. Philip Rice and Patricia Waugh. 4th ed. London: Arnold, 1989. Print.

Singh, Anita. "Githa Hariharan's *In Times of Siege*: A Symbolic Declaration of Human Rights." *Indian English Literature.* ed. Basavaraj Naikar. New Delhi: Atlantic, 2007. Print.

Soni M. Ronak. "A Review of Githa Hariharan's Fugitive Histories." *Githa Hariharan.* Rev. Web. 25 Apr. 2014. <http://www. githa hariharan.com/books/fugitive_histories.html

Chapter 4

THE SOCIETAL GHOSTS: *THE GHOSTS OF VASU MASTER* AND *THE ART OF DYING*

> I was dissatisfied sort of teenager-full of questions and undefined yearning. I was also a passionate reader, and my reading was wide and eclectic. So, writing came to me as the natural way to express what I felt, whether it was doubt, curiosity or bewilderment. From the very beginning, writing has been a way to make sense of the world around me. And after all these years, asking the right questions continues to be as much of a challenge as finding answers.
>
> **Hariharan "Discrete Thoughts" 213**

Hariharan's stories reflect the social restrictions or the oppression and suppression inflicted by the various social institutions which act as the societal ghosts. The social institutions actually paralyse the mind and body of the individuals thus reducing them to a mere puppet existence. Avery Gordon, who is currently a professor at the University of California, is well known for her first book *Ghostly Matters: Haunting and the Sociological Imagination*. She is a writer, social theorist and critic who has written about societal ghosts as well as about the ideas of complex relationships and complex personhood in her book. She expresses that life is complicated and the power relations that move any society are never simple or clear as the names which are given to them signify. Although theorists are forced to name these forces in order to describe them (patriarchy, nepotism, etc.) these names are too limited to express the power that permeates every relationship and too broad to express the unique ways in which power moves in particular relationships. Gordon takes on the concept of societal ghosts which frame our ways of thinking and acting. What Gordon means by the term personhood is the idea that people are shaped by multiple histories and personal agency, which is affected by the interaction of their multiple histories. Thus, the way in which people describe and tell stories about their lives and society at large is entangled in past personal history, experience, imagination and cultural tales. Gordon suggests that our lives are not as straightforward as they seem, to ourselves and also to others who observe our lives. She writes this in order to get at the bigger theoretical discussion of societal ghosts and the ghost stories which haunt us on a personal level, as well as societal level. She argues that ghosts and haunting are social phenomena, which affects the networks of power and society. She actually believes ghosts to be personal figures, social figures and institutions (shaped by history) that reproduce power relations and structures of inequality. She opines in her book, "A haunted society is full of ghosts, and the ghost always carries the message...that the gap between personal and social, public and private, objective and subjective is misleading in the first place."(*Ghostly* 98) Gordon questions contemporary methods of examining the relationships between knowledge, experience and power. She also opines the complexity of power relations where she talks about power structures via which we navigate daily without questioning it. Gordon opines about the societal ghosts, "It is a form of power or malificent magic, that is specifically designed to break down the distinction between visibility and invisibility, certainty and doubt, life and death that we normally use to sustain an ongoing and more or less dependable existence." (*Ghostly* 126)

Gordon expresses that the power relations can move any society and opines that they are not so simple as they appear to be. She agrees with Foucault's theory that power is not only an institution or a structure or an ideology, it is, in fact, a dynamic and productive force present in every interaction in society. Power never comes from a single direction or source and applied to the other. Rather it has a collective effect of different origins of power which could be a person, an institution, a value, perception, etc. Foucault's works are itinerant and are the outcome of different power relations and social dealings and thus encompass the social body. As he expresses,

> Power is everywhere; not because it embraces everything, but because it comes from everywhere... power is not an institution, and not a structure;

> neither is it a certain strength we are endowed with; it is the name that one attributes to a complex strategical situation in a particular society. (*History* 93)

The inequalities that exist in the society between men and women are not natural but created by men so that they can retain the myth of power and control. Power is retained by men as women are conditioned to believe that they are destined to be submissive and subjugated. Feminist cultural theory analyses prevalent gender roles as they are represented in different cultural constructs like literature, cinema, advertisements, etc. It is an approach that focusses on how such representations of women reflect and are connected to social conditions and the actual realities of life. It has become imbibed in our culture to label woman as vulnerable and weak. They are objectified with words that demean their existence by labelling them as the seductress, the other woman, the witch, the birthing machine and what not. The stories reflect upon the enslaving of men and women to the various roles thus losing their existence to the mere wheels of time and society. Her stories not only highlight the oppression faced by women but also men who willingly or unwillingly become a part of this suppression. She is equally sympathetic towards the men who are reduced to insignificance due to the vagaries of modern living.

This chapter undertakes a study of Githa Hariharan's two works *The Ghosts of Vasu Master* and *The Art of Dying* in the light of these observations. This novel and the collection of stories abound in a different set of power relations portraying the intellectually developed vis-à-vis the underdeveloped individuals. Both the works highlight the complexity of human relationships studied in the light of the dynamics of power. The chapter concentrates on the in-depth psychological analysis of the characters and situation of women who are colonised and are the victims of gender politics in Hariharan's novels. The present study is inspired by a scrutiny of Hariharan's works which calls for attention towards the women's issues and touches the socio-political and pedagogic concerns of modern India.

The Ghosts of Vasu Master aims to highlight the themes of self-discovery, marginalisation and empowerment. The novel can be understood as a psychological study of characters caught up in different sets of power relations attempting to discover themselves. The novel highlights the eclectic concerns pertaining to diverse and wide-ranging ideas like the modern education system, pervasive power relations, teacher-taught relationship and teaching-learning experience. As is prevalent in most societies, different groups interact with and control other groups and the resultant 'power relations' are sometimes clearly visible and sometimes ambiguous. While in some relationships, as in the master-slave relationship, it is obvious that the master will always dominate, in diverse situations, a 'power relationship' or 'exchange' rests on other factors. For example, two or more people may willingly consent to concede control or power of some facet of their relationship to another person and thus agree to accept domination. Social functioning also plays an important role in determining relationships whereby one group is able to exercise some authority and has the ability to have a desired effect on the other. These power relations tend to create a divide among people as a result of which the weaker group gets marginalised. At the same time, there is a streak of resistance ever present in these relations which make the weaker person/group strive for empowerment. *The Ghosts of Vasu Master* portrays the interaction between intellectually developed vis-à-vis the underdeveloped individual. It also depicts the man-woman relationship and reflects the attempt of women to emerge from the margins.

The novel is narrated on three parallel tracks. The first one comprises the fables told by Vasu Master to teach his mentally challenged student Mani. The second one is constituted of Vasu Master's encounters with the ghosts of his memories. The third track consists of the stories narrated by other characters of the novel in which Vasu Master becomes a listener. The chapters of the novel are organised independently as tales along with digressing asides. Personal myths, fables and allegories are narrated through Vasu Master leading to his analysis of himself and observations about their effect on Mani's mind. As Vikash Bhardwaj and Surender Kumar opine:

> Vasu Master begins to weave a web of fables and parables and tales of undigested 'karma' with more real-life images to inspire, to teach and to cure Mani of his unexplainable reticence and defiance. Through these

> fascinating and fantastic stories, he travels into his own childhood and also into his innermost recesses of fear and weaknesses. He recounts scenes from his past, trying to understand the present.

The Ghosts of Vasu Master, as is clear from the title itself, is not a woman-centric text. It may be pervaded by the ghosts and memories of the women in Vasu's life but it is basically the tale of a retired school master Vasu, who lives in Elipettai. The novel attempts to analyse the suffocating emptiness in the life of Vasu Master after superannuation and also addresses some other issues. Vasu Master, in the novel, is trying to come to terms with his retired life and is haunted by thoughts, dreams and memories of the past. His life has generally been simple and linear as a school teacher, and he is shaken out of his complacency by his retirement after which he embarks upon a journey of self-analysis and discovery. As Jasbir Jain writes in the essay "Men in the Minds of Women":

> It is not a simple confrontation between tradition and modernity, but a questioning of the moribund attitudes toward institutional practices, a questioning of the uses of both power and knowledge. In *The Ghosts of Vasu Master,* the theme is not of the lonely life of a retired schoolmaster who happens to be a widower, but a rediscovery of the lost art of living...The narrative, placed largely indoors, makes maximum use of memory and fables. It is the world of knowledge, the bringing together of different kinds of knowledge - traditional, experiential, herbal, fabulous, remembered pasts - and through them make an attempt at negotiating reality. (*Desert* 54)

Vasu Master undertakes the difficult task of teaching Mani, a twelve-year-old mentally retarded boy who cannot speak. As the epigraphs to the novel suggest, power relations prevail in every sphere of life including that of knowledge. The first by Charaka states: "*The entire world is teacher to the intelligent and foe to the unintelligent.*" The second one by Shakespeare articulates: "*We cannot all be masters,/nor all masters cannot be truly followed.*" It has been extracted from Act I, Scene I of the Shakespearean play *Othello*. The last one is a quotation from Gandhi "*I have nothing new to teach the world. Truth and non-violence are as old as/the hills.*"(ix) All three reflect upon the theme of knowledge and education in the novel. They also refer to the power relations between the intelligent individual and the mentally challenged individual. Vasu's courageous endeavour to educate a sub-normal child gradually turns into his quest to know and understand his own life and discover himself. He often wonders what could be the reason for their coming together and thinks of answers to certain questions such as "What Mani and I face together is our common need to make more sense of the world around us; so that we are able to do more in it. Together, can we prove that learning to live and knowledge are not two separate things?" (221) So, the link between life and knowledge is clearly established in his mind. The three epigraphs clearly emphasise that there is no need to create knowledge as it already exists in the world, it is for the seeker to find it. This becomes the basis for the story of Vasu Master and Mani. The epigraphs also represent the process of self-discovery through Vasu's final encounter with the teaching profession.

Vasu Master's contemplation on the role of a teacher reminds us of the methods of teaching which prevailed in ancient India. The *Gurukulam* method which existed in the past is revived by Vasu because it generates a direct teacher-student relationship. The teacher focusses total personal attention on the welfare of the pupil who in turn devotes himself completely to his tutor. As Hariharan writes:

> In this living relationship, the pupil imbibed the inward methods of the teacher; the secrets of his mind and the spirit of his life and work: all too subtle to be taught. The pupil belonged to the teacher, not to an institution of stone and mud. Learning was a lifelong task, not a brief sojourn in an exotic, artificial place. (199)

The Ghosts of Vasu Master thus questions the existing education system. It is a reassessment of the shallowness of the contemporary system of education where students confine themselves to a few prescribed texts. Throughout the narrative, the novel challenges the authoritative texts of western education and medicine. Hariharan propagates a system through Vasu that goes beyond the textual and traditional method of teaching. Living alone in a remote village of Elipettai, Vasu Master who is often haunted by feelings of loneliness decides to teach Mani to fill the emptiness and void in his life. It is at this belated juncture of his life that he accepts the challenge posed by Mani and begins to interrogate existing methods of teaching. He describes this challenge in the following words,

> But Mani was a puzzle; the kind you suspect has been given to you without all the pieces you need. And here was a puzzle I had to put together if I was to understand Mani, even in part; if I was to know what I was to him and he to me; and if I were to find myself before it was too late. (99)

Vasu's views on education and knowledge are portrayed in the words, "...all of us are pupils and teachers. While there is life in each of us, we learn and we teach."(28) Before the boy learns anything else, Mani needs to be brought out of the silence which has become a method of defence for him. Mani is not taught in the usual manner by using pencils, pens or notebooks as he feels irritated by it. Vasu lowers himself to Mani's level and finds innovative methods which kindle Mani's thoughts and imagination. Vasu denounces the education system he has been following for forty years and begins at an elementary level – telling stories and fables which remind one of the *Panchatantra* tales. Hariharan has acknowledged the influence of the famous *Panchatantra* Tales on this novel and how each story conveys a message which is also reflective of Vasu's increasing grasp over his own scattered existence. The challenge faced by Vasu Master is to educate Mani and make him a normal human being. Actually, when he teaches Mani, he himself undergoes a process of self-discovery as he is also trying to find answers to his own physical and personal problems. Hariharan's use of *Panchatantra* tales to teach Mani has an immense significance in the novel.

Another problem evident in Vasu's life is that of his health, the reason for his physical condition cannot be diagnosed. The opening chapter witnesses Vasu's visit to a doctor, "I sat on the chair, waiting for the old man to tell me what was wrong with me. I seemed to have sat there before, on a similar wooden chair, waiting for the man across to speak. The man held the key to the secrets of my body."(1) But the doctor admits defeat, "I can't find a thing wrong here...Maybe you should try something else...Have you considered homoeopathy? Or ayurveda?"(1) While Vasu is looking for methods to cure his physical condition, he is also exploring alternative methods of teaching and learning and the ways of healing the mind.

Vasu Master narrates the fables of Grey Mouse, Blue Bottle, Black Crow, Spider, Python, host of flies, etc and every story has a double meaning which relates to Vasu Master and Mani. The most significant among these stories is that of Grey Mouse and a fly Blue Bottle which signify Vasu and Mani respectively. The story moves parallel to that of Vasu whereby Grey Mouse stands for the Master. He is confined to his mouse hole and is cautious and fearful of the outside world. As Mahesh Kale opines, "the Grey Mouse is not a mouse, but a person in grey profession i.e. teaching." (*Contemporary* 200-202) The fly Blue Bottle resembles Mani in the story. Towards the end of the novel, Grey Mouse comes out of his hole and gets caught in the trap. His mind gets focussed and he begins to see and hear what he had shut out before. He realises that Blue Bottle is a part of himself. So, Mani becomes the representative of that part of Vasu's life about which he lacked clarity. While trying to teach him and through the revival of the lessons learned from his father, Vasu recognises his true self. Vasu's training of Mani is undertaken at a psychological level so that his pupil's mind is freed of the mental burdens that weigh upon his consciousness. In this endeavour, Vasu unburdens himself too.

In the chapter entitled "Two scenes in a Mousetrap," Vasu finally comes to terms with his situation and realises that he can end his story the way he likes:

> I could wrap it up neatly: come to terms gracefully with ancestral legacies; punish and banish Veera Naidu and his minions; spurn the Swami and save Venkatesan; cure my mutinous stomach and my head full of fantasies; or at least learn to keep decently quiet about it all. I could live up to my inherited tasks of healing, resurrecting Charaka, Shakespeare and Gandhi – my formidable trio of friends from Nageswaram. And I could put words, rich polysyllables into Mani's mouth, at long last. (260)

The chapter concludes with Vasu's understanding that "the trap comes with the bread. It is foolish to expect one without the other." (261) Life is a mixture of good and evil and every success has its share of pain within it. He no longer hears the buzz of the fly which has now become a tiny spark of blue leaping in and out of a weak sunbeam. This may simply mean that his inner fears and turmoil have reduced considerably and he is now confident that: "*(I have begun to plant thee, and will labour to make thee full of growing.)*"(260), as he muses.

Hariharan draws upon the pedagogic techniques prevailing in *gurukulas* to contrast the outcome of that kind of education with the contemporary system. The present education system has resulted in the degradation and deterioration of moral values in children as is seen in the behaviour of students of Class VI at PG School. The teaching method adopted by Vasu, when he is with Mani, is different from the western methods that he had been following blindly at PG School. Vasu shuns the postcolonial teaching style of 6B and adopts the traditional methods of teaching and storytelling. As Anjali Roy articulates in the essay "Visnu Sarma against Shakespeare: "Ghosts" of (Non) Dominating Knowledge in The Ghosts of Vasu Master", "Since the post-colonial and post-modern agendas often overlap, postcolonial restructurings of indigenous pasts or returns to "vernacular" roots are invariably subsumed within post-modernist resurrections of history or blending of the global and the local." (*Postmodern* 105)

Herein, Hariharan hints at the fact that we need to draw inspiration from our tradition to save people from degeneration. Vasu Master believes in Gandhiji's assertion that there is need to re-create the knowledge which already exists in the world, it is necessary to understand and revive it. Thus, the role of the teacher is shown as challenging and formal. Teaching is also a process which is influenced by the political and social background of a country, therefore teaching methods should also suit the environment. Vasu Master teaches Mani through his stories just as Vishnu Sharma taught the illiterate sons of King Amar Sakti. All these are basically allegorical presentations of Vasu's own life and existence. Mani responds positively to these communications. Mani learns to behave in a civil manner, his faith in humanity is restored and he even makes an attempt to talk and utters his own name 'Mani'.

Vasu, in fact, re-lives his past through Mani. The initial setbacks in his relationship with Mani remind him of his relationship with his father. Vasu recalls that his inability to grasp what his father wished to teach him had resulted in the latter's disappointment with him. He also recalls his father's assertion that a teacher has to be, above all, a mother. As Neelam Sanwal Bhardwaj avers:

> The effect of the fables on Mani is astonishingly positive. He learned to behave civilly, even learns to draw and paint. But most importantly, his faith in humanity is restored. Vasu's final success comes when Mani makes his first verbal communication with him and utters his own name, "Mani". Vasu, too, benefits from this relationship immensely. Mani is the mirror in which Vasu can see his own past...Vasu's father had told him that a teacher has to be, above all, a mother. Vasu has succeeded in creating a womb of fables and has, like a mother, delivered an evolved and educated Mani. (291)

This takes us back to the meaning of the three epigraphs and they get connected with Vasu's life and vocation. The first talks about the world being congenial and imparting knowledge to the people who are capable of learning it easily but unfriendly to those who are intellectually weak. It says that the intelligent get all the privileges. Mani's education thus becomes a challenging task for his teachers in school which they somehow prefer to avoid. Vasu accepts it and proves his mettle. The second quotation from Shakespeare about the difference in each individual's mental capacity not only to learn but also to teach is discussed. It also suggests that all scholars are not to be followed blindly. Vasu's father who often quotes Shakespeare and follows him cannot make his young son understand all that the 'master' says but the meanings become clear as Vasu grows and matures. The last quotation states that truth is eternal and there is no new knowledge "I have nothing new to teach the world. Truth and non-violence are as old as the hills." It shows the humility and the patience which is required. These epigraphs also remind us of the Foucauldian power/knowledge discourse which analyses the notion of knowledge and power and raises questions about their meaning. If Truth is absent from it, what does knowledge mean? Is there any absolute truth or do a group of people decide what it is? Can powerful minorities impose the idea of what is right or true on the majority? Is it correct to accept what is handed down to people by those who have exerted control over them?

Vasu too seems to be questioning whether the existing education system imposed by the colonial powers is suitable for the Indian setup. He and his pupil Mani begin to look at the world afresh. The freedom from the school system inspires Vasu to delve deep into his mind and evoke a new world for Mani who is influenced by his imaginative rendering of past experiences which are mingled with philosophical insights. Vasu's innovative stories and techniques are interspersed with memories of his childhood and youth. Vasu becomes a contemporary Vishnu Sharma who narrates stories from the *Panchatantra* to teach 'Papaya-Head Mani'(8) and to change him. Unconsciously, while teaching Mani, Vasu is learning more about himself and moving forward on the path of self-discovery. His own physical and psychological problems are being solved. As long as Vasu remains under the invisible influence of the power of societal forces, he is unable to discover his own potential. After his retirement, he is freed from the obligation of being an employee of the PG School and following its rules. Thus, he discovers his own self. He adopts new methods to arouse Mani's interest as Urvashi Butalia writes:

> Desperate to get reaction, Vasu tells Mani stories, and begins to supplement them with drawings, and gradually, Mani and his teacher (one might say a failed pupil - for Mani's parents hand him over to Vasu's as just that - and a failed teacher, failed only because he is assailed by a sense of his own inadequacy) establish some sort of communication. (*Peopled* 30)

As Mani starts understanding the various themes presented through the stories, fables, narratives and anecdotes, Vasu asks him to draw pictures of the stories narrated to him. The progress Mani's learning is reflected in his drawing pictures related to those stories. Mani converses through the language of marks and symbols on paper. Vasu Master is full of enthusiasm as he motivates Mani and says, "Come, Mani, let's create a new world. A better one."(262) Vasu Master, through his efforts, succeeds in improving Mani's condition, though partially. He also succeeds in creating a better world for himself by freeing himself from the constraints of societal barriers and emerging as a free individual. His success with Mani increases his confidence in himself.

The novel undertakes to reflect a psychological study of human nature and character. The structure and technique are also similar to the psychological literary texts in which episodes and situations are strung together through a single consciousness. Vasu Master educates Mani by narrating stories which he had heard from his grandmother. A series of tales, fables and allegories are woven into the text and with the completion of each, a greater clarity is attained by Vasu as well as his challenging and mentally challenged pupil Mani. Vasu Master's thoughts reveal him to be a man who has been forced to repress his instincts almost throughout his life, as a result of which his creative and fertile mind has never surfaced through his actions. As his character develops, his inherent intuitive capabilities become evident. This reflects the truth of the assertion that instincts are the motivating factors of behavioural patterns; by consummating them one can attain satisfaction, and also that denied instincts are not destroyed. They get pushed into the unconscious mind. The ideas and desires keep shuttling between the conscious and unconscious mind and enable the individual to liberate his mind. As Dr. Joseph Murphy opines:

> I have seen the power of the subconscious lift people up out of crippled states, making them whole, vital, and strong once more. Their minds made them free to go out into the world to experience happiness, health, and joyous expression. There is a miraculous curative force in your subconscious that can heal the troubled mind and the broken heart. It can open the prison door of the mind and liberate you. It can free you from all kinds of material and physical bondage. (3)

This happens in the case of Vasu. He becomes a teacher of traditional beliefs and system. Initially, he was not an independent-minded teacher but one who was influenced by the system and he played his role accordingly. Hariharan seems to suggest through Vasu that by rejecting our heritage of the *gurukula*, quality education has been diluted and distorted too. After forty years of teaching at PG School Elipettai, Vasu's retirement seems like the end of his profession as a teacher but it turns out to be a beginning. He begins to explore his inner psyche in order to identify the true aim and nature of his life. The novel thus highlights the psychological conflicts of Vasu Master and how he resolves them. He begins to contemplate upon the nature of teaching, the methods of teaching and evolves a new technique which proves his power to teach a child who is considered sub-normal, in a more satisfactory manner than he had ever taught the boys of class VI in PG School. Vasu is haunted by various 'ghosts' that frequently enter his mind seeking his as well as the reader's attention. As Urvashi Butalia articulates:

> *He is accosted by memories (ghosts) of his dead wife Mangala, his ayurvaid father, his long-dead grandmother. Rubbing shoulders with these characters are Vasu's two sons who hover in the background, Veera Naidu, the head of the school (PG) in which Vasu taught, Venkatesan, his onetime colleague and sort-of friend, and ever-present Mani, Vasu's last pupil, whose silent presence (he utters only one sound throughout the book, "Aaaaah") permeates the entire narrative. (Peopled 30)*

All these memories intrude upon his mind while he is deeply involved with Mani. Due to his disability, Mani was forced to leave the school where he learned nothing but distrust and self-defense. Vasu himself had never been very comfortable in his school. Mani does not speak at all and his silent suffering has an affinity with Vasu's loneliness. The biggest challenge for Vasu as a teacher is to restore Mani's self-confidence and emotional balance and in this attempt, he embarks on a process of self-exploration and recognition. Jasbir Jain writes about the effect which the haunting ghosts have on Vasu's mind. She writes in the essay "Men in the Minds of Women":

> These ghosts remind him of their words of wisdom, their tales, reprimands and nudge his memory, turning away his concentration from the present, the retirement and the speech to the past. He delves into this rich storehouse in order to unlearn the approaches used in the classroom, the empty reliance on a text or on the blackboard, the endless construction of sentences, the meaningless commands. (*Desert* 55)

Another aspect of power relations that is relevant to Vasu's case is that his subjectivity is also attained by the double relation of his interaction with himself and with others. While moving forward in the process of self-discovery, the subject becomes a target as well as the vehicle of power. This is evident through the growth that is witnessed in Vasu's character. He has been a target of the system but is now the vehicle of power. He engenders a new life in Mani.

Hariharan has devised a richly textured text in which various levels of Vasu's active consciousness are explored even though he is now at an age when activity should normally end. He is reminded of his father very often when he begins to teach Mani. His father was a well-educated man, with considerable knowledge of Ayurveda. He believed *"Life is nothing but one long balancing act. The minute you have an imbalance of air, a little too much phlegm, not enough bile, what happens? Disease,"(21)* The influence of his father is brought out at various points in the narrative in which his quotations from Shakespeare and other texts are remembered by Vasu. Experience has made him mature enough to understand them well now. He finds a concord in the liberal humanism of Shakespeare and the traditionalism of *slokas* and *rasayanams* as they are both universally significant. Vasu tries to trace the wisdom of India by adopting a change in the stereotypical method of education and delving deep into the indigenous texts his father used to refer to. His father has been his teacher in many ways. As is typical of the lives of most people, Vasu has drifted along in life struggling and striving to manage the problems he faced as he moved along but in the process, he missed some of the life's significant meanings and lessons which now dawn upon him through the effect of his memories and the so-called 'ghosts' that work upon his mind.

On one hand, there is the description of the intellectually strong individual's power over the underdeveloped consciousness through the characters of Vasu and Mani, on the other, marginalisation and empowerment is also described through the presentation of the women characters as 'ghosts.' The shift from the poetics of gender oppression towards the poetics of women empowerment is also an important issue taken up through the lives of Mangala, Jameela and other women characters such as Eliamma. As Hariharan has said in an interview with Arnab Chakladar:

> Talking about gender concerns being there, though not in an obvious way – *The Ghosts of Vasu Master* was my most ambitious attempt at looking at gender elliptically. And I think that is actually the most autobiographical of my novels. Which is why when people ask as if the first novel is the most autobiographical, I say, "no, no, Vasu Master is"...and they look at me if they are thinking, "My god, she's weirder than we thought." (Web. *www.anothersubcontinent.com*)

The kind of power relations presented in *The Ghosts of Vasu Master* reminds one of the ambiguities of their presence in the society. In this context, it is pertinent to recall that Foucault has explained in *The History of Sexuality* that the new methods are employed at all levels and go beyond the modus operandi of the state. The new form of power establishes relations that are more subtle, easier to miss and more difficult to resist, "...the new methods of power whose operation is not ensured by right but by technique, not by law but by normalization, not by punishment but by control, methods that are employed on all levels and in forms that go beyond the state and its apparatus."(*History* 89)

Patriarchy is one such power that has determined the roles of men and women and clearly defined them. It has, through its long reign, utilised the normalisation practices to create the gender differences and it determines the dynamics of man-woman relationship in particular. Women have been deeply affected by the marginalisation and exploitation they have experienced in society. Patriarchy or any other authority wields power with some aims and objectives and the results are taken for granted by those on whom the control is exercised. However, in this novel, it can be seen as a productive force that enables women to understand themselves and others in the world they inhabit. Vasu recalls his grandmother - the only woman who is an authoritative figure - Mangala, his wife and Jameela, her friend are marginalised figures hankering for empowerment through their needlework and friendship. In their case, we can see a true reflection of the notion that power also breeds resistance which may not always surface in a violent and forceful manner. As Butler and other theorists have averred that power is not wielded over passive bodies but these bodies sometimes take the imperative and transform it in more or less conforming ways. *The Ghosts of Vasu Master* has also often been read as a novel that deals with women and their attempt to practice domestic arts for self-expression. This is evident in the depiction of the women characters in the novel. They appear only briefly through Vasu's consciousness and dreams, thus emphasising their marginalised existence but their impact also hints at some element of empowerment.

Hariharan makes use of fantasy, fable, anecdotes and incidents to portray the plight of women characters. In the novel, Vasu Master's mother Lakshmi and his wife Mangala represent the stereotype of the traditional Indian women. These characters represent the modus operandi of the psyche of millions of Indian women who undergo the experiences of helplessness. Hariharan has, in a unique manner, highlighted women's issues through the mind of a man – Vasu Master. His association with his wife's friend Jameela is noteworthy. Even though he is attracted to her, he pretends to be unaware of her presence. Jameela is a more outgoing woman as compared to Mangala. In fact, at one point in the novel, she seems to make a friendly advance towards Vasu which he does not accept because he is a reticent person. On the other hand, Vasu's only memories of his wife are about her emotional support to him after the death of his father, her mending of the children's clothes and the sound of her conversation and laughter when she was with Jameela. Both created beautiful pieces of needlework. The shift in the designs from simple flowers to complex landscapes which they stitched on the tapestry describes their evolution as women. Vasu Master, however, mentions his wife Mangala and her friend Jameela's friendship which somehow enabled them to rise above the world. Mangala's friendship with Jameela is of a unique kind. The childhood memories that Mangala shares with Jameela are carefree and happy in nature as compared to her life after marriage which is burdened with duties and responsibilities. The relationship between Jameela who is earthy as compared with Mangala's ethereal nature is described by Vasu as follows:

> It was their completion of each other that held me, the coexistence of earthy and ethereal, cocoon and butterfly. A perfect pair, team or couple. Who was the Mangala Jameela knew? Jameela could not have known her as I did; as a man, as a husband does. But this woman Jameela could draw out with expert ease; or I should say, the woman with two faces, bodies, whose double-scaled laughter had tantalized me in the other room: who was she? (43)

It reminds one of the ideas of female bonding that have been discussed by some feminist thinkers and pertain to a relationship of deep sympathy which women have for one another. It is a relationship in which women are closely related to each other through friendship and attachment. They feel free to discuss all those matters which they cannot talk about with men, however closely they may be related to them. This bonding provides them with psychological space through which they unite and discover a feeling of healing and intimacy with each other. It is a movement which provides new social consciousness and opens new vistas to liberate women from the suffocating conditions so as to emerge as new beings. This friendship is invigorating and energising according to Mary Daly who is one of the propagators of the idea of this kind of bonding. Daly attempts to transcend all culturally specific models of female power and talks of creating cross-cultural communities of women or what she describes in her "New Intergalactic Introduction" to *Gyn/ Ecology* as "biophilic bonding with women of all races and classes, under varying oppressions of patriarchy"(*Gyn/Ecology*, xxxi) She writes:

> Women loving women do not seek to lose our identity, but to express it, discover it, create it...The presence of Enspiriting Female Selves to each other is a creative gynergetic flow that may assume different shapes and colors. The sparking of ideas and the flaming of physical passion emerge from the same source. The bonding of woman-loving women survives its transformations because its source is the Sister-Self. It survives because the very meaning of this bonding is Surviving, that is Super-living. It is biophilic bonding. (*Metaethics* 234)

Eliamma's story is another indirect reference to the fate of an enterprising woman in a patriarchal setup. It is the story of a woman named Eliamma who bartered her body to attain the freedom of mind. She is a ghost in a story; which Mangala conveys to her sons. The moral of this tale is that any woman who wants to achieve something that is forbidden to her would be doomed to invisibility and annihilation in this society. Eliamma is fascinated by the vast ocean and is not allowed to accompany the men on fishing boats to fulfil her desire to explore what lies beyond the horizon. So, she trades her body with a ghost, becomes invisible and travels to a rock in the midst of the ocean, remains there till she is satiated, but when she returns, she no longer has a body to return to. She remains invisible and has become a ghost who is roaming the beach alone. The story seems to suggest that women who transgress patriarchal rules are doomed to suffer. This is covered by the element of suspense that excites the children whom the story is told to. Eliamma's story also describes that factor of power which punishes the non-conformer but rewards the conformer. Eliamma can never attain success because she is a non-conformer. Mangala, the narrator of her story is capable of thinking independently but she has imbibed the values of patriarchy through normalisation and acculturation and does not transgress them openly like Eliamma.

Jameela also narrates the story of 'The Three Caterpillars' which reflects the attitude of the novelist towards women. The three caterpillars are named Ammukutty, Nanikutty and Ummikutty in the story who unite together to live and work with "sisterly togetherness":

> They looked at each other and liked what they saw, so the eldest, Ammukutty, said to the younger caterpillars: Nanikutty, Ummikutty, we don't know if we have a common mother, but it doesn't matter. Let's be friends and live on this tree always. Nanikutty and Ummikutty agreed, and without wasting time on further discussion the three immediately began to chomp leaves in sisterly togetherness. (132)

Ammukutty sheds her skin and gets the blue colour skin underneath, a process which she teaches to her sisters as well. All the three shed their skin and continue with the chomping of leaves. Soon they learn new patterns and designs from each other and spin more thread. Exhausted of their continuous hard work, they get into their cocoons and sleep soundly only to get trapped and become victims of men's desires. The first woman caterpillar Ammukutty becomes the victim of men's desire which portrays the realistic plight of women as they are destroyed for men's gratification. The second caterpillar Nanikutty is brought up and taken care of (by men), to be sacrificed at a later stage for men's selfish motives. The third caterpillar watches the plight of her two elder sisters and ponders over their ordeals. As a result, she makes a plan not to succumb to the men and evolves a design to get liberated from their clutches. As a result, she succeeds and flies away from men's company and emerges as a liberated individual. Jameela says:

> Ummikutty, as far as I know, is still in hiding somewhere in the forest, weaving on her old spinning loom. Year in and year out she designs a tapestry full of meaning; but whatever she weaves is also ever-dissolving. If you saw her creations, the colours and shapes she uses, you would understand why she is no longer called Ummikutty; why she has grown into Begum Three-In-One. The stories she spins, you see, are not all her own; and not always easy to unravel; because all of them weave in, with the finest of silk threads, the ghosts of her lost sisters. (136-37)

Women empowerment has been a pivotal theme in almost all of Hariharan's novels. The process of awakening of women to the gradual journey of self-empowerment is evident in the novel *The Ghosts of Vasu Master* as well. The grandmother is shown as a strong-willed, powerful and assertive old woman who is a born ruler. She rules the kitchen and can argue with her son too. She says to Vasu, "What is a husband, Vasu? Just a hungry stomach and a few other things, never mind what. But all equally greedy, swallowing like a big red swollen mouth, then chewing and belching."(174) After attaining widowhood, his grandmother finds her prophet in Mahatma Gandhi and she donates her gold bangles for India's freedom. Vasu's grandmother and Jameela are two women in the novel who have managed to attain some power. However, it is ironic that these women attain liberation only in their old age or after attaining widowhood in the novel.

The husband-wife relationship depicted in the novel follows the traditional patriarchal norms where, more often than not, the husband and wife move together but hardly have any common interests. Men are educated and underestimate women's capability of understanding their intellectual passions and desires. Women are pressurised into adopting the roles of caretakers and sexual objects and to the performance of child-bearing tasks. Both Vasu Master and Mangala have been living under the same roof, but they remain detached. Vasu and Mangala have been married for many years still they are unable to share their memories and experiences with each other. Neither is Vasu Master able to share his teaching experience and problems with Mangala nor is she able to share her childhood memories. Mangala lives a life of submission in her husband's home, and quietly accepts her duties as a wife who places her husband on the same pedestal as a God who is to be respected and worshipped. It is ironical that Vasu Master, even after Mangala's death does not even remember her - his wife and the mother of two sons. She is merely a cloudy memory, more than being an individual. While Vasu Master remained too busy and focussed on his job and school, she always remained in the background. "I always saw her in my mind against a vast seashore in the background, the monotonous slosh and thud of waves against rock and sand drowning out all possibility of words."(41)

Vasu's consciousness is the binding link in these feminist stories in the novel. The patriarchal power structure is also being subverted and questioned through Vasu's relationship with his sons. His father is undoubtedly a dominating figure under whose influence Vasu has remained subdued, quiet and incapable of any self-assertion. How patriarchy can affect a person belonging to any gender is clearly evident in Vasu's character. However, his sons who are now grown up and independent are trying to support him in this new phase of his life and they also try to control his life. The elder son, Vishnu, always tries to act as a protective and concerned parent who keeps directing Vasu to go to the doctor and to leave Elipettai. While the younger one, Venu, makes similar suggestions though he ultimately accepts whatever his father says. There are hints of other psychological and social pressures that control the human psyche but the conclusion Vasu arrives at is that no outside force can prompt a person much, one has to undertake the voyage of self-discovery alone and enlightenment comes from within.

The names assigned to the characters in the novel also seem to have their own significance. The name of the protagonist Vasu is the short form of "Vasudeva", who was the father of the eighth incarnation of Vishnu. He was the person who took care of the young Lord Krishna in his childhood. In the novel too, Vasu takes care of the young child Mani. Mani means "Parasmani" or Elixir which is a touchstone or a stone that turns iron to gold. Vasu is the one who is tested through Mani's consciousness and turns into gold as he discovers himself. Mani proves to be the touchstone which judges the value of gold. Mangala means "Mangalam" or auspicious. Her presence in Vasu's life is auspicious as she is an excellent caretaker – looking after Vasu and his children. Though her presence is quiet, she is always helping everyone with her domestic chores. Jameela is a Muslim name which means "beautiful" and graceful. Jameela not only refers to the physical beauty but believes in inner beauty as well. Jameela, as the name suggests, has an unmatched beauty and a virtuous heart as shown in the novel. Eliamma means "earth-mother" who stares at "some remote point in the distance" "always intent as if straining to see something at a great distance."(124) "Something as yet unknown, hidden perhaps in the depths of the waters mid-sea." (126)

The Ghosts of Vasu Master is a text in which Hariharan portrays the situation of women through a man's observations and consciousness. As the author acknowledges, she was dealing with the issue of women deliberately in a more indirect manner than in her other novels. As the title also suggests, the central character and consciousness are that of Vasu but various significant issues of identity and self – are resolved through his thoughts. From being an obscure and insignificant school teacher, he emerges as an effective individual. His intuitive and insightful journeys into his past enable him to overcome some shortcomings in his own nature. So, the novel becomes a complex rendering of the issues in the lives of both men and women. The novel ultimately culminates with the chapter "Terminal Examination" which highlights what Hariharan says in "Acknowledgements" given at the end of the novel:

> Some of the ideas Vasu grapples with reflecting my own rather eclectic course of reading over the last six years for this novel. The list included readings on education, alternative methods of teaching, ancient Indian education, Indian healing systems and healing in general. (275)

It is this last chapter that in some ways clarifies the writer's intentions in writing this novel. Hariharan talks about the universality of healing approaches which are "in reality bound by their relativity."(266) They are "springboards" to be used by individuals to find answers to the enigmas of life. It concludes that the only trial teaches the proper lessons in this world. The last question paper set by Vasu is unique because it intends not to uncover deficiencies and losses but to light up one or more of the manifold paths that confront the examinee. The individual needs to confront the truth and the very ambiguity of existence. The examinee is placed at many of the crossroads and his/her response would reflect how he perceives this world. This is also a new method of educating the individual and empowering him/her to make choices and take decisions on his own. Hariharan has also posited in an interview with Joel Kuorrti that this examination raises questions that should inspire others to contemplate and dwell upon them. She says,

> I think at the end of *The Ghosts of Vasu Master* I also say that the story is not quite over. It seems to be over, but it will continue. There is always this quality of the retold tale that is never quite finished. It is as if you are saying, I've done this and I've put here and somebody can come along and pick up and continue. (22)

The open-ended conclusion leaves behind some unanswered questions because it is a story which will be carried on. A storytelling has no end and thus it will lead to telling of many other stories that will have new beginnings. Thus, it may be concluded that Hariharan's novel *The Ghosts of Vasu Master* has been explored from different perspectives. Feminism, human psychology and self-discovery are some major concerns of this text. Besides, *The Ghosts of Vasu Master* traverses India's progress as an independent nation and also deals with psychological and physical maladies and the process of healing. Though indirectly, it gives a fresh look at the postcolonial issues including education system and feminist concerns. The novel is written at a time when India is marked with the cultural and social change due to the advent of globalisation and other technological advances. It highlights issues of the identity crisis, questions the education system and the human condition through the loneliness of Vasu and his grappling with the existing value system and returns to a preference for the old value systems.

Hariharan's collection of short stories *The Art of Dying* has abundant examples of her understanding the realistic human ideals which she upholds through all her fiction. The stories portray the realistic view of how the relationship between men and women have existed over the centuries and even today in the so-called modern times. Hariharan highlights the struggle of individuals through the characters of Revati, Rukmini, Patricia, Brenda, Chellamma, etc. who are the protagonists of her stories. The stories selected for study are 'The Art of Dying', 'Untitled Poem', 'The Remains of the Feast', 'Reprieve', 'Revati', 'Gajar Halwa', 'Virgin Curry', 'Repeat Performance', 'The Will', 'Halfway Animals' and 'Forefathers' which highlight the emptiness, rootlessness, yearning, temptation and suppression of humans. The pathetic plight of individuals has been evoked through these short stories which clearly represent the marginalisation of men and women in the domestic as well as the social sphere. As Prabha Pant opines in the essay 'Variations on a Theme: Humanism in Arundhati Roy's *The Cost of Living* and Githa Hariharan's *The Art of Dying*':

> Githa Hariharan's *The Art of Dying and Other Stories* is a slim volume of brilliantly etched stories. The twenty-odd stories cover a whole range of contemporary life showcasing the common man's dreams and aspirations, highs and lows, laughter and sorrow. The vivid imagery and the lucid prose add to the sense of immediacy of each story. She captures the very nuances, the incandescent glow of each individual. The technique is of allowing each character to take over the narration. Nowhere does one feel the presence of the omniscient author. (*Humanism* 99)

Social evils like casteism, child marriage, dowry system, orthodoxy and widowhood which are evidently responsible for the sorrowful condition of women are also often condemned by Hariharan. As Jasbir Jain writes, she uses this genre to sketch out the 'inner workings of the protagonists who are enmeshed in the lateral mappings and the relationships which reveal the cartography of power and social control.'(*Indian* 226)

The stories in *The Art of Dying* give us a variety of images taken from all spheres of human life, the domestic as well as the business world. The author describes the struggle of mankind to survive in the hostile environment of suppression from various undesirable influences. The advent of machinery and technology has reduced the humans to a pitiable condition resulting in unemployment. The subjugation of weak individuals by the powerful is also prevalent in Hariharan's stories. Women are also suppressed and oppressed in various phases of their lives as wives, daughters and even as social beings. They have to make sacrifices from childhood until their old age. Hariharan, in her stories, has tried to bring out the influences of various social taboos which woman may experience in the society. She lays stress on the different gendered discourses on widowhood, sati, dowry deaths and child widows through her collection of stories.

'The Remains of the Feast' is an effective portrayal of a Brahmin family. Hariharan highlights the suppression of women and the false customs and rituals of the Brahmin culture. The struggle between fundamentalism and humanism is clearly portrayed through this story. It is a story of Rukmini, a ninety years old dying grandmother, narrated by her great- granddaughter Ratna. She is a young girl of twenty-two, who is studying medicine. In spite of the generation gap, there seems to be a special bonding between the two. The story reflects upon the warm and lovely bond between the grandmother and granddaughter. It shows a cheerful grandmother who has accepted and lived with the various societal pressures that come from being a widow, old age and a mother who has lost her son and his wife. She resolves to survive the shock of losing her son with the help of her granddaughter and tries to live her life without any societal inhibitions.

Rukmini has a craving for food as she had been suppressing her desires for quite some time. She had been prohibited by her religion to take certain food after she was widowed and thus her desires had not been fulfilled. Now, she is suffering from deadly cancer and decides to indulge in all types of food to fulfil her physical and psychological cravings including that which has been prohibited to her by her religion. She eats food prepared by people who her class of society considers to be untouchables. Rajul Bhargava writes:

> This old woman, now living the last days, of her life, the body licked away by a cancerous goitre, hands puckered by needles and tied to the IV pole, legs outstretched on a raised bed, could not resist the temptations of the heart, the yearnings of the mind and the craving of the tongue – the three precious organs that have to be muted in the name of domestic harmony and familial peace. A week before she died she even broke through the shackles of being a brahmin widow. She conspired with her granddaughter to smuggle her cakes and ice creams, biscuits and samosas made by non-brahmin hands. (*Indian* 228)

In a very short span of time she tastes all the food that she had been deprived of- Lemon tarts, garlic, three types of aerated drinks, fruit cakes laced with brandy, bhelpuri from the fly-infested bazaar and peanuts with chilli powder deep fried in oil. She also wants to be draped in a red silk saree with a wide border of gold. She has been craving for these trivialities in her lifetime and has not even been able to express her wishes for the fear of social criticism. When her husband dies, the traditional Hindu wife has to succumb to the age-old customs. She changes into a living ghost and is deprived of her human rights as a widow. She must wear white clothes and is allowed to eat only vegetarian food-epitomized by boiled rice. She is so much repressed by the rigid patriarchal system that she is unable to express her natural longings. Ratna goes against the age-old customs and breaks the conventional rules and covers Rukmini in her best red silk saree. Ratna's gesture, in the words of Sunitha Srinivas.C, shows "the loving reverence for the dead, with recognition of the continued relation of the dead with the living."(107) She airs her grandmother's room after she passes away and replaces the dull, grey clothes with new ones which indicate the gradual social change that has come about in the attitude of the new generation women regarding the traditional discriminatory practices. It is actually her way of opening the room to new ideas and thoughts. As Ratna expresses in the text, "Then I open all the windows and her cupboard and air the rooms. I tear her dirty, grey saris to shreds. I line the shelves of her empty cupboard with my thick, newly-bought, glossy-jacketed texts, one next to the other. They stand straight and solid, row after row of armed soldiers."(16) The greyness and monotony of a widow's life, her confined suffocated existence is described in the story. Ratna's replacement of the old widow's belongings with her books is a gesture which suggests progression.

The title story 'The Art of Dying' is yet another story which deals with a dying woman. The narrator is the daughter of the dying woman. The story is based on flashbacks and the crux of the story is the same as 'The Remains of the Feast.' It is about the women grieving and trying to handle the loss of their only sons. The inexplicable grief of the parents at the loss of a child is highlighted in the story. They confront the cycle of the grief process, several stages of grief such as shock, denial, resentment, guilt, sadness, dejection and finally acceptance. Guilt which is at the peak stage of the grief cycle is experienced by all the grieving parents at one time or other. It is immaterial whether they are really responsible for their child's death, the feeling of guilt always persists.

A close reading of the stories of Hariharan hints at the theme of death that surfaces even though feminist concerns comprise key issues in most of her stories. Death is the central concern in her anthology. It plays an important role in the stories and is described as a painful process. Death is a metaphor used to describe physical or psychological starvation where human beings are forced to curb all their heartfelt desires. Many of the stories are about people dying or inhabiting hopeless universes of boredom and social decay. Death is not shown merely as an event but as a shadow looming large over life. Life is like a journey and death is its only destination. Hariharan's skill at describing the process of death/dying is reflected through her characters. Her characters possess immense courage in accepting the inevitability of death and that becomes the author's prime concern. Krishna Daiya writes, "She shows her characters fading away, thinning away to embrace a slow, sure death. They are also aware of this unavoidable end towards which they are advancing."(*Post-Independence* 47) In the title story, 'The Art of Dying', the dying mother tries to explain to her daughter that death is not a mere end of your breath but an act for which your strength and understanding are required. The mother lying on her death-bed tells her daughter "Death, she says, the word rolling off her tongue with intimacy, demands strength, not a final weakness." (70)

'The Art of Dying' is the story of a woman who loses a healthy son in the prime of life, a son who still was unmarried. The news was shocking because he was hale and hearty. He was a practising doctor in Australia who collapsed "on his own examining table." The news came as a shock to the mother. "...she was completely dry-eyed. Without a whimper or a moan, she groped for her widow's narrow bed."(67) A mother, who in throes of her grief, becomes listless and her body fights with the grief for three days with no water and food. But on the fourth day, her daughter forcibly feeds her before she leaves for Australia to bring the body of her brother. The mother confronts several stages of grief and guilt. The dying mother's confession is also reflective of her feelings towards her dominating husband. Her speech clearly shows the bitterness and hatred in her voice. Her husband had been subjugating and dominating the children all his life. She is not ready to forgive him even at her deathbed. Both the mother and the daughter had grudges against him. A few days before her death, the dying mother seems to have a contented look on her face. It is certainly not the acceptance of her son's death but a strange happiness that she is going to join him in the other world. So death is not a suffering for her, rather it becomes a salvation. It is an escape from the present physical suffering which she is undergoing.

The story 'The Art of Dying' perfectly highlights the post-feminist culture. It states how women adopt a peaceful and gentle existence. It also shows the monotonous life of women which leads to a feeling of emptiness and frustration. It is not by any other means but by the art of self-negation, pushing their feelings, emotions and desires to a second state. It talks about the stereotypical tenor of women's lives through the narrator which is so monotonous that it leads to a feeling of emptiness and frustration. The narrator is a therapist by profession, healing people, working for hours at the Counselling Centre to bring people back to normal, looking after her teenage children and also coping with the distractions from her husband. The society looks at it as a "peaceful, gentle existence" (64) but to women it is a "contraption" which moves only in one direction – negation of the self, leading to a "yawning emptiness". It is an art they learn best from nobody else but their own moms and other female relatives in the household, which they have to acquire throughout their lives. The more they control their desires, they are appreciated by society. As the protagonist reflects

> Death – or madness – is far too sudden, dramatic. The tenor of my life – wifing, childbearing – has been determined by the subtle, undulating waves of progress creeping over my body. Bleed, dry up; expand with life, contract with completion. A peaceful, gentle existence; motion, not quite blunt-edged change. (64)

The story 'The Art of Dying' showcases feminist strains where women are hegemonised by agencies of power. Feminist theory has several theoretical approaches and positions, whether socio-eonomic, psychological or literary, it primarily concentrates on power and freedom which have traditionally been denied to women.

Susan Faludi examines the strategies of equality and freedom and writes: "The truth is that the last decade has been a powerful counter – assault on women's rights, a backlash, an attempt to retract the handful of small and hard-won victories that feminist movement did manage to win for women....The backlash is at once sophisticated and banal, deceptively 'progressive' and proudly backward." (qtd in *Indian*) Women are often placed on the margins. Sometimes women tend to go beyond the traditional boundaries laid down by the institutions. It is these margins which are being redefined or renegotiated to prevent feminist literary aesthetics from being trapped in confessional and victim-centered narratives which is evident in some of Hariharan's stories. Gayatri Spivak in her essay "Marginality and the Teaching Machine" has observed:

> There can be no universalist claim in the human sciences. This is most strikingly obvious in the case of establishing "marginality" as a subject-position in literary and cultural critique. The reader must accustom herself to starting from a particular situation and then to the ground shifting under her feet. (*Outside* 53)

Thus post-feminism is not merely a phase but an aspect of feminist strategy to reframe the margins and to prevent feminist aesthetics from reaching a dead end. Jasbir Jain opines that post-feminism is a move which talks about feminism in a different perspective. It releases the movement from the stereotypical women's matters and presents a more contemporary perspective. She talks about feminism which explores the self or the identity of an individual. Postfeminism moves a step ahead as it is free from the stereotypical image of the woman and shows its concern towards humanism:

> Feminism is about the self, about rights and about difference; post-feminism is a move towards reciprocal change, and expresses a need to look anew at the harsh political realities. It is motivated, to my mind, by the need to put feminism in a forward gear, to free it from its woman-to-woman dialogue, and prevent it from being devalued by repetitive, superficial analysis. Post-feminism, in its impact on literary aesthetics, shifts the issue from identity to relationships, from a concern with oppression to one with the concept of freedom. (*Indian* 91)

Though the women live apparently full lives dedicated to housekeeping and other activities of the body, their minds and hearts yearn for much more. They want to break away from the cocoon of being tagged as one-dimensional figures. The plight of a young innocent child widow is highlighted in the story 'Revati' where she has to undergo trials at a tender age.

The story 'Revati' presents the plight of a child widow who strives for her identity within the age-old rigid patriarchal system. Revati is a girl who has been a victim of a social evil, i.e., child marriage at the tender age of ten and ironically, she becomes a child widow within a year. It's a story about a girl who not only loses her childhood but also her life to the evil practice of society. Revati's blessing came in the form of a liberal father who wanted that his daughter should not take her life as a stigma but as a challenge. He got her a tutor who comes home to teach her. As she grows old, she is sent to Madras for further education. Finally, she attains the degree and becomes a teacher who is financially independent. Years after, she comes home hungry and sweaty. "She was an unpleasant reminder of a world gone by. A child-widow was a thing of the past, a page from a history textbook that should be safely contained between cardboard covers. Not what she was, as large as life, walking, talking, eating huge mouthfuls of our food."(93) As the narrator states, she would eat to her heart's content, unaffected by the details as to how much she left for the rest of the family. "Eat, so that you're strong. So the ghosts don't get you, she said."(94) The ghosts signify the social pressures predominating over women. One needs to become physically and mentally strong to combat them.

Revati does not indulge in any kind of formalities. She does not wait like other women for the children and men to finish their food. She does not believe in the societal formalities of women eating last or eating the leftovers. She eats to her heart's content and with children, she would gulp like them making "great big balls of it all mixed up, into her mouth."(94) It has been ten years since her retirement from her teaching career when a poor distant cousin is sent for to live with Revati, as companion and bodyguard. But the imbecile idiot is sent away when Revati and he were found alone in the upstairs room.

> Oh, press my legs, press my head, I heard her moan. I saw him squeeze her ankle, and she burped, a tentative, bird-like cheep. He massaged her legs and I heard a long, hissing burp. He pressed down hard on her thighs and kneaded her flabby midriff like dough. She made a huge, full-throated noise – a belching sound that went on and on.
>
> It was all innocent, of course. She was an old woman, at least seventy. He was only an imbecile. But I still thought I should let my mother-in-law know. (96)

In spite of being independent, Revati has a fit in the middle of night where she would scream. The social stigma and fear of being mocked at left her in bodily discomfort. She is scared, her body jerks and eyes roll wildly as she mutters "There, he's there. He's laughing at me, she screamed."(97) Revati's plight showcases the social suppression which gets ingrained in the mind of women. She feels afraid of being subjugated or mocked at. It's an insecure feeling which has made its way into the mind's crevices."Together , through the night, my mother-in-law and I sat on either side of Revati, stroking the trembling body back to stillness, enticing her wandering mind back to us." (97)

Both 'Revati' and 'The Remains of the Feast' reflect the plight of women who are deprived and undernourished not only physically but also emotionally. The stories portray women who always bring peace and harmony by compromising a bit of themselves all the time in their lives. They yearn to eat well, be respected, be involved in decision-making but are left on the outskirts as secondary citizens. The stories highlight the struggle of both the women whose desires remain unfulfilled and also fail to achieve a respectable place in the family. Both of them represent women who are unable to express themselves and fulfil their basic needs because of the restrictions that are imposed on widows. Both the women shun the traditional norms and customs inflicted on women and try to make a way for themselves. They also suggest the idea that an individual's desires can be curbed due to repression but will not lie latent once the cup of tolerance overflows. Being merely reduced to playthings, they yearn to make a place in the household and attain independence and self-fulfillment which is as important as the fulfillment of sexual needs for an individual. This idea is clearly expressed through Betty Friedan's opinion, For women as for men, the need for self-fulfillment – autonomy, self-realization, independence, individuality, self-actualisation – is as important as the sexual need, with as serious consequences when it is thwarted. (*Feminine* 282)

'The Will' is the story of Raghu and his wife Sushila and is based on husband-wife relationship full of love and faith. The story is about the challenge faced by a woman whose husband Raghu dies leaving behind a will. He has divided everything he owned amongst his three kids, leaving his widow with just a letter. It transforms her into a philosophical individual. The story is about how that letter becomes the woman's strength and how on the basis of that letter she takes her other relationships forward The letter remains a kind of motivation for Sushila to guide her children in their lives 'stand apart like a friendly, tranquil island.'(148) The story showcases the mental state of a widow and the anguish, adjustments and compromises made by her. The author portrays the Indian woman and her hapless existence in a state of widowhood. Sushila's attempt to stay alive with the good thoughts handed to her by her late husband goes ahead of death."Don't breathe down their necks, Raghu had written to her. No one wants a nagging mother an inch behind him all the time. But watch carefully, from a distance, and step forward when you must." (149)

Her son is impressed with her wisdom and confidence and is amazed and intrigued how the woman who was always like his father's shadow and had never taken a decision could have such a major personality shift. She transforms into a woman who is full of poise and is even admired by other people for her wisdom. Nobody knew what is in the letter that causes this change. She reads the same letter every day and inhales its fragrance every night before she goes to bed. She has become so confident that she volunteers to help her daughter with her kids. She accidentally loses the letter and the impact of this mishap leads her back to her old subdued self:

> It was not torn, snatched, stolen or misplaced. It simply slipped out of her hands, floated out of the window, and wafted down seven storeys. She ran down the stairs, forgetting the lift in her agitation, and searched every inch of the compound.
>
> Then she slowly went back upstairs, her legs like lead, a stupid, baby-like emptiness in her mind. (150-151)

Losing the letter has an adverse effect on her personality. She feels lonely and dejected. She hardly has anything to say now. She tries to think but nothing comes to her mind now. She becomes "an aging invalid."(151) It is only when she is with her seven-year-old grandson who pleads her to help him with his homework that she realises her own self. Her grandson reads:

> A cheerful wife is the joy of life, he chanted. Standing pools gather dirt. Spare the rod and spoil the child. A good husband makes a good wife.
>
> Ah, she said, and suddenly, like a rebirth, she remembered who she was. She looked at the child, who had stopped his sing-song recitation, and was looking at her expectantly.
>
> Did I make a mistake? he asked.
>
> Oh no, she said, her mind filling up again, in grateful, familiar little trickles. What noble sentiments! Wonderful! Please, please go on. (152)

This is when she is transformed and uplifted psychically. She is full of gratitude for her grandson who revives her desire to participate in the process of life once again. It is like a rebirth for her as she discovers her true self and realises the motive of her being.

In an Indian society, a woman is dependent on the male family members. Before her marriage, she is dependent on her father and then her brother, after her marriage it is the husband, her son and grandson who continue to dominate her. The woman who is the child- bearer, the nurturer of mankind, is considered a goddess in the Indian culture but she never gets her due respect. She lives in a fear of losing her respect in the society if she tries to exert herself. The same emotion is beautifully expressed in the story.

Gajar Halwa is a story of a girl who is sent to Delhi by her mother in anticipation of a better life. It is the story of Chellamma, a servant girl from a small-town family who learns to survive in a big city. She brings in Perumayee, a poor sixteen-year-old girl from her village who comes with the hope of leading a good life in Delhi. Amma, Perumayee's mother, had been a labourer who had been feeding the family with hard work. But she could no longer find any work, so she sends her daughter to the city as she sees a promise in Chellamma. Perumayee is one of those millions of migrant labourers who come to the city looking for work and leave their village and homes behind. But her dreams are shattered when she enters the small, smelly house of Chellamma. All the dreams and aspirations of the girl are shattered when the hard reality knocks her down. Women in Indian society are often reduced to mere non-existent individuals who struggle all their lives to attain a respectable place in the society.

They forget their little desires and ambitions and have to undertake menial jobs to make their living. The story *'Gajar Halwa'* expresses the condition of present-day women as they struggle to lead respectable lives in the society. Perumayee actually has to work hard because she wants to send some money to Amma in the village. She has an obligation to work for her mother and also to live a respectable life. Despite being tired of grating, washing, cooking, etc., she has to keep slogging to fulfil her aims. The mechanical movement of her arms symbolises the back and forth movement of her mind. The narrator comments that the society drains an individual internally:

> The *gajar*, absorbing, sucking in like a greedy round red mouth, swallows the sugar, the ghee and the milk. It sucks in everything, and the earlier spluttering becomes a faint but steady heave of red, like a heartbeat, then gentle sighs. (84)

In the story, the process of making *gajar halwa* is used as a simile to describe the struggles of a woman to become a patient, loving housekeeper. The way a carrot is grated and cooked with sugar and other ingredients to make it tasty and aromatic is how a woman goes through various struggles of self-negation, self-depreciation to reach the standards of being good and homely. Women actually have to absorb all the problems of their lives without complaint as they are socially trained to do so. Prabha Pant opines,

> Like the *gajar halwa* she is cooking she will be sucked down into the morass of life just as the carrots absorb all the various ingredients turning into a gooey sticky mass. Perumayee represents the millions of nameless voiceless people who constitute an important part of the concrete jungle. (*Humanism* 100)

The '*gajar*' in the story is symbolic of women's plight because like the carrot they are also subjected to all kinds of peeling, grating procedures in the course of their struggle through this life. As the narrator says, one has to be "peeled off their fine skins" (80) in the due course of struggle and work. Our society has laid the standards for social norms, customs and traditions which each individual is bound to follow. '*Gajar Halwa*' and 'Forefathers' is actually a portrayal of such norms and customs where women are confined to a certain social boundary and they are not allowed to cross the limit even psychically.

Hariharan's story 'Forefathers' describes the state of three sisters who are awaiting the death of their father, A father who is paralysed physically but mentally quite active and continues to act as the head of the family and keeps the family under total domination. The story gives the views of each daughter and how they gather patience to handle this situation. As one of the daughters reflects:

> My father is the lawmaker. Our flat defines the circumference of his kingdom. Except for the terrace, which strictly speaking belongs to the entire building, there is not a single corner in the house which offers privacy. But the word exists in our vocabulary. (50)

He acts as the supreme power in the house and his daughters are "automated menials" (48) who can be summoned and dismissed at the ring of his bell. He also tries his best to seek attention by ringing the bell very often and as the daughter narrates, he wants them to be by his side all the time so he emotionally blackmails them by describing it as neglect on their part and desire to make him die alone.

> The sound of the bell can mean anything, it can ring any time of the day or night. It can mean the bedpan (I vomited only the first time), the tray filled with smaller and smaller portions of at least four dishes for him to choose among, or it could be just a plain summons. Sit here, do you want me to die alone? (51)

He had been a 'cunning tyrant' (49) since the day he became an invalid. He would make the eldest daughter play the role of a nursemaid. She asks the crow, the oracle to tell her how long the father will continue with the domination. Though the attitude of the daughter is not sympathetic, one can understand the frustration she experiences because all her desires and needs have to be sacrificed at her father's bedside. When her patience has reached the end of its tether she feels,

> I reach for a stone. If I hit the crow the first time, my father will die next week. A second attempt means a delay of a month. If the third shot misses the crow, or if the bird takes fright and flies away, my father will live for at least another six months. (48)

His extended life will mean another six months of helplessness, one hundred and eighty nights of sleeplessness and an eternity of watchfulness. She will have to suffer the domination of her father like her mother and survive 'like a pastel – shaded, grimy, badly-daubed wall-hanging her father's kingdom absorbing the dust of years.'(50) The narrator and her sisters yearn for privacy in the confines of the circumference of their father's kingdom. There is not even a single corner in the two-roomed flat they can call their own. Yet the three sisters are obsessed with the word,

> ...they have learnt the art of slyly dressing in public. They put on some of their clothes in the narrow, wet bathroom – a fine balancing act – and then rush to the kitchen to finish dressing behind the open doors of our steel cupboards. (50)

Hariharan describes how women have to suffer at all costs and take up their pain with a mask of humbleness, dutifulness that "absorbs the sharpest sarcasm and hides the angriest of tears."(52) The relationship between the daughters and the father depict power relations of patriarchy prevalent in the society where the institutions curb the desires of individuals and they undergo a feeling of suffocation. Many men and women, in fact, are forced to live their lives, unlike their will.

The story 'Virgin Curry' portrays the streaks of post-feminism through the protagonist Patricia Menezes who stays with her best friend Brenda in the hostel and the caretaker is Sister Phyllis. Both Patricia and Brenda are secretaries and have joined a computer course for their career advancement. Patricia is involved with a married man, Samit and likes to spend time with him. She also is a strong believer that Sister Phyllis had big dreams for her life which she had to give up because of her austere vocation and because of some pressure she has become a nun. Patricia is shown as a person who does not care for what people have to say and likes to live life on her terms and this attitude of hers also makes her leave the hostel and stay as the other women in the flat provided by her lover. She does not like the restrictions which Sister Phyllis inflicts on them and goes away to lead an independent life. Brenda, on the other hand, is left alone in the dull environment of the hostel. The story concludes with Brenda going to the dining hall, where she has that dejected and neglected feeling:

> I went up to the counter and piled a big heap of rice on to my plate, then reached for the dish of mutton curry. There wasn't a single piece of meat left in it. It was all gravy, oily and slimy, and I was only twenty minutes late!
>
> Spooning the gravy on to the rice, I remembered Pat's laughter. Virgin Curry again, she would pretend to growl on meatless days. (110)

Individuals like Brenda who are not as bold as Patricia has always been left to suffer the pangs of loneliness due to the deprivation of one kind or another. Life is like a virgin curry for them-sans fun, frolic or enjoyment. The security of a routine life does not compensate for the feeling of deprivation that haunts them. The feeling of deprivation, discontentment and monotony of Brenda may be likened to the plight of Sarala who also undergoes the same feelings of loneliness, seclusion and dejection in the story 'Untitled Poem.'

Hariharan's 'Untitled Poem' portrays the discontentment of Sarala and her husband, who is the narrator, a retired salesman and an aspiring and creative writer. The story shows the dull, monotonous, incomplete, dejected and discontented life of the couple. The couple in the story has recently shifted into their newly built house. This house lends Sarala a feeling of satisfaction because she now possesses a real though small garden. She nurtures and takes care of her garden very well.

> She has spent a lifetime growing minute, self-contained gardens in pots. When she saw the small stretch of land in front of the house, she didn't even want to go inside. 'I won't have a single pot here,' she said. 'No more pretend-gardens in the balcony on the seventh floor. Everything I grow now will dig its roots deep into the soil.'(1)

This shows Sarala's discontent because all her life she has not been able to establish roots, and acquire a feeling of belongingness. They do not have children who could help to strengthen their mutual relationship and they lead drab disparate lives. He passes his time bent over his sheet of paper and she busies herself in her garden. Being deprived of natural companionship she confides and has some kind of bonding with her old gardener. 'They make a good team. She is the navigator, he the oarsman.'(4) But her bad luck is that a rodent creeps into her garden of Eden to destroy her paradise.

> This rodent is no ordinary enemy. He picks on the most lush, the most fecund of her plants. He digs deep into the soil and pulls wildly at the roots. He leaves no tracks but Sarala and the gardener find the uprooted, torn shreds of stalks and leaves every day. He does not eat any of it. It is a song of pure destruction.(5)

The unseen rodent is symbolic of the invisible power that is disturbing the peace and beauty of life. So many forces work upon the minds of men that every individual is under stress. Each individual has to suffer, torn, ripped apart, broken and stalked yet condemned to live. Sarala and her husband are living in a similar kind of situation where individuals face adverse kind of situations in the form of the rodent who spoils their paradise. Rajul Bhargava states in the essay 'Post-Feminist Configurations in Githa Hariharan's Short Stories in *The Art of Dying*'

> In most stories, on first reading, there seems to be some internal disconnectedness, some disjointedness, the ending as much as the beginning as the first line, but there is always an internal design, some oblique reference which combines into a rich texture of trope – exposing a pattern of feminist meaning within the symbolic structure. Her short stories are but shells of a story, fragile containers of composed meaning, metonymic structures of understatement that help in overstanding the suppression that women have to suffer. (*Indian* 230)

The story 'The Reprieve' is a portrayal of Nagaraj, a senior advocate, who is the dominating controller of the house. Mangala, who is his wife, was married off to him at a tender age of fifteen. "If she missed her parents, her brothers and sisters, the games of her recent childhood, her husband heard nothing of it." The feelings of his young wife Mangala are of no consequence as he is not supposed to know them. She was overburdened with work in Nagaraj's thirty-member joint family consisting children, cousins, the widowed aunt, the bachelor grand uncles and retired nephews. She had painstakingly and unquestioningly taken care of the whole family but never bothered about her own health.

> For fifty years, she had been a good, or at least unobtrusive wife in the background. She had run the machinery of a thirty-member household, had oiled its creaky joints, though Nagaraj Rao had been responsible for the larger, more obvious task of providing the components of the machinery, the family members who would be part of the fold, the hierarchy. (42-43)

In a few years, the machinery built so painstakingly and with such unquestioned belief in the family, lay idle and obsolete. Mangala and Nagaraj were left alone as all the others were dead. Later she too took seriously ill, as if "the basis of her existence had been questioned, the purpose of her womanhood destroyed."(43) She suffers from undiagnosed diabetes, high blood pressure and suspected cancer. She dies as she had lived, nothing ugly or sudden, just a "slow, lingering inconspicuous bundle of well-disguised pain, the flesh slowly but not offensively disintegrating." Rajul Bhargava opines,

> Hariharan points out that in handling the many problems of the household she very quickly forgets her own joys and blurs her dreams. It is only in the seclusion that sleep affords does the girl's smile sometimes stretch across her pinched wrinkled face. Despite all this, Mangala knows, she understands and quickly comes to Nagraj, her face full of tender concern, her hand outstretched promising dark safety. It is the woman to whom men come for solace, peace and completion. (*Indian* 229)

It is evident that howsoever the women have been treated they are expected to help men in their hour of need and distress.

The story 'Repeat Performance' portrays the life of a woman who falls in love with a married man Shyam, twenty years senior to her. He had come for a week's tour to Bombay and they spent hours together and shared intimate moments. But it couldn't go on for long.

> I can't go on like this, Shyam said to me, his hands holding mine across the table. I seem to remember the most intense of romantic moments between us only in the safe setting of public places.
>
> When I miss you now, it is like physical pain. He took off his glasses and wiped them, something he did every time he was deeply moved. His eyes colourless and myopic, held mine till I began to tremble. (112)

She loses touch with Shyam, does not even see him for at least twenty-five years. She starts indulging in painting as a hobby. After bearing a son, she takes on painting as her full-time profession. She paints a copy of the painting of Rembrandt's *The Stone Bridge* which depicts an approaching thunderstorm. Later on, she switches over to painting Sisley's landscapes. She absorbs herself fully in her art "I spend at least two or three days just looking at the masterpiece first. I study it, absorb it; if it is a portrait of an old woman reading a book, it becomes the sum total of my perception of old women. No other image, mood or light enters my picture." (115)

She becomes a great artist whose interview clipping in the newspaper says 'Housewife turns expert reproducer.' She puts up her photograph of Van Gogh's *Vase with Sunflowers*. Years later, her masterpiece is bought by a wealthy buyer who owns a garment factory. Conversing with the buyer, it is revealed that she is actually Shyam's second wife. This time again the protagonist goes back to Rembrandt and paints *Landscape with Ruins*. The paintings that she makes on canvas minutely express the mood and psyche which she actually experiences and undergoes. Life lends her some happy moments with Shyam which are shortlived and later she has to live a life of seclusion. She doesn't stagnate, rather moves ahead professionally exhibiting her painting talent.

> I grew up, continued, one track suspended in waiting, totally independent of the other that moved ahead, inevitably, and survived. We did not wait for each other; there were no plans afoot. The secrecy, the briefly-evoked air of doomed passion, became permanent. It slipped down a long, deep, well-like tunnel, and settled at the bottom. We lost each other when it congealed into a memory.(118)

Hariharan shifts from feminism to humanism through some of her stories like 'Halfway Animals' and 'Retrospective.' The stories portray the oppression, repression, dejection of the individuals as a whole by the callous societal ghosts/institutions. 'Halfway Animals' is the story of a male stenographer who works hard like an animal. He had been given the lessons of hard work and sanctity by his father. "'How is the work going, boy? Remember, Work is Worship!'"(17) He becomes the victim of the social system which subjugates the weak individuals. He feels stressed, lonely and neglected to indulge in excessive hard work. "The stenographer is a peculiar kind of animal that does not hunt. It lies in wait for a more strong-hearted animal to come by and find its prey."(17)

With the advent of technology, he is reduced to a man having no importance, a mere plaything at the hands of the society. He is relieved of his job but cannot disclose it to his wife or family. He gets up at the same time and gets ready for his office. He follows his daily routine and finds his respite in the zoo, watching the animals.

> Then I found the zoo. It was convenient, it opened the same hour as the office, and there were not too many people on most weekdays. I had my newspaper, and when that was finished, I could watch the animals.
>
> I still thought of them as animals then. That was before I became an eager student. It was the gharial that first initiated me as a disciple. (19)

He would watch the animals for hours-gharial, apes, monkeys, thus invoking atavism i.e. the tendency to go back to the ancestors. He finds an association with them and calls them companions. "'Apes are man's nearest cousins. Like us, they have no tail, and can stand upright, although normally they walk about on all fours.'"(21) He studies and observes the Primates closely and believes in Darwin's Theory of Evolution,

> As long as an animal fitted into its surroundings, like a worm in the ground, a fish in water or a monkey up a tree, it would survive. But surroundings change constantly. To live successfully in an ever-changing world, life itself might change as well. (20)

In the end, he narrates a sick baby chimpanzee's plight and needs to be taken for a medical aid. When the mother chimp resists, she is shot dead. The stenographer observes pain in the eyes of the father chimpanzee and realises that it is time to get back to work.

The story gives the idea through the description of the life of animals and the Darwinian Theory that individuals have to adapt to the environment in order to survive and lead a comfortable life. The world is changing forever and we have to adapt ourselves and change our lifestyle accordingly. The last few lines sum up the idea of the story,

> I decide to leave the zoo though I have not put in a full day. I leave earlier than usual, having received my forefather's legacy a second time around. Even unemployed, redundant stenographers know when it is time to go back to work. (23)

A similar plight of Prem Lal is seen in the story 'Retrospective.' Prem Lal, who is a clerk in the Delhi Electric Supply Undertaking, is stuck in the dullness and monotony of his work. As he puts in the text, "A long, s-shaped queue stirred like a restless snake in front of my desk. I ignored it and went about my business, dusting my table, chair and files. I changed the page on my desk calendar."(101) The choked bathroom drain in Prem Lal's house is also symbolic of his brain also becoming dull, stale, dross and choked by the social system. Just like the stenographer in 'Halfway Animals,' he too, becomes the victim of the deteriorating system which compels a person to submit and resign from his job against his will.

> 'Prem Lal,' he said more gently. 'I know you have worked here for years. You have been a steady, reliable worker. But you're now – let me see – how many years of service do you have left?'
>
> 'Two, sir,' I whispered, my feet slipping now, the small rocks in my way tumbling in a landslide as I fell.
>
> 'That will be all,' he said, brisk again. 'You can take the afternoon off and apply for leave tomorrow.' (103-104)

Prem Lal couldn't do anything except nod and submit to the will of his boss. The story showcases the helplessness of the individuals who have to sacrifice their will under varied social and institutional pressures. These pressures often block the freedom and growth of the individuals. Society is likened to the gardener who prunes the tentacles of the plants when they try to grow according to their sweet will.

The story 'Voices in the Twilight' is about the recently orphaned siblings. Through the technique of stream of consciousness, the author has portrayed the deep recesses of the minds of two daughters Vidya and Shakuntala and a brother Arjun. The binding thread of their relationship had snapped. Instead of developing a closer and a warmer bonding with each other, the siblings argue with each other and look forward to leading their independent lives. They stop all communication and an atmosphere of gloom and misery prevails. The three symbolise the lost and isolated individuals swallowed by the huge city. Vidya takes up a bank job, Shakuntala gets married in a wealthy family and Arjun looks for emotional security in short-lived relationships. His relationship with Rita ultimately proves to be a lifeline of his wandering, meaningful existence. Hariharan portrays the power of compassion through the story which can transform even the ordinary lives. It can also help one to escape from the clutches of the "loving tarantula",

> The city is a big insect with its beady, wandering eyes. Nothing escapes its hunger. It sucks golden honey. It smells of sweat and rotten tears. It grows an evil flower in its heart of deeply-scarred stone. Everything is found in the sweet, heady poison that oozes out of the loving tarantula. (145)

The story 'Love poem' centers around Neeta, who has come to Bombay for studying in a women's college. She is portrayed as a "Bookworm"(120), a girl with "oily hair" and "thick spectacles." Neeta recalls how her father had left her inside the hostel. He was relieved to see that no single man except the watchman was allowed inside the hostel. Her father was not even allowed to go and see Neeta's room and he left her in the "custody of rules, wardens, and the constant, suspicion-sharpened company of women."(122)

Neeta feels lonely and secluded and this seclusion does not keep her confined to the gender roles given to women. "The girls were friendly, as long as you looked like them and spoke like them. They queued up for hours at the pay phone; they read one Mills and Boon romance a day; and they chatted endlessly about clothes and boys. Watching them, from the fringes of their charmed circle, Neeta felt her tongue curl in her mouth. She spoke less and less."(122) She felt as if she is an anomaly and did not talk much. She discovers Dr. Sharma, another "anomaly"(122) who is her English teacher. He was a man "who read poetry as if it flowed with the blood in his veins and lit up his beady little eyes with their fire!...he could make any word sound exciting; and alive. Inspiration. Lyrical. Muse. Metaphor. And of course, love."(122) Neeta enjoys the poetry and the style of delivery of Dr. Sharma. She enjoys being 'outside' the periphery of her existence through the poetry narrated by Dr. Sharma.

On the contrary, Dr. Sharma's gender identity has been formed by portraying him as "something of an anomaly"(122) in the women's college. There is a rumour among the girls that he "separated from his wife"(123), a polygamist or a homosexual 'man'. The situation becomes problematic when he invites Neeta to his room. Neeta is quite relaxed to demonstrate her love for poetry, which makes her different from others. But she is surprised to see him undress before her and arranging his naked body on the bed "as if he was a poet's muse."(126) Moreover, he asks Neeta, "Are you moved now? Does the image of my body excite you? The symbol of my desire?"(126) Neeta was frozen in the chair. She felt a kind of horror and wetness on her cheeks. She rushed to the door, "not so much to escape his nakedness, but to hide her own."(126)

Most of the writers and critics of the feminist school have discussed gender as a definite category and for them, the body of women becomes the basic criteria for research and practice. They consider the body as matter, but critics like Judith Butler through her seminal works like *Gender Trouble* and *Bodies That Matter* oppose the idea strongly. The stories in *The Art of Dying* reflect that although sex and gender have an impact on women, men too cannot remain completely unaffected by their pressure. The feminist discourse may lay emphasis on the bodies of women but gender studies reveal that if women are vulnerable, so are men. The conventional roles assigned to both sexes on the basis of their bodies may not necessarily satisfy them. As the analysis of the stories 'Love Poem' and 'Revati' show that bodies and gender constructs do not always determine human behaviour. Men may be as prone to be oppressed by masculinity as it is practised in the social setup they belong to. Both in *The Ghosts of Vasu Master* as well as *The Art of Dying*, Hariharan like Butler, raises queries about the construction of 'sex' and gender as natural constructs. As early as 1928, Virginia Woolf had also spoken about a "man-womanly" and "woman-manly"(82) in *A Room of One's Own*. She asserted that biological sex should not be the basis on which a person should be expected to perform his/her role in a patriarchal setup. The fact that sex and gender are both cultural constructs is highlighted by Butler as well. With the support of critics engaged in the discussion of gender, Hariharan's work can be studied from an approach which is not purely feministic in intent and purpose. As a postmodern feminist, she has the potential of a writer who understands that the external pressures are equal in all cases. In fact, a whole research project can be undertaken on the depiction of gender and sex and their relationship with the male/female body in Hariharan's works.

Hariharan is an activist as well as a novelist and deems it her duty to sensitise people to the contemporary issues. She presents the actualities of life and whatever she observes in the society. She raises issues pertaining to the everyday life. In an essay titled "The Power Within" Shashi Deshpande elucidates on the art of writing. She says:

> All good writing is socially committed writing, as it comes out of a concern for the human predicament. I believe, as Camus says, that the greatness of an artist is measured by the balance the writer maintains between the values of creation and the values of humanity....Writing that probes with honesty and artistry into the human situation. (*Creating* 212)

Being a committed writer herself, Hariharan shows her concern for human beings who are haunted by societal ghosts. She does not limit her work to the experiences of women but also understands and portrays the predicament of men. As Rajul Bhargava aptly remarks:

> In her stories Hariharan chooses to describe what are perhaps everyday happenings, things taken for granted about a woman's life, her living and universality of woman's condition and capacity. These stories create a one to one correspondence between the singular and the universal, the part and the whole, the trivial and the significant, what appears to be a trifle is potently important. (*Indian* 230)

Her short story collection describes everyday occurrences and incidents pertaining to women's lives and their behaviour. She also explores the lives of men and their relationships with women and society and the world in which they live. How globalisation and technological advancement have influenced their lives adversely is also reflected in her stories. *The Art of Dying* focusses on the problems of men and women and highlights their suffering meted out by the orthodox society. Hariharan's stories reflect the social restrictions which act as the societal ghosts and create trouble in the lives of people. In fact, various social institutions render individuals incapable of thinking for themselves and reduce them to mere puppets in the hands of different socio-political forces. These societal ghosts curb the aspirations of individuals. Everyone has to act according to the norms laid down by the society. Even men are not spared of societal ghosts who are the invisible entities controlling their lives. These ghosts suppress and oppress individuals, preventing them from living a life of their own. In fact, there is still a long struggle to achieve the status of autonomy. However, the invincibility of the human spirit is emphasised by the silent resistance that Hariharan's characters practise.

Works cited

Bhardwaj, Neelam Sanwal. "Enlarging the Limits of the Canvas: Feminist Perspective in Githa Hariharan's *The Ghosts of Vasu Master*" *The Criterion: An International Journal in English*. Web. 5.2 (2014) 290-295.

Bhardwaj, Vikash and Surender Kumar. "*The Ghost of Vasu Master:* Exploring the Self through Teacher-Taught Relationship." *International Journal of English and Education*. Web. 2.4 (2013).

Bhargava, Rajul "Post-Feminist Configurations in GithaHariharan's Short Stories in *The Art of Dying*" eds. Jain, Jasbir and Avadesh Kumar Singh. *Indian Feminisms*. New Delhi: Creative, 2001. Print.

Bhutalia, Urvashi. *Peopled by Ghosts and Absences*. The Book Review. 19.3 n.d. March 1995.

Butler, Judith. *Bodies That Matter: On the Discursive Limits of Sex*. New York & London: Routledge, 1993. Print.

Daiya, Krishna. *Post-Independence Women Short Story Writers in Indian English*. New Delhi: Sarup & Sons, 2006. Print.

Daly, Mary. *Gyn/Ecology: The Metaethics of Radical Feminism*. Boston: Beacon Press, 1978. Print.

Deshpande, Shashi. "The Power Within." *Creating Theory: Writers on Writing*. ed. Jasbir Jain. Delhi: Pencraft, 2000. Print.

Faludi, Susan. *Backlash: the Undeclared War Against Women*. London: Vintage, 1992. Print.

Foucault, Michel. *The History of Sexuality: The Will to Knowledge*. London: Penguin, 1978. Print.

Friedan, Betty. *The Feminine Mystique*. Harmondsworth: Penguin, 1971. Print.

Gordon, Avery F. *Ghostly Matters: Haunting and the Sociological Imagination*. 2nd ed. London: U of Minnesota P, 2008. Print.

Hariharan, Githa. *The Art of Dying and Other Stories*. New Delhi: Penguin, 1993. Print.

---. *The Ghosts of Vasu Master*. New Delhi: Penguin, 1994. Print.

Githa Hariharan. "The Double Burden: The Continual Contesting of Tradition and Modernity": Githa Hariharan interviewed by Joel Kuorrti. *The Journal of Commonwealth Literature*. Web 36.1 (2001): 7-26.

---."Discrete Thoughts" ed. Meenakshi Bharat. *Desert in Bloom: Contemporary Indian Women's Fiction in English*. Delhi: Pencraft, 2004. Print.

---."A Conversation with Githa Hariharan." Interview by Arnab Chakladar. *Another Subcontinent: South Asian Society and Culture*, 2005. 12 Aug 2005. Web. 8 July 2013. http://www.anothersubcontinent.com/gh3.html

Jain, Jasbir. "Positioning the 'Post' in Post-Feminism: Reworking of Strategies" eds. Jain, Jasbir and Avadesh Kumar Singh. *Indian Feminisms*. Delhi: Pencraft, 2004. Print.

Jain, Jasbir. "Men in the Minds of Women: Women writers and Male Narrators in the Fiction of Nayantara Sahgal, Anita Desai and Githa Hariharan." *Desert in Bloom: Contemporary Indian Women's Fiction in English*. ed. Meenakshi Bharat. Delhi: Pencraft, 2004. Print.

Kale, Mahesh. "The Ghost of Vasu Master: Case Study of an Indian Teacher." *Contemporary Research in India*. 2.1 (2012): 200-02. Web. 8 Mar.2013.

Murphy, Dr. Joseph. *The Power of Your Subconscious Mind*. London: Simon & Schuster, 1977. Print.

Pant, Prabha. "Variations on a Theme: Humanism in Arundhati Roy's *The Cost of Living* and Githa Hariharan's *The Art of Dying*." ed. T.S. Anand. *Humanism in Indian English Fiction*. New Delhi: Creative, 2005. Print.

Roy, Anjali. "Visnu Sarma against Shakespeare: "Ghosts" of (Non) Dominating Knowledge in The Ghosts of Vasu Master." *The Postmodern Indian English Novel: Interrogating the 1980s and 1990s*.ed. Vinay Kirpal. Bombay: Allied, Vol.VIII, 1996. Print.

Spivak, Gayatri Chakravarty. "Marginality in the Teaching Machine", *Outside in The Teaching Machine*. London: Routledge, 1996. Print.

Srinivas, C. Sunitha. *Functionalism and Indian English Fiction From Cradle to Grave*. New Delhi: Atlantic, 2010. Print.

Woolf, Virginia. *A Room of One's Own*. 1928. London: Harmondsworth, 1945. Print..

CONCLUSION

> My novels would be impossible without plurality in many ways – of narrative voices, alternative scenarios, reinterpreted tales and so on. Perhaps this is also a comment on the nature of the eternal tale. My novels have been, so far, preoccupied with the powers of the simple – but not simplistic – tale. And it is in the nature of these stories all of us hear and retell that they are never finished. There is no authoritative version; they must be twisted and retold for our times and lives.
>
> **Hariharan "A new take on power"** ***Pioneer***

Hariharan is one of those prominent writers whose non-fictional prose writings and interviews not only explain but also give us food for thought regarding her fictional works. The plurality of narrators, situations, interpretation of tales without always giving them a conclusive ending make it difficult for any research project to come to any complete finality about her work. The present study focusses on the fiction that depicts different types of power relations and their social, political and psychological impact on the society. Power structures have remained a vital part of our day to day life and they exist in every sphere of our existence – economic, political, personal, social, religious and cultural. Hariharan's works elucidate how the hidden power structures assume different shapes and facades and create turmoil in the lives of ordinary people.

The project studies the pluralistic themes brought out in Hariharan's novels and short stories collection that include political, social and cultural topics, marginalisation of women suppression, empowerment, female bonding, communalism and religious prejudices. Hariharan's works reflect her resistance to the existing systems and traditions by offering a subversion of ancient texts. She takes the reader into a different world of imagination and creativity. She deals with simple issues, portraying everyday happenings re-told in her unique narrative and objective style. She is a writer who is an enlightened citizen, an activist who brings to light all that she observes around her. She is a courageous critic of the contemporary Indian polity and legal system. While speaking to Suhasini Haidar in an interview, she states:

> The law, if I may say so, is an amoeba riddled with parasites. We have so many laws that applied at earlier times and are now obsolete. There is no question, for example, that across the classes, women are functioning as financial providers to their families, and even so, this law had persisted. So we have to continually look at the validity of our laws. It is an ongoing process. And people are doing that. (web *www.rediff.com*)

This is authenticated by the fact that Hariharan approached the court when she came to know that women were denied the right of being sole guardians of their own children (as mentioned earlier). Her works are written with objectivity, though her omniscient presence can be felt in them because they are brimming with her views and ideas. She acknowledges the inquisitiveness of a writer in the article, "New Voices, New Challenges," "All of us know that though we lead rather solitary lives when it actually comes to the writing, the raw material is from the world around us - and understanding this world, so as to ask the questions writers must, is perhaps the biggest challenge we face even before we put pen to paper." (web *www.jstor.org*) Hariharan asserts that the writers should reassert their commitment to society and should be the voices that question. They should oppose whatever injustice or inequality they see around them.

In all her works, Hariharan portrays the man-woman relationship. While emphasising the truth that patriarchal society pushes women into the margins, Hariharan also portrays the efforts of women to reject the position of 'other' and become subjects in their own right. She claims to have feminist inclinations and at the same time, she reflects humanistic concerns through her writing. Some texts primarily focus upon the condition of women and their contemporary roles are studied against the backdrop of the traditional, stereotypical, mythical frameworks that promote the Sita, Sati, Savitri and Draupadi images. Like their traditional counterparts, contemporary women are struggling hard to survive in this antagonistic and hostile environment. Some of them are in the midst of the crisis and trying to seek a way out (*The Thousand Faces of Night* and *When Dreams Travel*) others like Mangala in *The Ghosts of Vasu Master* and many in *The Art of Dying*, Meena in *In Times of Siege* and Mala, Bala, Sara and Yasmin in *Fugitive Histories* have taken things in their stride and managed to maintain the balance between tradition and modernity. They are not portrayed as unwilling slaves of the men in their lives, but as women who understand the dynamics of power relations and come to terms with them. Men have assumed sovereign positions and it is women's duty to compromise and adjust to create a congenial atmosphere.

Hariharan's fiction captures the angst of women and describes how the roles they play as mothers, daughters and wives in the society are very taxing on them. Her fiction and non-fiction portray the marginalisation and repression of women and their consequent attempt to attain self-discovery and self-realisation. It has been observed that men have always kept all the essential powers in their hands by setting up the patriarchal system. They have wielded power over women as masters over slaves. In his "On the Subjection of women", J.S.Mill has pointed out that if slavery still exists in any form in the world, it is in marriage because married women are no better than slaves. Most women writers lament and complain about the women's condition but Hariharan manages to rise above the petty differences and understands that emphasis needs to be laid on the human predicament and not just on the condition of women. Hariharan's growth as a writer and as an individual is evident through the manner in which she moves from being a feminist to becoming a humanist. This shift gives evidence of her wider vision as she migrates from the study of men and women in society to a study of society with all its economic, political and religious frameworks that have their repercussions on men and women alike.

While analysing her novels, chronologically it becomes clear that her characters also mature from being men (male) and women (female) to acquire androgynous sensibilities. How well women know and understand men and how men realise that women have their own lives and individualities is particularly evident in *The Ghosts of Vasu Master*. In fact, women's issues have been portrayed through the mind of a man in this novel. Hariharan's close observation of life also enables her to grasp the truth that if patriarchy oppresses women, it also has its expectations and demands of the men. So, men are equally repressed and haunted by 'societal ghosts' and patriarchal concepts.

Hariharan experiments with various narrative techniques in her novels. All of her novels have a different technique. Though all of them have common elements like storytelling, embedded stories, poetic language yet each differs in narrative technique and expression. She takes myths and references from the epics of *Ramayana* and *Mahabharata* in her novels, stories from *Panchatantra* and the *Arabian Nights* to enhance and narrate the texts in her own way. As she says about the narrative skill of a writer:

> I don't see my writing as an introduction to India and I am not self-conscious about being "Indian" in my writing. For some reason all of us like to imagine that a writer is a writer because she has a great deal to say (message!) or is a good egg (social concern!). Both these should be there, but really, in the ultimate analysis, a writer is a writer because she has a narrative skill - a balancing act she can perform. (*Desert* 214)

Hariharan acknowledges that having a message and a social concern are necessary pre-requisites to become a good writer but these need to be coupled with narrative skills and the ability to maintain a balance. *The Thousand Faces of Night* and *When Dreams Travel* have utilised the concept of revisionist myth-making and she transforms the characters from their traditional mythical versions to modern women. Revisionist myth-making is perhaps the after effect of Rich's contentions in "When We Dead Awaken." Feminists advocate the re-reading of literature from the perspective of women and to subvert and transform the stereotypical representations of women and bring her to the centre. *When Dreams Travel* also employs the technique of magic realism.

Reality is presented in an imaginative manner and it is the dream of helping women to attain freedom from all constraints that is the driving force behind the story. In *The Thousand Faces of Night,* it is mostly the story telling technique that is employed. *In Times of Siege* and *Fugitive Histories* are written fictional records of the communal differences among people and the rise of fundamentalism. *The Ghosts of Vasu Master* strings together a number of short stories through the consciousness of Vasu. The stories are interspersed with the analysis of Vasu Master's journey through life. The Art of Dying also reflects a variety of narrative techniques that only a skilful writer can fully utilise.

It is noteworthy that all the nouns in the titles of Hariharan's novels are 'plural', e.g., 'faces', 'ghosts', 'dreams', 'times' and 'histories', signifying pluralist attributes of the heterogeneous society of India. 'Faces' signify the different faces/roles of Devi from childhood to adulthood and married woman to a liberated woman. The 'ghosts' are the characters in Vasu Master's life who haunt his memory. They also help him to devise new methods to teach Mani. The 'dreams' signify Shahrzad's stories. The novel seems like a dream as the stories are a continuation of *The Thousand and One Nights*. The novel *Fugitive Histories* hints at the fact that these 'histories' will continue if there is no end to the mad politics prevailing in our country. Hariharan comments in her interview with Arnab Chakladar:

> The medley of voices is a common strand. Someone observed once, very cleverly, that all the titles of my novels are plural – it had never occurred to me...I might become the writer who adds "S"s to everything. But perhaps it does say something...Perhaps one of the strong points of my work, or perhaps one of the curses of my vision, is that I can never quite see one part of the story or imagine one voice without hearing something in the background. I think multiplicity and the mutability of stories will always hold me in thrall...I love the idea of the same story being told by ten different people. (Web *www.anothersubcontinent.com*)

The use of plurals thus signifies another aspect of Hariharan's analysis of life – that it can never be understood from a single perspective. It is multi-faceted, multi-vocal and has a relative meaning to suit each individual's mindset and his/her understanding of life. One incident may be interpreted in as many different ways as the number of people narrating it or even experiencing it.

The formal decolonisation of our country was consummated with the unfurling of the flag of independence which granted the nation economic and political freedom. India is a free, democratic, globalised nation which boasts of political freedom, legal equality and the rule of law. Democracy literally means 'rule of the people', 'for the people' and 'by the people.' India has a Constitution based on the principles of democracy which are enumerated in the Preamble. The Preamble writes about a democratic republic that ensures Justice, Liberty, Equality and Fraternity. It promises liberty of thought and expression, belief, faith, equality of status and of opportunity, the dignity of the individual and to secure social, economic and political justice to all citizens. But, the post-independence history of India belies the assurances given to the people and questions the claims of secularism and democracy laid down in the Constitution. It is ironical that even after seventy years of independence, individuals have not attained complete freedom. They are being suppressed and marginalised by various agencies of power. It is paradoxical that while boasting of growth and progress, Indians ignore the truth that moral values are being bypassed and human rights are being violated. A process of degeneration and deterioration is incessantly taken place and Hariharan laments that the country is becoming rich in hypocrisy, fundamentalism, communalism and religious prejudices and poor in human values and secularism. So, the basics of the Indian Constitution are being flouted. Admiral Laxminarayan Ramdas (Retd.) raised his voice against the 'religious hyper nationalism' being practised in India. He wrote an open four-page letter to the President Ram Nath Kovind wherein he wrote:

> "the country's constitution "faces grave threats" from the forces of "religious hyper nationalism" who could "endanger the fundamental constitutional provisions and promises of a tolerant nation..."The increased intolerance at all levels, the shocking assault and treatment of our minority communities – especially Muslims, the growing tendency to take law into their own hands by lynch mobs and Gau Rakshaks – and the continuing impunity with which your own community,...are

> targets of physical, sexual and verbal abuse and attacks brings no credit to our proud heritage and tradition." (Web *www. indianexpress.com*)

He further views his fears about the future of the youth of the nation in which the "monster of religious tolerance" is damaging the "plural, syncretic and secular democracy." He urged the President to take the nation away from the narrow path of nationalism towards the path leading to Dharma. He says, "We are inhabiting an India where there is growing discrimination, and also growing alienation of our youth and unrest in the temples of learning - our universities." (Web *www.indianexpress.com*) History endorses the fact that communal conflicts have affected and injured the lives of countless people in India, especially minority communities and women have been the worst sufferers. They have been the victims of rape, mutilation, brutal murder, exploitation and have been used as pawns in political games. They have been playthings in the hands of patriarchal, colonial and today the political powers that exist are prone to becoming victims in every critical moment of history. These adverse experiences affect their minds and downgrade them socially, economically, politically and also psychologically.

Communalism and religious prejudices is a thinly-disguised superficial discourse that is given out for public consumption. It is the surface structure. What is the deep structure? At a less overt, underlying level operates the discourse of religious and cultural cleansing, the racial purges. It is to make India a Hindu *Rashtra*. Obviously one of the ways this can be done is to bulldoze the minorities, their lifestyles, their daily praxis into extinction and oblivion. For this reason, the petit narratives and histories of the minorities, the non-Hindus need to be highlighted. This is, in a way, what Hariharan is doing. She, via her fictional works, is trying to string together a narrative of stories and characters trapped, silent and thus unrecognised. Where does it leave democracy and democratic scaffoldings? They, every day, prove to be redundant; ridden wantonly and arbitrarily by the power players who over the years have mastered the craft of raping democracy and making it a mute brutalised witness. It's a spectacle that glares intellectuals and liberals in the eye. It asks them: Think

Reflect Articulate. Let there be a national debate on the workings of the democratic model? Where are we heading? How can we proceed from being a dumbfounded weakening, crumbling democracy to a mature, responsible democracy? How can we proceed to follow our constitutional provisions and promises in a proper way? As Arundhati Roy puts in her essay "Democracy: Who's She When She's at Home?":

> Every political party has mined the marrow of our secular parliamentary democracy for electoral advantage. Like termites excavating a mound, they've made tunnels and underground passages, undermining the meaning of 'secular'until it has become just an empty shell that's about to implode. Their tilling has weakened the foundations of the structure that connects the Constitution, Parliament and the courts of law - the configuration of checks and balances that forms the backbone of a parliamentary democracy. (*Listening* 18)

Thus, the study is not only confined to the plight of individuals but talks about the present times, portraying the negative effects of fundamentalism, communal divides, obscurantism, terrorism and conservatism. In this context, one is reminded of some pertinent questions raised by Arundhati Roy in her essay "Democracy: Who's She When She's at Home?":

> Can we not find it in ourselves to belong to an ancient civilization instead of to just a recent nation? ...The Sangh Parivar understands nothing of what civilization means. It seeks to limit, reduce, define, dismember and desecrate the memory of what we were, our understanding of what we are and our dreams what we want to be. What kind of India do they want? A limbless, headless, soulless torso, left bleeding under the butcher's cleaver with a flag driven deep into her mutilated heart? Can we let that happen? Have we let it happen? (*Listening* 16)

It seems that democracy is a 'failing light'(ix) in the Indian context and it cannot be relied upon to provide freedom, justice, stability which is needed to fulfil the dreams that Indian leaders envisioned when they fought for the country's independence. Arundhati writes:

> We have to accept that there is a dangerous, systemic flaw in our parliamentary democracy that politicians will exploit. And that's what results in the kind of conflagration that we have witnessed in Gujarat.

> There's fire in the ducts. We have to address this issue and come up with a systemic solution...Every 'democratic' institution in this country has shown itself to be unaccountable, inaccessible to the ordinary citizen and unwilling or incapable of acting in the genuine interests of social justice. (*Listening* 18-19)

Hariharan thus emerges as a writer who is concerned with the preservation of life, maintenance of heterogeneity and resistance as a measure to preserve the rich cultural heritage and past traditions of India. She seems to be issuing warnings to people not to fall prey to the divisive forces that are bent on ruining peace but to celebrate diversity as a welcome feature of our culture and society. She aims to build awareness among people as to how to make the nation stronger and not leave it to the mercy of negative forces. She, no doubt, highlights the problems of the marginalised people and minorities. She also questions the validity of the Indian government and democracy. She focusses single-mindedly on the problems of contemporary India and wishes to awaken people to the exigencies of the situation and to look for the appropriate solutions. In her fictional as well as non-fictional writings, all her concerns point towards her inherent desire to control the damage being caused to the nation. The connection and commonality between her fictional and non-fictional work clearly show her sincere intent and purpose to save humanity from the hazards of modern life. She is one of the persons who practises what she preaches, and this is revealed through her constant interest in activism and involvement in various causes.

After having written a variety of fiction on children, women and fugitives, she has now shifted to writing non-fiction as it provides her with more space to take things headlong. She says in the interview "My voice is a medley" with Sangeetha Devi Dundoo,

> You can't help the voice you have as a writer. It's a given. My voice is a medley. Plurality engages me and I want to hear many voices – focusing on a variety of issues. Fiction is a gift; it's home. I am now writing non-fiction since it allows me to raise questions I want to ask as a result of learning over the years. (web *www.thehindu.com*)

The ideas presented by Hariharan in two of her essays "New Voices, New Challenges" (2005) and "In Search of Our Other Selves: Literature as Resistance" (2007) bear out what is discovered during the study of her fiction. She believes that writers need to resist and oppose irrational, fundamental, stereotypical elements. She is an advocate of heterogeneity as the use of plurals in her titles suggests. She believes that diversity must be maintained or else essentialism will destroy the capacity of finding multiple responses and perspectives on particular incidents. As an individual, each human being is a part of a community as well and needs to see life from a personal as well as a universal angle. She also warns against resistance turning essentialist. She talks of jingoism - how it is shrinking spaces and how Indian and Hindu identity have been clubbed together in the name of patriotism. Hariharan also highlights through *In Times of Siege* and *Fugitive Histories* how historical and cultural landmarks become 'disputed structures.' As she writes in "In Search of Our Other Selves",

> It's inevitable perhaps that with physical sites being paved over, with history itself becoming a contested site where memories are erased or retold or new memories invented, the ongoing, real target of the disputing exercise is that large and amorphous thing called culture. (web *www. tandfonline.com* 127)

She laments that the right-wing ideology is reducing the once complex cultural site in India to a disputed site. She says that by laying so much significance on monolithic Hindu culture: "The culture that has become the right-wing rallying point reduces the myriad shades and nuances of real cultural sites to a "singular" Indian culture. This shrunken site is called cultural nationalism of the Indian variety." (web *www.tandfonline.com* 128) She pertinently observes that by naming periods of history as Hindu, Muslim, the legacy of the colonial experience is being reinforced. Texts are being written with a greater emphasis on the caste system, *sati* and foeticide "while demonising Islam or Christianity." Ironically, Basavanna in *In Times of Siege* is 'passionately anti-caste', who is to be protected by the 'History Protection Brigade' - an institution that upholds caste. Hariharan is upset by the fact that despite the process of globalisation, every community in India seems to be heading towards a more narrow-minded outlook. She also feels that every new work of fiction or character a writer creates is another 'self' which he/she embraces, so a writer has many 'selves', not one 'self.'

At the end of most of her fictional writings, Hariharan leaves an open ending perhaps to suggest that in this country and world, various options are open to people. It is for them to decide what is best for them and how to face the crises in their lives. As pointed out in the chapter entitled "The Societal Ghosts: *The Ghosts of Vasu Master* and *The Art of Dying*", Hariharan believes that no story should be completely unfolded or told because readers also have the capacity to reinterpret and continue those stories and provide them with a fresh perspective. As she says in "In Search of Our Other Selves":

> So for a writer, for a reader, and for the literary work itself, it's best not to sanctify the compartmentalization of different tools of analysis, different aspects of resistance. It's an exercise in impoverishing oneself, I think, to produce literature that is only about gender to the exclusion of say caste, or vice-versa. (web *www.tandfonline.com* 131)

Hariharan is a writer with a committment whose aim is to keep "the Great Indian Experiment" going while celebrating its diversity and still maintaining its unity. She is conscious of the difficulties in this path and every piece that she writes makes an appeal to the people and writers of India that they must commit themselves to the improvement of the nation. Courage and fearlessness will enable the writers to question the system and break the walls that are threatening to divide people. The final message of her works is to save humanity, salvage India and protect the world from disintegration at the hands of the 'ghosts' and power relations that threaten to annihilate it.

Works cited

Hariharan. Githa. "A new take on power." Interview by Anuradha Marwah Roy. *Pioneer*. 7 Feb.1999.

---. "The law is an amoeba riddled with parasites." Interview by Suhasini Haidar. *The Rediff Interview.* web 13 Mar 1999. http://www.rediff.com/news/1999/mar/13gita.htm

---."Discrete Thoughts" ed. Meenakshi Bharat. *Desert in Bloom: Contemporary Indian Women's Fiction in English.* Delhi: Pencraft, 2004. Print.

---."New Voices, New Challenges." *Indian Literature.* 49.4 (2005): 31-37. Web. 9 Oct 2017. http://www.jstor.org/stable/23340768

---."In Search of Our Other Selves." *Journal of Postcolonial Writing.* 43.2 (2007): 125-132. Web. 9 Oct 2017. http://www.tandfonline.com/action/journalInformation? journalCode=rjpw20

---."A Conversation with Githa Hariharan." Interview by Arnab Chakladar. *Another Subcontinent: South Asian Society and Culture,* 12 Aug 2005 web. 8 July 2013. http://www. anothersub continent.com/gh3.html

---."My voice is a medley." Interview by Sangeetha Devi Dundoo. *The Hindu.*Web. 27 Jan. 2014. http://www.thehindu.com/books/books-authors/my-voice-is-a-medley/article5623104.ece

Mill, John Stuart. "On the Subjection of Women." *Princeton Readings in Political Thought.* Ed. Mitchell Cohen and Nicole Fermon. New Jersey: Princeton UP, 1996. Print.

Ramdas, Admiral. "Constitution facing 'grave threats' from forces of 'religious hyper nationalism" *Indian Express.* New Delhi: Express Web Desk, 1 Sept 2017. http://indianexpress.com/article/india/in-letter-to-president-kovind-admiral-ramdas-alleges-constitution-facing-grave-threats-from-forces-of-religious-hyper-nationalism-4824338

Roy, Arundhati. "Democracy: Who's She When She's at Home?" *Listening to Grass Hoppers: Field Notes on Democracy.* New Delhi: Penguin, 2009. 1-21. Print.

BIBLIOGRAPHY

Primary Sources

Books

Hariharan, Githa. *The Thousand Faces of Night*. New Delhi: Penguin, 1992. Print.

---. *The Art of Dying and Other Stories*. New Delhi: Penguin, 1993. Print.

---. *The Ghosts of Vasu Master*. New Delhi: Penguin, 1994. Print.

---. *When DreamsTravel*. New Delhi: Penguin, 2001. Print.

---. *In Times of Siege*. New Delhi: Penguin, 2003. Print.

---. *The Winning Team*. New Delhi: Rupa and Co., 2004. Print.

---. *Fugitive Histories*. New Delhi: Penguin, 2009. Print.

---. *Almost Home: Cities and Other Places*, Fourth Estate, Harper Collins, New Delhi, 2014; Restless Books, Brooklyn, 2016.

Edited collections

---.ed. *A Southern Harvest*. New Delhi: Katha-Rupa, 1993. Print.

---.,and Shama Futehally, eds. *Sorry, Best Friend!* Chennai: Tulika, 1997. Print.

---. *From India to Palestine: Essays in Solidarity* (ed.), LeftWord, New Delhi, 2014.

Interviews

---."Interview with Githa Hariharan." Prema Vishwanath. *Indian Express Sunday Magazine*, Web.12 Sept. 1993.

---."A new take on power." Interview by Anuradha Marwah Roy. *Pioneer*. 7 Feb.1999. Print.

---."The law is an amoeba riddled with parasites." Interview by Suhasini Haidar. *The Rediff Interview*.Web. 13 Mar. 1999. http://www.rediff.com/news/1999/mar/13gita.htm

---."Our Spaces Are Shrinking All the Time." Interview by Preeti Verma Lal. *Literary World.* 19 Mar. 2003. Print.

---."Multiple Choice." Interview by Chitralekha Basu. *Sunday Statesman* 13 Apr.2003. Print.

---."Plea for pluralism." Interview by Gowri Ramnarayan. *The Hindu* 22 Apr. 2003. Print.

---."The Siege Of The Mind." Interview by Vaishna Roy. *Outlook* 23 Apr. 2003. Web. 22 May 2014. <http// www.outlookindia.com/ article.aspx?219912>

---."A Conversation with Githa Hariharan." Interview by Arnab Chakladar. *Another Subcontinent: South Asian Society and Culture,* 2005. 12 Aug. 2005. Web 8 July 2013. http://www. another subcontinent.com/gh3.html

---.Interview by P. Anima. "Going Strong After Decades of Writing." *The Hindu.* 19 Mar. 2007. Web. 20 Nov. 2013.<http:// www. thehindu.com/2007/03/19/stories/200703190533 0200.htm>

---.Interview by Bageshree S. *The Hindu* N.p. 4 Aug. 2009. Web.10 Mar. 2013. <http:// www.thehindu.com/mp/2009/08/04/stories/ 2009080450050100.htm>

---."An Interview with Githa Hariharan." Luan Gaines. Web. 25 Feb. 2011. <http://www.curledup.com/githaint.htm >

---."Resisting Regimentaton." Interview by Anuradha Roy. *The Hindu* nd. Web. 8 July 2013. http://www.anothersubcontinent. com/ gh3.html

---."My voice is a medley." Sangeetha Devi Dundoo. *The Hindu.* Web. 27 Jan. 2014. http://www.thehindu,com/books/books-authors/my-voice-is-a -medley/article5623104.ecehariharan/ 1/206692.html>

Articles/ Contributions (short fiction/extracts)

---."Shrinking Spaces in Times of Globalisation." in *JSL,* Spring 2004, *Journal of the School of Language, Literature and Culture Studies,* Jawaharlal Nehru University, New Delhi.

---."New Voices, New Challenges." *Indian Literature,* vol. 49.4 (2005) *JSTOR,* www.jstor.org/stable/23340768.

---."In Times of Siege: Shrinking Spaces in Times of Globalisation." *Littcrit: An Indian Response to Literature.* Web. Vol. 31.1 (2005)

---. "When Bodies Speak." *World Literature Today*, vol. 91.2 (2017) *JSTOR*, www.jstor.org/stable/10.7588/worllitetoda.91.2.0016.

Secondary Sources

Abrams, M.H. *A Glossary of Literary Terms.* 7th ed. Heinle: Thomson, 2005. Print.

Agamben, Giorgio. *Homo Sacer: Sovereign Power and Bare Life.* trans. Daniel Heller-Roazen. Stanford: Stanford UP, 1998. Print.

---. *State of Exception.* trans. Kevin Attell. Chicago: The U of Chicago P, 2005. Print.

Allen, Graham. *Intertextuality.* London: Routledge, 2007. Print.

Ashcroft, Bill, et al. eds. *The Post-Colonial Studies Reader.* 2nd ed. London: Routledge, 2006. Print.

Bajrangi, Babu. "'After Killing Them, I Felt Like Maharana Pratap'." *Tehelka.* 1 Sept. 2007.

Balachandran, K. *Critical Essays on Diasporic Writings.* New Delhi: Arise, 2008. Print.

Baldick, Chris. *The Oxford Dictionary of Literary Terms.* New York: OUP, 2008. Print.

Barry, Peter. *Beginning theory: An introduction to literary and cultural theory.* 2nd ed. Manchester: Manchester UP, 1995. Print.

Beasley, Chris. *What is feminism? An Introduction of Feminist Theory.* New Delhi: Sage, 1999. Print.

Beauvoir, Simone de. *The Second Sex.* trans. H.M.Parshley. 1949. London: Vintage, 1983. Print.

Bertens, Hans. *Literary Theory: The Basics.* London: Routledge, 2001. Print.

Bhabha, Homi K., ed. *Nation and Narration.* London: Routledge, 1990. Print.

---. *The Location of Culture.* London: Routledge, 1994. Print.

Bharat, Meenakshi. ed. *Desert in Bloom: Contemporary Indian Women's Fiction in English.* Delhi: Pencraft, 2004. Print.

Bharti K.S. *Thoughts of Mahatma.* Nagpur: Dattsons, 1995. Print.

Bhargava, Rajul."Post-Feminist Configurations in Githa Hariharan's Short Stories in *The Art of Dying.*" eds. Jain, Jasbir and Avadhesh Kumar Singh. *Indian Feminisms.* New Delhi: Creative, 2001.Print.

Bhargava, Rajul and Shubhshree. eds. *Of Narratives, Narrators*. Jaipur and New Delhi: Rawat, 2004.

Bhutalia, Urvashi. *Peopled by Ghosts and Absences*. The Book Review. Web. 19.3 March 1995.

Bowers, Maggie Ann. *Magic(al) Realism*. London: Routledge, 2007. Print.

Bradbury, Malcolm. ed. *The Novel Today*. London: Manchester UP, 1977. Print.

Brahma, Rustam. "Gender, Identity and Politics: A Study of Githa Hariharan's *When Dreams Travel* and *The Thousand Faces of Night*." *The Criterion*.Web. 6.2 (2015): 179-185.

Butler, Judith. *Bodies That Matter: On the Discursive Limits of 'Sex'*. New York: Routledge, 1993. Print.

---.*Gender Trouble and the Subversion of Identity*. New York: Routledge, 1990. Print.

Chaturvedi, Vinayak.ed. *Mapping Subaltern Studies and the Postcolonial*. 2000. Jaipur: Rawat, 2015.

Christopher, Rollason and Rajeshwar, Mittapalli. ed. *Modern Criticism*. New Delhi: Atlantic, 2002.

Daiya, Krishna. *Post-Independence Women Short Story Writers in Indian English*. New Delhi: Sarup & Sons, 2006. Print.

Daly, Mary. Gyn/Ecology: *The Metaethics of Radical Feminism*. Boston: Beacon, 1978. Print.

Das, Bijay Kumar. *Twentieth Century Literary Criticism*. New Delhi: Atlantic, 2005. Print.

De, Shobha. *Shooting from the Hip: Selected Writings*. New Delhi: UBS, 1994. Print.

Deshpande, Shashi. "The Power Within." *Creating Theory: Writers on Writing*. ed. Jasbir Jain. Delhi: Pencraft, 2000. Print.

Durairaj, A. Joseph. *Myth and Literature*. Palayamkottai: FRRC, 2003. Print.

Dhawan, R.K., ed. *Indian Women Novelists*. Set III. Vol. IV. New Delhi: Prestige, 1995. Print.

Dhiman, O.P., *Gandhian Philosophy*. Ambala: Indian Publications, 1971. Print.

Doniger, Wendy. *The Hindus: An Alternative History*. New Delhi: Penguin, 1999. p. 200-298. Print.

Eagleton, Terry. *Marxism and Literary Criticism*. London: Methuen, 1976. Print.

Eliot, T.S. *Selected Poems*. Great Britain: Penguin, 1951. Print.

Faludi, Susan. *Backlash: The Undeclared War Against Women*. London: Vintage, 1992. Print.

Fanon, Frantz. *Black Skin, White Masks*. Trans. C.L. Markman. London: Pluto, 1986. Print.

Fillingham, Lydia Alix. *Foucault for Beginners*. Chennai: Orient, 2000. Print.

Firestone, Shulamith. *The Dialectic of Sex: The Case for a Feminist Revolution*. New York: Bantam, 1970. Print.

Foucault, Michel, *Madness and Civilization: A History of Insanity in the Age of Reason*. London: Routledge, 1989. Print.

---.*The Archaeology of Knowledge*. London: Tavistock, 1972. Print.

---.*Power/Knowledge: Selected Interviews and Other Writings*. 1972-1977. Ed. Gordin Colin. New York: Pantheon, 1980. Print.

---.*Discipline and Punish: The Birth of a Prison*. London: Penguin, 1991. Print.

---.*The History of Sexuality: The Will to Knowledge*. London: Penguin, 1998. Print.

Friedan, Betty. 'The Feminist Mystique.' *America since 1945*. ed. Robert D. Marcus and David Burns. New York: St. Martin's Press, 1991. Print.

Fulkerson, Mary McClintock and Susan J. Dunlap. "Michel Foucault (1926-1984): Introduction" *The Postmodern God: A Theological Reader*. ed. Graham Ward. U.S.A: Blackwell, 1997. Print.

Gamble, Sarah, ed. *The Routledge Companion to Feminism and Postfeminism*. 1998. London: Routledge, 2001. Print.

Gandhi,Leela. *Postcolonial Theory: A Critical Introduction*. Edinburgh: Edinburgh UP,1998. Print.

Gandhi, Madan G. *Gandhi and Marx*. Chandigarh: Kewal Krishan, 1969. Print.

Gaventa, John. *Power after Lukes: a review of the literature*. Brighton: Institute of Development Studies, 2003. Print.

George, Rosemary M. *The Politics of Home*. New Delhi: Cambridge UP, 1995. Print.

Ghosh, Mohua. "*When Dreams Travel*: 'Writing Back' to *The Arabian Nights*." *Studies in Women* Writers *in English*. Vol II. ed. Mohit K.Ray & Rama Kundu. New Delhi: Atlantic, 2005. Print.

---."Feminist Interrogation of a Patriarchal Text: Intertextual Echoes and Departures." *Studies in Women Writers in English*. Vol II. ed. Mohit K.Ray & Rama Kundu. New Delhi: Atlantic, 2005. Print.

Gibaldi, Joseph. *MLA Handbook for Writers of Research Papers*.7th ed. New Delhi: EWP, 2009. Print.

Gordon, Avery F. *Ghostly Matters: Haunting and the Sociological Imagination*. 2nd ed. London: U of Minnesota P, 2008. Print.

Gowalkar, Madhav Sadashiv. *We or Our Nationhood Defined*. Nagpur: Bharat, 1939. Print.

Gramsci, Antonio. *Selections from the Prison Notebooks of Antonio Gramsci*. ed. and trans. Joseph A Buttigieg. New York: Columbia UP, 2007. Print.

Greer, Germaine. *The Female Eunuch*. London: Harper Perennial, 2006. Print.

Guerin, Wilfred L., et al. *A Handbook of Critical Approaches to Literature*. 4th ed. Oxford: OUP, 1999. Print.

Gutting, Gary. *Foucault: A Very Short Introduction*. New York: OUP, 2005. Print.

Jain, Jasbir, and Avadhesh Kumar Singh, eds. *Indian Feminisms*. New Delhi: Creative, 2001. Print.

Hornby, A.S. ed. *Oxford Advanced Learner's Dictionary 8th*. Oxford: OUP, 2010. Print.

Hutcheon, Linda. *A poetics of Postmodernism*. New York: Routledge, 1988. Print.

Indira, S. "Walking the Tight Rope: A Reading of Githa Hariharan's *The Thousand Faces of Night*" ed. R.K. Dhawan. *Indian Women Novelists*. Set III. Vol. IV. New Delhi: Prestige, 1995. Print.

Jain, Jasbir. "Discrete Thoughts" ed. Meenakshi Bharat. *Desert in Bloom: Contemporary Indian Women's Fiction in English*. Delhi: Pencraft,

2004. Print.

---."Men in the Minds of Women." *Desert in Bloom: Contemporary Indian Women's Fiction in English.* Delhi: Pencraft, 2004. Print.

---."Positioning the 'Post' in Post-Feminism: Reworking of Strategies" eds. Jain, Jasbir and Avadesh Kumar Singh. *Indian Feminisms.* Delhi: Pencraft, 2004. Print.

Kala, A., "Flying in New Skies: Githa Hariharan's *The Thousand Faces of Night*: A Feminist Perspective" ed. K. Balachandran. *Critical Essays on Diasporic Writing.* New Delhi: Arise, 2008. Print.

Kalpana, R.J. *Feminism and the Individual.* New Delhi: Prestige, 2005. Print.

Kaur, Iqbal. ed. *Gender and Literature.* Delhi: B.R. Publishing, 1992. Print.

Kaur, Dr. Sarabjit. "Journey of Women Characters in Githa Hariharan's *The Thousand Faces of Night* and Manju Kapur's *Home.*" *IQSR Journal Of Humanities And Social Science.* Web. 20.3 (2015): 79-82.

Kaushik, Abha Shukla. "Changing Faces of Indian Woman: Bharati Mukherjee's *Jasmine* and Githa Hariharan's *The Thousand Faces of Night.*" eds. Malti, Agarwal. *Women in Postcolonial Indian English Literature.* New Delhi: Atlantic, 2011. Print.

Khan, A.G., "*The Thousand Faces of Night:* An Epic "Capsulized". eds. Khan, M.Q. and A.G.Khan, *Changing Faces of Women in Indian Writing in English.* New Delhi: Creative , 1995. Print.

Kirpal, Vinay. ed. *The Postmodern Indian English Novel: Interrogating the 1980s and 1990s.* Vol. VIII. Bombay: Allied, 1996. Print.

Kourtti, Joel. and Rajeshwar, Mittapalli. *Indian Women's Short Fiction.* New Delhi: Atlantic, 2001. Print.

Kristeva, Julia. "The Powers of Horror: An Essay on Abjection." Trans. Leon S. Roudiez. New York: Columbia UP, 1982. Print.

---.*Revolution in Poetic Language.* New York: Columbia UP, 1984. Print.

Kumar, Girja. "Bhakti Movement and politics in Karnataka." *Censorship in India: Studies in Fundamentalism, Obscenity and Law.* New Delhi: Har-Anand, 2009. Print.

Lazarus, Neil, ed. *Postcolonial Literary Studies.* London: Cambridge UP, 2004. Print.

Lodge, David.ed. *20th Century Literary Criticism.* London: Longman, 1972. Print.

---.ed. *Modern Criticism and Theory: A Reader*. London: Longman, 1988. Print.

Loomba, Ania. *Colonialism/Postcolonialism*. London: Routledge, 1998. Print.

Marx, Karl, and Friedrich Engels. *The Communist Manifesto*. trans. Samuel Moore. London, 1888. New Delhi: Penguin, 2002. Print.

McLeod, John. *Beginning Postcolonialism*. Manchester: Manchester UP, 2000. Print.

Mellor, Mary. *Feminism and Ecology*. New York: New York UP, 1997. Print.

Mill, John Stuart. "The Subjection of Women" *Princeton Readings in Political Thought*. ed. Mitchell Cohen and Nicole Fermon. New Jersey: Princeton UP, 1996. Print.

Millet, Kate. *Sexual Politics*. 1969. Illinois: U of Illinois P, 2000, Print.

Mishra, Binod. *Critical Responses to Feminism*. New Delhi: Sarup, 2006. Print.

Mitchell, Juliet. *Psychoanalysis and Feminism*. New York: Vintage, 1975. Print.

---.*Women's Estate*. London: Penguin, 1971. Print.

Mittapalli, Rajeshwar and Allesandro Monti. *Post-Independence Indian English Fiction*. New Delhi: Atlanlic, 2011. Print.

Mohanty, Chandra Talpade. "Under Western Eyes: Feminist Scholarship and Colonial Discourses" eds. Ashcroft, Bill, et al. *The Post-Colonial Studies Reader*. 2nd ed. London: Routledge, 2006. Print.

Moi, Toril. *Sexual/Textual Politics: Feminist Literary Theory*. New York: Metheun, 1985. Print.

Morris, Pam. *Literature and Feminism: An Introduction*. Oxford: Blackwell, 1993. Print.

Mukhopadhyay, Arpita. ed. Sumit Chakrabarti. *Feminisms*. Hyderabad: Orient. 2016. Print.

Murphy, Dr.Joseph. *The Power of Your Subconscious Mind*. London: Simon & Schuster, 1977. Print.

Naik, M.K. *Aspects of Indian Writing in English*. New Delhi: Macmillan, 1979. Print.

---. *A History of Indian English Literature*. New Delhi: Sahitya Akademi, 1982. Print.

Naikar, Basavaraj. *Indian English Literature* . Vol VI. New Delhi: Atlantic, 2007. Print.

---.*Critical Response to Indian English Literature*. Rohtak: Shanti Prakashan, 2009. Print.

Nair, Rama. "The Art of Fiction: A Note on the 'Prelude' of Githa Hariharan's *The Thousand Faces of Night*" ed. R.K. Dhawan. *Indian Women Novelists*. Set III, Vol.4. New Delhi: Prestige, 1995. Print.

Narasimhaih, C.D. ed. *Awakened Conscience: Studies in Commonwealth Literature*. New Delhi: Sterling, 1978. Print.

Nawale, A.M. ed. *Reflections on Post-Independence Indian English Fiction*. New Delhi: Anmol, 2011. Print.

Nayar, Pramod K. *An Introduction to Cultural Studies*. 2008. New Delhi: Viva, 2009. Print.

Newman, Michael. *Socialism: A Very Short Introduction*. Oxford: OUP, 2005. Print.

Nityanandam, Indira and Reena Kothari. eds. *Indo-English Fiction: The Last Decade*. New Delhi: Creative, 2002. 41-46. Print.

Nityanandan Indira, "A Search for Identity: *The Thousand Faces of Night*" ed. R.K. Dhawan. *Indian Women Novelists*. Set III. Vol. IV. New Delhi: Prestige, 1995. Print.

Pandey, Surya Nath. *Contemporary Indian Women Writers in English: A Feminist Perspective*. New Delhi: Atlantic, 1999.Print.

Pant, Prabha. "Variations on a Theme: Humanism in Arundhati Roy's *The Cost of Living* and Githa Hariharan's *The Art of Dying*." ed. T.S. Anand. *Humanism in Indian English Fiction*. New Delhi: Creative, 2005. Print.

Paranjape, Makarand. "A Cathartic Exercise", Rev. of *The Thousand Faces of Night*. The Book Review, Vol. 17.4 (1993): 19. Print.

Poddar, A. ed. *Indian Literature*. Shimla: Indian Institute of Advanced Study, 1972. Print.

Prasad, Amar Nath. ed. *Indian Women Novelists in English*. New Delhi: Atlantic, 2001. Print.

Prasad, Madhusudan. ed. *Indian English Novelists*. New Delhi: Sterling, 1982. Print.

R.J.Kalpana. *Feminism and the Individual*. New Delhi: Prestige, 2005. Print.

Rabinow, David, ed. *The Foucault Reader*. New York: Random House, 1984. Print.

Rabinow, Paul, ed. *The Foucault Reader*. London: Penguin, 1991. Print.

Rao, K.Damodar. "Penance as Multiple Response in Githa Hariharan's *The Thousand Faces of Night*" ed. R.K.Dhawan. *Indian Women Novelists*. Set III, Vol.4. New Delhi: Prestige, 1995. Print.

Rich, Adrienne. "When We Dead Awaken: Writing as Revision." *College English*, 34.1(1972): 18-30. 11 Sept 2008. Print.

Roy, Anjali. "Rev. of *The Ghosts of Vasu Master*", *The Literary Criterion*. 33.3 (1998).

---. "Visnu Sarma against Shakespeare: "Ghosts" of (Non) Dominating Knowledge in *The Ghosts of Vasu Master*." *The Postmodern Indian English Novel: Interrogating the 1980s and 1990s*. ed. Vinay Kirpal. Bombay: Allied, Vol.VIII, 1996.

Roy, Anuradha. *Patterns of Feminist Consciousness in Indian Women Writers*. New Delhi: Prestige, 1996. Print.

Roy, Arundhati. "Listening to Grass-hoppers: Genocide, Denial and Celebration" *Listening to Grass-hoppers: Field Notes on Democracy*. New Delhi: Penguin, 2009. Print.

---."Introduction: Democracy's Failing Light" *Listening to Grass-hoppers: Field Notes on Democracy*. New Delhi: Penguin, 2009. ix-xxxvii. Print.

Roy, Mohit K.ed. *Indian Writing in English* New Delhi: Atlantic, 2003. Print.

Rustam, Brahma. "Myth, History and Identity: A Study of the major works of Githa Hariharan." *Research Journal of English Language and Literature*. Web. 4.1 (2016): 164-172.

Said, Edward W. *Orientalism*. London: Routledge and Kegan Paul, 1978. Print.

---.*Culture and Imperialism*. New York: Vintage, 1993. Print.

Selden, Raman, ed. *The Cambridge History of Literary Criticism*. Vol 8 (From formalism to Poststructuralism). Cambridge: Cambridge U.P, 1995. Print.

Selden, Raman, Peter Widdowson, and Peter Brooker, eds. *A Reader's Guide to Contemporary Literary Theory*. 5th ed. New Delhi: Pearson, 2005. Print.

Seshadri, Veena. "Overloaded with Messages." Rev. of *The Ghosts of Vasu Master, Indian Review of Books*. 4.6 (1995) Print.

Sharma, Brahma Dutta and Susheel Kumar Sharma. *Contemporary Indian English Novel*. New Delhi: Anamika, 1991. Print.

Showalter, Elaine. *A Literature of their Own: British Women Novelists from Bronte to Lessing*. Princeton: N.J. Princeton U.P, 1979. Print.

---.ed. *The New Feminist Criticism*. New York: Pantheon, 1985. Print.

Singer, Peter. *Marx-A Very Short Introduction*. Oxford: OUP, 1980. Print.

Singh, Anita. *Indian English Novel in the Nineties and After: A Study of the Text and Its Context*. New Delhi: Adhyayan, 2004. Print.

---."Githa Hariharan's *In Times of Siege*: A Symbolic Declaration of Human Rights." *Indian English Literature*. ed. Basavaraj Naikar. New Delhi: Atlantic, 2007. Print.

Singh, Sushila. ed. *Feminism and Recent Fiction in English*. New Delhi: Prestige, 1991. Print.

Singh, Sushila. *Feminism: Theory, Criticism, Analysis*. New Delhi: Pencraft, 1997. Print.

Spivak, Gayatri Chakravarty. "Marginality in the Teaching Machine", *Outside in The Teaching Machine*. London: Routledge, 1996. Print.

Srinivas, C. Sunitha. *Functionalism and Indian English Fiction From Cradle to Grave*. New Delhi: Atlantic, 2010. Print.

Tandon, Neeru. *Feminism: A Paradigm Shift*. New Delhi: Atlantic, 2008. Print.

Tidd, Ursula. *Simone de Beauvoir*. London: Rouledge, 2004. Print.

Tikoo, Prithiv Nath. *Indian Women (A Brief Socio-Cultural Survey)*. New Delhi: B.R. Publication, 1985. Print.

Tiwari, R.S. "Feminism and Globalisation versus Indian Women Empowerment."eds. Avasthi, Abha. and Srivastava, A.K. *Modernity, Feminism and Women Empowerment*. Delhi: Rawat, 2001. Print.

Tolan, Fiona. "Feminisms". ed. Patricia Waugh. *Literary Theory and Criticism: An Oxford Guide*. Oxford: OUP, 2007. Print.

Tripathi, Shubha. "Voice of Protest and Assertion: A Comparative Study of Githa Hariharan's *The Thousand Faces of Night* and *In Times of Siege*." Binod Mishra. *Critical Responses to Feminism*. New Delhi: Sarup, 2006. Print.

Waugh, Patricia. *Literary Theory and Criticism-An Oxford Guide*. Oxford: OUP, 2006. Print.

Williams, Raymond. *Marxism and Literature*. Oxford: OUP, 1977. Print.

Woolf, Virginia. *A Room of One's Own*. 1928. London: Harmondsworth, 1945. Print.

Young, Robert. *White Mythologies: Writing History and the West*. London: Routledge, 1990. Print.

Young, Robert J.C. *Colonial Desire: Hybridity in Theory, Culture and Race*. London: Routledge, 1995. Print.

Internet Sources and Journals

Bhardwaj, Vikash and Surender Kumar. "*The Ghost of Vasu Master:* Exploring the Self through Teacher-Taught Relationship." *International Journal of English and Education*. Web. 2.4 (Oct 2013)

"Carl Schmitt." *Wikipedia, the free Encyclopedia.* Wikipedia Foundation Inc. Web. 22 June. 2011. <http://en.wikipedia.org/wiki/Carl_Schmitt>

Cixous, Helene. "The Laugh of the Medusa." Tr. K. Cohen and P. Cohen. *Signs*. Web. 1.1 (1976): 875-99.

Deshpande, Shashi., "I'm not a feminist." *Times of India*. 22 July 2001.Web. <http://articles.timesofindia.indiatimes.com/2001022/hyderabad/27243928_1_shashi-deshpande-slow-change-issues>

Foucault, Michel. "The subject and power." *Critical inquiry* 8.4 (1982): 777-795. Web. 26 Oct. 2016.

"Giorgio Agamben." *Wikipedia, the free Encyclopedia.* Wikipedia Foundation Inc. Web. 22 June. 2011. <http://en.wikipedia. org/wiki/Giorgio_Agamben>

Jacob, Bindu. "A Study of the Evolution of Three Generations of Women in Githa Hariharan's *The Thousand Faces of Night*." *International Research Journal*. 1.5 (2010): 81-84. Print.

Kale, Mahesh. "The Ghost of Vasu Master: Case Study of an Indian Teacher." *Contemporary Research in India*. 2.1 (2012): 200-02. Web. 8 Mar.2013.

MacKinnon, Catherine A."Feminism, Marxism, Method and the State: An Agenda for Theory." *Signs.* 17.3 (1982): 516-17 Feminist Theory The U of Chicago P. Web. 30 Oct. 2014. <http://www.jstor.org/stable/3173853>

Mahaprashasta, Ajoy Ashirwad and Venkitesh Ramakrishnan. "Wounds of 1984." *Frontline.* 26.24 (2009): Web. 28 Nov. 2017. <http://www.frontline.in/static/html/fl2624/stories/20091204262410000.htm>

Mehala, A.S. "Art-An Act of Liberation in Githa Hariharan's *The Thousand Faces of Night* and *When Dreams Travel." Research Journal of English Language and Literature*. Web. 4.2 (2016): 865-867.

Nair, Anita. "Dissenting Motif" Rev. *India Today.* Web. 24 Feb.2003. <http://indiatoday.intoday.in/story/book-review-of-in-times-of-siege-author-githa-hariharan/1/206692.html>

Navarro Tejero, Antonia. *The Fiction of Arundhati Roy and Githa Hariharan: Another World is Possible.* Diss. U de Huelva, 10 July 2003. Web. 24 Oct. 2013.

Ramamoorthy, Mohan. "A novel discord." Rev. n.d. Web. 2009. 12 Oct. 2013. <http://www.indianexpress.com>

Ramdas, Admiral. "Constitution facing 'grave threats' from forces of 'religious hyper nationalism." *Indian Express.* New Delhi: Express Web Desk, 1 Sept 2017. http://indianexpress.com/article/india/in-letter-to-president-kovind-admiral-ramdas-alleges-constitution-facing-grave-threats-from-forces-of-religious-hyper-nationalism-4824338/

Sankaran, Chitra. "Narrating to Survive: Ethics and Aesthetics in Githa Hariharan's *When Dreams Travel." Asiatic.* Web. 2.2 (2008): 65-72.

Soni M. Ronak. "A Review of Githa Hariharan's *Fugitive Histories." Githa Hariharan.* Rev. Web. 25 Apr. 2014. <http://www. githa hariharan.com/books/fugitive_histories.html>

Zaheer, Noor. "*Fugitive Histories* as Fiction." Rev. 21 Feb 2009. Web. 15 May 2014. http://infochangeindia.org/human-rights/books-a-reports/fugitive-histories-as-fiction.html.